A Functional Approach to the Legal Review of /

International Humanitarian Law Series

Editors-in-Chief

Professor Timothy L.H. McCormack

Editorial Advisory Board

VOLUME 72

The International Humanitarian Law Series is a series of monographs and edited volumes which aims to promote scholarly analysis and discussion of both the theory and practice of the international legal regulation of armed conflict.

The series explores substantive issues of International Humanitarian Law, including:

- Protection for victims of armed conflict and regulation of the means and method of warfare
- Questions of application of the various legal regimes for the conduct of armed conflict
- Issues relating to the implementation of International Humanitarian Law obligations
- National and international approaches to the enforcement of the law and
- The interactions between International Humanitarian Law and other related areas of international law such as Human Rights, Refugee Law, Arms Control and Disarmament Law, and Intenational Criminal Law.

The titles published in this series are listed at *brill.com/ihul*

A Functional Approach to the Legal Review of Autonomous Weapon Systems

By

Damian Copeland

BRILL | NIJHOFF

LEIDEN | BOSTON

Cover illustration: Lethal drone. Image of Skyborne Technologies Pty Ltd Cerberus MI UAV armed with HAVOC 40 mm Grenade Launcher.

Library of Congress Cataloging-in-Publication Data

Names: Copeland, Damian, author.
Title: A functional approach to the legal review of autonomous weapon systems / by Damian Copeland.
Description: Leiden ; Boston : Brill, 2025. | Series: International humanitarian law series, 1389-6776 ; 72 | Includes bibliographical references and index. | Summary: "Autonomous Weapon Systems (AWS) are no longer limited to science fiction. Conflicts in the Ukraine and Gaza demonstrate an increased trend toward the use of autonomy in the use of force in armed conflict"– Provided by publisher.
Identifiers: LCCN 2024033604 (print) | LCCN 2024033605 (ebook) | ISBN 9789004707030 (hardback) | ISBN 9789004707047 (ebook)
Subjects: LCSH: Autonomous weapons systems (International law) | Weapons systems–Automation. | Humanitarian law.
Classification: LCC KZ5645.5.A98 C67 2024 (print) | LCC KZ5645.5.A98 (ebook) | DDC 341.6/3–dc23/eng/20240723
LC record available at https://lccn.loc.gov/2024033604
LC ebook record available at https://lccn.loc.gov/2024033605

Typeface for the Latin, Greek, and Cyrillic scripts: "Brill". See and download: brill.com/brill-typeface.

ISSN 1389-6776
ISBN 978-90-04-70703-0 (hardback)
ISBN 978-90-04-70704-7 (e-book)
DOI 10.1163/9789004707047

This book is printed on acid-free paper and produced in a sustainable manner.

Contents

PART 2
How Can a State Determine the Legality of an AWS?

Foreword

There is important work to do operationalising how international law applies to regulate the use of autonomous weapon systems (AWS) in armed conflict. It cannot wait as AWS are no longer limited to science fiction. In March 2021, the final report of the United Nations Panel of Experts on Libya included a reference to the Libyan Government of National Accord Affiliated Forces' use of a Turkish made STM Kargu-2 autonomous drone to attack the logistics convoys and retreating Haftar Affiliated Forces.[1] The report states that the AWS 'were programmed to attack targets without requiring data connectivity between the operator and the munition'.[2] While this was the first officially recorded use of an AWS in armed conflict, it occurred against the background of a so-called AI arms race.[3] Currently, the Russian invasion of the Ukraine and ongoing conflict in Gaza have accelerated the development of increasingly uncrewed technologies towards autonomous capabilities.[4] In particular, Israel's use of AI to inform human targeting decisions is evidence of this trend.[5]

AWS and the prospect of algorithms making life and death decisions in armed conflict raise complex legal, ethical, technical, moral and operational challenges for those states and private industry developing them for use in armed conflict. The urgency of dealing with this is evidenced by the United Nations General Assembly calling upon states to consider the regulation of AWS.[6] This call is against the background of nearly a decade long debate on the need for new regulation under the auspices of the *Convention on Certain*

1 United Nations, *Final Report of the Panel of Experts on Libya Established Pursuant to Security Council Resolution 1972*, UN Doc S/2021/229 (2011) [63] ('UN Report on Libya') <https://undocs.org/Home/Mobile?FinalSymbol=S%2F2021%2F229&Language=E&DeviceType=Desktop&LangRequested=False>.

2 Ibid.

3 D Mauri, *Autonomous Weapons Systems and the Protection of the Human Person: An International Law Analysis* (Edward Elgar Publishing, 2022) 119.

4 M Meaker, *Ukraine's War Brings Autonomous Weapons to the Front Line* (23 February 2023) https://www.wired.co.uk/article/ukraine-war-autonomous-weapons-frontlines.

5 A Safadi, *Israel's AI can produce 100 bombing targets a day in Gaza. Is this the future of war?* (8 December 2023, The Conversation Website), https://theconversation.com/israels-ai-can-produce-100-bombing-targets-a-day-in-gaza-is-this-the-future-of-war-219302>.

6 United Nations General Assembly, Resolution 78/241 on lethal autonomous weapon systems (28 December 2023), <https://documents.un.org/doc/undoc/gen/n23/431/11/pdf/n2343111.pdf?token=Co3gOJZVzJbAt1Jx1Q&fe=true>.

Conventional Weapons (CCW).[7] While some states party and elements of civil society seek a prospective ban on LAWS by creating a new Protocol under the CCW, the forum is yet to achieve consensus on the need for new international law either prohibiting or restricting the use of AWS in armed conflict.

In the absence of new international law regulating AWS, an important question is how can states ensure that their development and use of AWS is consistent with their existing international law obligations? The central question addressed by this book is: How can states party to AP 1 fulfil their art 36 legal review obligation to determine the legality of AWS? This is a challenging question. While there is academic discourse and evidence of state practice on the legal review of conventional, human operated weapons, there is little in relation AWS. Many states have called for the voluntary exchange of best practice for the legal review of AWS[8] however few states have publicly disclosed their national approach to the legal review of AWS. This book seeks to contribute to the knowledge of the art 36 legal review (referred to as the 'legal reviews') obligation as it applies to AWS.

This book provides insights for both academics and practitioners in bridging the gap between law and practice. It uniquely provides a step-by-step process to undertake the review, in consideration of the unique challenges that autonomy places upon the conduct of such a review. This material has contributed to the development of confidence building measures, in the form of the Expert Meetings instigated by Damian; and provides those States yet to adopt a legal review process with a practical starting point to adopt for incorporating AWS into their military arsenals in a considered, and lawful way. The universalisation of legal reviews is critical in a time of increasing non-compliance with the laws of armed conflict, and a key confidence building measure in light of the uncertainties posed by AWS. This book provides practical guidance, well-grounded in State practice and with academic rigour to support this universalisation process.

Dr Lauren Sanders, CSC
Adjunct Associate Professor
University of Queensland

7 *Convention on Prohibitions or Restrictions on the Use of Certain Conventional Weapons Which May be Deemed to be Excessively Injurious or to Have Indiscriminate Effects* (10 October 1980) and Amendment to Article 1 (21 December 2001) 1342 UNTS 137 ('CCW').

8 See, e.g., for Argentina, *Questionnaire on the Legal Review Mechanisms of New Weapons, Means and Methods of Warfare*, GGE on LAWS, UN Doc CCW/GGE.1/2019/WP.6 (29 March 2019) (Argentina Questionnaire).

Acknowledgements

This book was originally written as my doctoral thesis at the Australian National University. I would like to express my sincere gratitude to my supervisors, Professor Robert McLaughlin, Professor Hitoshi Nasu and Dr William Boothby, for their patience, guidance, support and advice.

I am also very grateful to my colleagues within the Australian Department of Defence, Military Legal Services. In particular, thank you to Air Commodore Patrick Keane for his generous support and to Colonel Penny Saultry and Wing Commander Julian Tattersall for their support, suggestions and feedback.

Thank you also to my colleagues at the University of Queensland's Law and Future of War Team; Professor Rain Liivoja for his calm wisdom, guidance and insight; and Dr Lauren Sanders, Dr Simon McKenzie, Dr Eve Massingham and Dr Tim McFarland for their expertise, collegiate and generous support.

Many others have influenced my thinking and research, including Dr Vincent Boulanin from the Stockholm Institute for Peace Research, Ms Netta Goussac of Lexbridge Lawyers, Dr Natalia Jevglevskaja from the University of New South Wales, Dr S Kate Conroy from the Trusted Autonomous Systems Defence Cooperative Research Centre.

Most importantly, thank you to my darling wife Lise and children Manning, Taran and Timothy, who have shared this journey with me. All of you are a constant source of support, motivation and inspiration.

Tables

Abbreviations

ADF	Australian Defence Force
AI	Artificial Intelligence
AP 1	1977 Additional Protocol I to the Geneva Convention
AP 2	1977 Additional Protocol II to the Geneva Conventions
ATT	Arms Trade Treaty
AWS	Autonomous Weapons Systems
BCW	Biological Weapons Convention
CCW	United Nations Convention on Certain Conventional Weapons
CIL	Customary International Law
DARPA	Defence Advanced Research Projects Agency
DCDC	Development Concepts and Doctrine Centre
DSTG	Defence Science and Technology Group
EOTS	Electro-Optical Targeting System
ERW	Explosive Remnants of War
GGE	Group of Governmental Experts
GPS	Global Positioning System
IAC	International Armed Conflict
ICC	International Criminal Court
ICJ	International Court of Justice
ICRC	International Committee of the Red Cross
ICTR	International Criminal Tribunal for Rwanda
ICTY	International Criminal Tribunal for the Former Yugoslavia
IHL	International Humanitarian Law
IHRL	International Human Rights Law
LAWS	Lethal Autonomous Weapons Systems
LOAC	Law of Armed Conflict
MoD	Ministry of Defence
NLW	Non-lethal Weapons
NATO	North Atlantic Treaty Organization
NGO	Non-governmental Organisation
NIAC	Non-International Armed Conflict
ROE	Rules of Engagement
SI/US	Superfluous Injury or Unnecessary Suffering
SIPRI	Stockholm International Peace Research Institute
TASDCRC	Defence Trusted Autonomous Systems Defence Cooperative Research Centre
TTPS	Tactics, Techniques and Procedures

UAVs	Uncrewed Aerial Vehicles
UK	United Kingdom
UN	United Nations
US	United States
WW1	First World War
WW2	Second World War

Glossary

Artificial Intelligence (AI)	Artificial intelligence includes a broad class of techniques in which seemingly intelligent behaviour is demonstrated by machines.
Autonomous Weapon System (AWS)	There is no internationally agreed definition of an 'autonomous weapon system'. One view is that autonomy in weapons exists on a scale ranging from automatic through to fully autonomous. International debate focuses primarily on 'fully' autonomous weapons being those that, once activated, can select and engage targets without direct human intervention. This book focuses on this category of AWS rather than existing semi-autonomous weapons (e.g., US Navy's Phalanx Close-In Weapon System) that have been in military service for decades.

PART 1

Is the Traditional Approach to Legal Reviews Sufficient to Determine the Legality of Autonomous Weapon Systems?

Introduction to Part 1

> If man does not master technology, but allows it to master him, he will be destroyed by technology.[1]

Part 1 of this book addresses the fundamental question, is the traditional approach to the legal review of weapons sufficient to determine the legality of AWS? In doing so it sets the foundations for the key conclusions and findings of this book. It contains five chapters that analyse the existing process for legal reviews, referred to as the traditional legal review process, and considers whether this process is insufficient to determine the legality of AWS.

After this introductory chapter, Chapter 2 analyses academic literature and state policy across three broad periods since the inception of the legal review obligations. It identifies several important scholarly works that define the scope of the legal review obligation and considers how these apply to autonomy in weapons.

Chapter 3 analyses how international law regulates a state's possession and use of AWS by surveying the specific and general international law prohibitions and restrictions reveals that determines the legality of weapons *per se*. It notes that international law does not expressly prohibit or restrict autonomy in weapons and argues that the predominant risk in the legality of AWS relates to its use. Recognising that, in addition to legal risks, AWS raise ethical, moral and operational challenges Chapter 3 also considers the Martens clause and its role in considering national AWS policy in the conduct of a legal review.

Chapter 4 analyses the sources and scope of the legal review obligation. In doing so, it identifies a number of traditional interpretations that influences the scope of the legal review and considers whether these are sufficient to address autonomy in weapons. It also asks whether these interpretations require reconsideration in light of the increased role of defence industry and research organisations, the potential for AWS capable of machine learning to change

1 Y Sandoz, C Swinarski and B Zimmerman (eds), *Commentary on the Additional Protocols of 8 June 1977 to the Geneva Conventions of 12 August 1949* (ICRC and Martinus Nijhoff, Geneva, 1987) ('*ICRC Commentary*') art 36 [1476].

 DOI:10.1163/9789004707047_002

method of use and therefore become 'new', and finally the possibility of AWS performing normal or expected uses in unpredictable and unintended ways.

Finally, Chapter 5 analyses the 'traditional legal review' process and concludes that this approach focusses primarily on a weapon's legality *per se* without in depth analysis of relevant targeting law. It identifies a legal review dichotomy between weapons law and targeting law and argues that the traditional legal review process is insufficient to determine the legality of AWS as it presumes, rather than determines, that the weapon will be used lawfully in armed conflict. Where an AWS design includes functions that are governed by IHL, the traditional approach does not determine its ability to do so in compliance with targeting law.

CHAPTER 1

Introduction

Military weapons technology has always influenced the way in which armed conflict is conducted. From the invention of the longbow and crossbow to gunpowder, cannon, rifles, artillery, machine-gun and guided and precision-guided weapons, the nature of armed conflict has reflected developments in weapon technology. In the past decades, new weapons technology has enabled combatants to be increasingly separated from their adversaries.[1]

While advances in weapon technology are not new, humans have traditionally been directly in control of and responsible for weapon use in armed conflict. This paradigm is changing using artificial intelligence (AI) to augment or even replace human decision-making on the battlefield.[2] This presents significant legal, moral, ethical and philosophical challenges for states developing autonomous weapon systems enhanced by AI (hereafter AWS) for use in armed conflict.

The drivers for the automation of force on the battlefield are many. They include the need for rapid decision-making in response to immediate threats, the desire to fulfil the humanitarian obligation to protect victims of armed conflict by reducing human errors that lead to unintended collateral damage and the military desire to develop weaponry that is more effective. These drivers were enabled in the past two decades by significant advances in computer power, data availability and computer programming improvements.[3] These have combined to allow rapid developments in military AI applications. Since 2012, advances in AI machine learning, particularly deep learning, have seen developments in AI image understanding, intelligent decision-making, artificial creativity, natural language processing and physical automation.[4]

1 For example, during the US Operation Enduring Freedom (2001–2014), US drone pilots remotely flew uncrewed aircraft in Afghanistan and Iraq from the Creech Air Force Base in Nevada, US: <https://www.cbsnews.com/news/air-force-anti-terrorism-drone-program-behind-the-scenes/>.

2 G Moy et al, *Technical Report: Recent Advances in Artificial Intelligence and their Impact on Defence* (Defence Science and Technology Group, May 2020) vii ('DSTG Report') <https://www.dst.defence.gov.au/publication/recent-advances-artificial-intelligence-and-their-impact-defence>.

3 Ibid iii.

4 Ibid.

 DOI:10.1163/9789004707047_003

Such advances in technologies have generated what is described as an autonomous arms race, with the United States (US), Russia and China all making significant progress.[5] These countries are closely followed by the United Kingdom (UK), France and Israel.[6] While there is a proliferation of automatic 'fire and forget' weapons,[7] it is likely that there will be an increased use of AI to achieve greater autonomy in the use of force in armed conflict. The Australian Defence Force (ADF) predicts that the use of AI in military capabilities will progress from enhancing humans' use of existing technology to augmenting and finally replacing elements of human decision-making in machine-teaming operations.[8]

Automating the use of force in armed conflict is not new. Land and sea mines and booby traps are methods of warfare that, for more than a century, have separated human decision making and control from the actual weapon effect. This separation can be measured in days, years and, regrettably, even decades. International humanitarian law (IHL) has a long history of addressing new weapons technologies.[9] However, there is a distinction between automated methods of warfare and the use of AWS to perform tasks governed by IHL. For example, there is a clear link between the human decision to deploy a mine or booby trap and its harmful effect. The development of increasing autonomy in weapons threatens this link and may create a gap in human responsibility where an AI system is interposed between the human and a weapon effect.

In the past 40 years, technology has enabled greater temporal and geographic separation between those who plan or decide upon an attack and the weapon effect. This trend includes the development and use of increasingly sophisticated automated weapons that, once activated, are capable of automatic operation without direct human control. Weapons such as the US Navy's Phalanx Close-In Weapon System (C-IWS) are principally defensive weapons designed to defend warships against fast-moving anti-ship missiles and other close-in threats.[10] The C-IWS integrates vertical-launch missiles and the Phalanx point

5 D Mauri, *Autonomous Weapons Systems and the Protection of the Human Person: An International Law Analysis* (Edward Elgar Publishing, 2022) 119.

6 Ibid.

7 See, eg, IAI, *IAI Harpy* (Website) <https://www.iai.co.il/p/harpy>.

8 Australian Government, Australia Defence Force, *Concept for Robotic and Autonomous Systems*, Version 1 (25 November 2020) 28 ('ADF RASAI Concept').

9 For example, *Hague Convention (VIII) Relative to the Laying of Automatic Submarine Contact Mines*, opened for signature 18 October 1907, 205 CTS 331 (entered into force 26 January 1910).

10 Raytheon Missiles and Defence, *Phalanx Close In Weapon System* (Web Page) <https://www.raytheonmissilesanddefense.com/capabilities/products/phalanx-close-in-weapon-system>.

defence Gatling gun into an anti-air warfare and anti-ballistic missile suite that can automatically track, target, and destroy incoming missiles and aircraft.[11] Such weapons operate within narrow operational and technical parameters and target objects with specific signatures that enable accurate, although not infallible,[12] target identification. These weapons are automatic and, as they rely on programming rather than AI, are not considered to be AWS for the purpose of this book.

However, in March 2021, the final report of the United Nations (UN) Panel of Experts on Libya described the Government of National Accord Affiliated Force's use of an AWS, an STM Kargu-2 drone, to attack logistics convoys and retreating Hafter Affiliated Forces.[13] The AWS 'were programmed to attack targets without requiring data connectivity between the operator and the munition'.[14] This report records one of the first uses of an AWS in armed conflict, which occurred against the background of an AI arms race involving military nations, including Russia, China and the US.[15] The use of AI and autonomy in the ongoing conflicts in Ukraine and Gaza are further evidence of their impact on the conduct of hostilities.

States party to the First Additional Protocol to the Geneva Conventions of 1949 (AP 1) are required by art 36 to determine the legality of new weapons, means or methods of warfare. Article 36 states:

> In the study, development, acquisition or adoption of a new weapon, means or method of warfare, a High Contracting Party is under an obligation to determine whether its employment would, in some or all circumstances, be prohibited by this Protocol or by any other rule of international law applicable to the High Contracting Party.[16]

11 Kraska, J & Pedrozo, R. A., *Disruptive Technology and the Law of Naval Warfare* (2022) Oxford University Press, 109.

12 The 1988 incident where an Iranian civilian Airbus was accidentally shot down in the Persian Gulf by the *USS Vincennes* via Aegis C-IWS, killing 290 passengers and crew: <https://www.usni.org/magazines/proceedings/1989/may/vincennes-incident>.

13 United Nations, *Final Report of the Panel of Experts on Libya Established Pursuant to Security Council Resolution 1972*, UN Doc S/2021/229 (2011) [63] ('UN Report on Libya').

14 Ibid.

15 Mauri (n 5) 119.

16 *Protocol Additional to the Geneva Conventions of 12 August 1949, and relating to the Protection of Victims of International Armed Conflicts (Protocol I)*, opened for signature 8 June 1977, 1125 UNTS 3 (entered into force 7 December 1978) ('AP 1'), art 36.

Despite there being 174 states party to the AP 1, fewer than 20 states are known to have implemented national art 36 legal review processes.[17]

The term 'AWS' is used throughout this book to describe the range of weapons that use AI to enable autonomous functionality enabling the use of force in armed conflict. This book identifies several definitions of AWS but does not discuss the need for or content of a universal definition. The book distinguishes AWS from other automated weapons that operate on pre-programmed instructions to perform specific, well-defined tasks in controlled environments. Accordingly, weapons such as the Phalanx C-IWS ship defence system and the land-based version known as the Counter-Rocket, Artillery and Mortar (C-RAM) system[18] are not considered to be AWS and within the scope of this book.

1 Aim

The aim of this book is to analyse how a state party to AP 1 can fulfil its art 36 legal review obligation to determine the legality of AWS.

To achieve this aim, the book considers two broad questions. First, is the traditional legal review process sufficient to determine the legality of AWS? Second, how can a state conduct a legal review to determine the legality of an AWS?

To answer these questions, this book argues:

1. there is limited academic discourse or evidence of state practice relating to the legal review of AWS;
2. in the absence of international law specifically or generally regulating AWS, the primary IHL risk relates to their use. As such rules governing the lawful use of a weapon are critical to determining the legality of AWS;
3. the current interpretations of several of art 36's operative terms are challenged by the use of autonomy in weapons;
4. AWS raise ethical, moral and operational challenges, e.g., human control, that states may address through national policy and consider during a legal review under the Marten clause;
5. there is a dichotomy in the traditional legal review analysis between weapons law (concerned with the legality of a weapon *per se*) and targeting law (concerned with the lawful use of weapons in specific

17 Asia-Pacific Institute for Law and Security, (2024) *Portal on the Legal Review of Weapons* (Website) <https://apils.org/>.

18 See Counter-Rocket, Artillery and Mortar System (website) <https://asc.army.mil/web/portfolio-item/ms-c-ram_lpws/>.

circumstances). The traditional legal review analysis focusses primarily on a weapon's compliance with weapons law and does not consider compliance with targeting law;

6. if an AWS is designed to perform functions that are governed by targeting law, e.g., distinguish between lawful and unlawful targets, the AWS' ability to perform this function in compliance with targeting law must be determined during a legal review;
7. the legal review of AWS raises interpretive and methodological challenges that need to be addressed in the legal review;
8. an additional 'functional review' step is required in the legal review of AWS to determine its compliance with both weapons law and targeting law. This step should also consider compliance with national policies addressing other ethical, moral and operational challenges raised by AWS; and
9. the legal review process for an AWS should be expanded beyond the military acquisition process to include informing the early study and development, determining the legality prior to acquisition and governing its ongoing legality during its in-service use.

2 Methodology and Scope

Consistent with its aim, this book is in two parts. Part 1 analyses the existing process for legal reviews and concludes that it is insufficient to determine the legality of AWS. Following this introductory chapter, Chapter 2 reviews the literature that has shaped the interpretation of the art 36 terms and the legal review obligation. It illustrates how, until very recently, academic literature has not examined the legal review of AWS nor questioned whether the traditional interpretations of the art 36 obligation remain suitable for weapons which rely on AI to perform tasks. It also identifies the absence of state practice in the legal review of AWS. To help explain why the traditional legal review process is insufficient for the legal review of AWS, Chapters 3 and 4 describe how international law regulates weapons and the sources and scope of the legal review obligation, respectively. These chapters are followed in Chapter 5 by a survey of state legal review practice and identification of a common steps referred to as the traditional legal review process. These chapters demonstrate that the traditional legal review process is focused on determining the legality of weapons per se and presumes that a weapon user will use the weapon in accordance with IHL. This book questions whether this is appropriate for AWS that make decisions governed by IHL and is the basis for arguing that the traditional legal review process is insufficient to determine the legality of AWS. Part 1 concludes that the traditional legal review process is insufficient to determine the legality of AWS as it does not consider the weapon's ability to be used in compliance with targeting law. This conclusion provides the basis for proposing in Part 2 modifications to the legal review process to determine the legality of AWS functions that are governed by targeting law.

Part 2 contains four chapters. Chapter 6 analyses the interpretive and methodological questions that arise in the art 36 obligation as it relates to AWS, including the dichotomy in the traditional legal review process between weapons law and targeting law. It argues that the legal review process must assess the AWS' ability to perform its autonomous functions in compliance with IHL targeting rules. This requires states to identify which rules govern the AWS' functions and decide what standards are required to determine compliance with IHL. To address these challenges, Chapter 7 proposes an additional step in the traditional legal review process called the 'functional review' step. This step is designed to analyse each AWS function that is governed by IHL rules. This analysis includes consideration of quasi-legal considerations, including the appropriate level of human control of AWS functions based on a legal risk assessment. Chapter 8 then proposes the traditional legal review process be expanded beyond 'study, development, acquisition or adoption' to include informing industry research into AWS technology and during the AWS in-service life. Finally, Chapter 9 reiterates the findings and conclusions of the book.

3 Why Is This Important?

There is a significant gap in academic discourse and state practice concerning the legal review of AWS. This is recognised by the participants in the ongoing UN GGE on lethal autonomous weapon systems (LAWS), where states have called for a compendium of relevant principles, best practices and interpretations of existing law.[19] This includes identifying the elements of best practice

19 Australia, Canada, Japan, the Republic of Korea, the UK and the US, 'Principles and Good Practices on Emerging Technologies in the Area of Lethal Autonomous Weapons Systems' (GGE LAWS, 7 March 2022) <https://reachingcriticalwill.org/images/documents/Disarmament-fora/ccw/2022/gge/documents/USgroup_March2022.pdf>. See also United Kingdom, 'Proposal for a GGE Document on the Application of International Humanitarian Law to Emerging Technologies in the Area of Lethal Autonomous Weapon Systems (LAWS)' (GGE LAWS, March 2022) <https://reachingcriticalwill.org/images/documents/Disarmament-fora/ccw/2022/gge/documents/UK_March2022.pdf>.

for the conduct of art 36 legal reviews.[20] Some elements of civil society even question states' ability to conduct legal reviews of AWS at all.[21]

At the time of writing, a detailed study of the art 36 legal review of AWS has not been published.[22] This is concerning given the events in Libya, Ukraine and Gaza and the so-called autonomous arms race.[23] This book argues that the purpose of the legal review is not only to assess the legality of such systems at the very early stages of their development but also to inform their study and development. This is to ensure that the IHL rules and principles relevant to their autonomous function are understood by those programming their algorithms and training their artificial neural networks.

To help resolve this gap, this book analyses the law and its application in determining the legality of a new weapon, means or method of warfare under art 36 of AP 1. It proposes an amended legal review process during the lifecycle of an AWS. In arguing for such an approach, this book challenges existing interpretations of the art 36 obligation to address the technical, legal and ethical issues raised by autonomy in weapons.

4 Conclusions and Findings

The key conclusions and findings of this book are:

a. there is limited academic discourse or evidence of state practice relating to the legal review of AWS;
b. in the absence of international law specifically regulating AWS, IHL rules governing the lawful use of a weapon are critical to determining the legality of AWS;
c. in addition to legal challenges, AWS raise ethical, moral and operational challenges that states may address through national policy and consider during a legal review;

---

20 *Draft Report of the 2019 Session of the Group of Governmental Experts on Emerging Technologies in the Area of Lethal Autonomous Weapons Systems*, UN Doc CCW/GGE.1/2019/CRP.1/Rev.2 (21 August 2019) <https://www.unog.ch/80256EDD006B8954/(httpAssets)/5497DF9B01E5D9CFC125845E00308E44/$file/CCW_GGE.1_2019_CRP.1_Rev2.pdf>.

21 See, for example, Human Rights Watch, *Making the Case: The Dangers of Killer Robots and the Need for a Preemptive Ban* (2016) 33 <https://www.hrw.org/sites/default/files/report_pdf/arms1216_web.pdf>.

22 The ICRC plans to publish an updated version of its 2006 Guide to the Weapons review of New Weapons, Means and Methods of Warfare in 2024.

23 Mauri (n 5) 119.

d. the traditional interpretations of the art 36 obligation are challenged by the use of autonomy in weapons;
e. there is a dichotomy in the traditional legal review analysis between weapons law, concerned with the legality of a weapon per se, and targeting law which regulates the lawful use of weapons in specific circumstances;
f. the legal review of AWS raises interpretive and methodological challenges that may be addressed via a revised legal review process;
g. an additional 'functional review' step is required in the legal review of AWS to determine the AWS' ability to operate in compliance with IHL, including targeting law;
h. the traditional legal review process is not sufficient to determine the legality of AWS as it does not determine the legality of AWS functions governed by IHL or consider the other quasi-legal issues raised by AWS. Considering this finding, this book proposes:
    i. an expanded approach to the legal review of AWS. This expanded approach consists of a functional review step in addition to the traditional legal review process, and
    ii. an expanded scope of the legal review process that spans the entire lifecycle of the weapon.

CHAPTER 2

A Survey of Academic Discourse on Legal Reviews

In contrast to the broader body of IHL, academic discourse and state practice concerning the art 36 legal review of AWS is scarce and comparatively recent. The dearth of state practice is unsurprising as AWS are a relatively new military capability and few states are known to have established formal national processes for the conduct of legal reviews.[1] The academic debate is in equal parts influenced by and reflective of this fact. It is important that these contextual foundations are properly established before embarking upon a more detailed analysis of legal reviews and AWS. There are three discernible periods of academic discourse concerning legal reviews identified in this chapter. These are described in this book as the International Committee of the Red Cross (ICRC) period, the LAWS period and the Convention on Certain Conventional Weapons (CCW) Group of Governmental Experts (GGE) period.

The ICRC period, from 1987 to 2006, set important foundations for how states conduct weapon reviews. It is characterised by the ICRC's efforts to broaden state awareness and understanding of the art 36 legal review obligation and to encourage compliance by states party to AP 1. This period was followed by academic literature written in the context of the UN debate on LAWS and is divided into two phases. The initial period of CCW, broadly during the period of expert meetings from 2014 to 2018, was influenced by, among others, reports from the Stockholm International Peace Research Institute (SIPRI)[2] representing the first academic efforts to consider the legal review obligation in the context of AWS. The final CCW GGE period, from 2018 to the present, saw a proliferation of academic literature concerning the legal review of AWS. It included blog posts by academics on the ICRC's Humanitarian Law & Policy website[3] and

1 Asia-Pacific Institute for Law and Security, (2024) *Portal on the Legal Review of Weaponsl* (Website) <https://apils.org/> ICRC, *A Guide to the Weapons Review of New Weapons, Means and Methods of Warfare: Measures to Implement Article 36 of Additional Protocol I of 1977* (2006) ('ICRC Guide') fn 8; V Boulanin and M Verbruggen, *SIPRI Compendium on Article 36 Reviews* (SIPRI, December 2017) <https://www.sipri.org/publications/2017/sipri-background-papers/sipri-compendium-article-36-reviews>.

2 Stockholm International Peace Research Institute (Website) <https://www.sipri.org/>.

3 D Copeland and L Sanders, 'Engaging with the Industry: Integrating IHL into New Technologies in Urban Warfare', *International Committee of the Red Cross: Humanitarian*

 DOI:10.1163/9789004707047_004

others.[4] Notably, this period included the publication of important texts by Dr Tim McFarland[5] and Dr Diego Mauri,[6] analysing the compatibility of AWS with IHL and by Dr Natalia Jevglevskaja on legal reviews generally.[7]

1 The ICRC Period (1987–2006)

Legal reviews are a comparatively new obligation in international law. While states such as the US[8] and Sweden[9] have formally assessed the legality of weapons since the early 1970s the express international law obligation did not exist prior to AP 1 entering into force on 7 December 1978.[10]

The ICRC period, between 1987 and 2006, reflects the ICRC's efforts to encourage states party to AP 1 to complete legal reviews in compliance with art 36. The challenges posed by the legal review of AWS were not a feature of the literature of this period as international debate concerning AWS did not emerge until the early 2010s.[11]

The ICRC was thus highly influential in the early academic literature concerning the art 36 legal review obligation. Their initial aim was not only to illustrate the nature and scope of the legal review obligation but to encourage states to

---

Law and Policy Blog (Blog Post, 7 October 2021) <https://blogs.icrc.org/law-and-policy/2021/10/07/industry-ihl-new-technologies/>.

4 L Sanders and D Copeland, 'Holding Autonomy to Account: Legal Standards for Autonomous Weapon Systems', *West Point: Articles of War Blog* (Blog Post, 15 September 2021) <https://lieber.westpoint.edu/holding-autonomy-account-legal-standards-autonomous-weapon-systems/>.

5 T McFarland, *Autonomous Weapon Systems and the Law of Armed Conflict: Compatibility with International Humanitarian Law* (Cambridge University Press, 2020).

6 D Mauri, *Autonomous Weapons Systems and the Protection of the Human Person: An International Law Analysis* (Edward Elgar Publishing, 2022).

7 N Jevglevskaja, *International Law and Weapons Review: Emerging Military Technology under the Laws of Armed Conflict* (Cambridge University Press, 2021).

8 US Department of Defense, Instruction 5500.15 *Review of Legality of Weapons under International Law* (16 October 1974).

9 *Förordning om folkrättslig granskning av vapenprojekt* [Ordinance on the International Law Review of Arms Projects] SFS 2007:936 (15 November 2007) <https://www.riksdagen.se/sv/dokument-lagar/dokument/svensk-forfattningssamling/forordning-2007936-om-folkrattslig-granskning_sfs-2007-936>.

10 United Nations, Audiovisual Library of International Law <https://legal.un.org/avl/ha/pagc/pagc.html>.

11 International Human Rights Clinic and Human Rights Watch, *Losing Humanity: The Case Against Killer Robots* (IHRC and HRW, 2012) ('Losing Humanity') <https://www.hrw.org/report/2012/11/19/losing-humanity/case-against-killer-robots> was an early catalyst for international debate on autonomous weapons.

develop internal processes to conduct legal reviews. The ICRC authored or published several important studies, culminating in the 2006 release of the *Guide to the Legal review of New Weapons Means and Methods of Warfare: Measures to Implement Article 36 of Additional Protocol I of 1977* ('ICRC Guide').[12]

The ICRC's 1987 Commentary on AP 1 records some of the formal debate during the Diplomatic Conferences held to draft the Additional Protocols to the Geneva Conventions between 1974 and 1977.[13] Importantly this included a detailed explanation of the nature and scope of the art 36 obligation. This source is significant as it clarifies several important issues concerning the interpretation of art 36. First, it confirms that the nature of art 36 is one of internal state self-assessment, and as such, it 'impl[ies] the obligation to establish internal procedures with a view to elucidating the problem of illegality'.[14] Article 36 does not require a particular approach. Second, the ICRC affirms that a determination of the legality of a particular weapon is made based on the weapon's normal use as anticipated at the time of evaluation.[15] The commentary adds that a state 'is not required to foresee or analyse all possible misuses of a weapon for almost any weapon can be misused in ways that would be prohibited'.[16] This is an important issue that is discussed in Chapter 4 and one that this book challenges in the context of AWS. The ICRC Commentary on AP 1 confirms that the nature of a state determination of legality is not intended to create a subjective standard and is not internationally binding. Consequently, a state is not obligated to make its findings public.[17] Interestingly, although this view remains valid in contemporary debate concerning the regulation of autonomous weapons, there are increasing calls to states to, consistent with art 84 of AP 1,[18] communicate their laws and regulations adopted in the application of AP 1 obligations. Considering this obligation, the ICRC has called on states

12 ICRC Guide (n 1).

13 Y Sandoz, C Swinarski and B Zimmerman (eds), *Commentary on the Additional Protocols of 8 June 1977 to the Geneva Conventions of 12 August 1949* (ICRC and Martinus Nijhoff, Geneva, 1987) ('ICRC Commentary') [1463]–[1482].

14 Ibid [1466].

15 Ibid.

16 Ibid.

17 Ibid [1469].

18 *Protocol Additional to the Geneva Conventions of 12 August 1949, and relating to the Protection of Victims of International Armed Conflicts (Protocol I)*, opened for signature 8 June 1977, 1125 UNTS 3 (entered into force 7 December 1978) ('*AP I*'), art 84 states, 'The High Contracting Parties shall communicate to one another, as soon as possible, through the depositary and, as appropriate, though the Protecting Powers, their official translations of this Protocol, *as well as the laws and regulations which they may adopt to ensure its application*' [emphasis added].

to share national legal review mechanisms and procedures.[19] More recently, states participating in the UN GGE on LAWS have emphasised the need to exchange 'best practices to conduct legal reviews on a voluntary basis'.[20]

Finally, the ICRC's Commentary on AP I emphasises that the art 36 obligation is concerned with the legality of weapons in armed conflict and not their possession by a state. It distinguishes the latter as a disarmament issue, which is not the intended purpose of art 36.[21] Acknowledging the purpose of art 36 is to ensure a state's use of weapons complies with AP I and its other international law obligations and not create a mechanism for weapon disarmament, the ICRC's Commentary correctly identifies that a state legal review process must consider those arms control treaty obligations binding on a reviewing state.

The ICRC Commentary on AP I acknowledges 'the problem of evaluation' by posing the rhetorical question, 'On what basis can or should this evaluation be made?'[22] In doing so, the commentary deliberately avoids any discussion of possible legal review mechanisms.[23] This is appropriate given its intended purpose is 'commentary' rather than 'guide'. The ICRC's intention was to assist in the understanding of the law rather than advise on its practical application. However, this gap in practical understanding of the legal review obligation was recognised by the ICRC and addressed in the early 2000s.

Interestingly, the ICRC Commentary on AP I notes 'future arms', citing an expert's concerns with 'geophysical, ecological, electronic and radiological warfare as well as with devices generating radiation, microwaves, infrasonic waves, light flashes and laser beams'. It prophetically adds:

> The use of long-distance, remote-control weapons, or weapons connected to sensors positioned in the field, leads to the automation of the battlefield in which the soldier plays an increasingly less important role.[24]

---

19 28th International Conference of the Red Cross and Red Crescent, Geneva (2003) Res. 1, *Adoption of the Declaration and Agenda for Humanitarian Action* (Final Goal 2.5) 20. <http://www.icrc.org/en/doc/assets/files/other/icrc_002_1103.pdf>.

20 For example, Argentina, *Questionnaire on the Legal Review Mechanisms of New Weapons, Means and Methods of Warfare*, GGE on LAWS, UN Doc CCW/GGE.1/2019/WP.6 (29 March 2019) ('Argentina Questionnaire').

21 ICRC Commentary (n 13) [1471].

22 Ibid [1472].

23 Ibid.

24 Ibid.

The ICRC Commentary asserts, without citation, 'all predictions agree that if man does not master technology, but allows it to master him, he will be destroyed by technology'.[25]

The ICRC addressed the issue of legal review practice during the 27th Conference of the Red Cross and Red Crescent, held in Geneva in 1999. Recognising that only a few states had national legal review mechanisms or procedures, they adopted a Plan of Action to enable the ICRC to consult with states on legal reviews.[26] This initiative was followed in 2001 by an expert meeting on the legal review of weapons and their Superfluous Injury and Unnecessary Suffering ('SIrUS') Project.[27] The meeting was intended to promote the establishment of national legal review mechanisms and to consider the nature of injuries caused by weapons.[28]

In the early 2000s, several authors published scholarly papers on legal reviews in the ICRC journal, *The International Review of the Red Cross*. These papers expanded on the ICRC's Commentary concerning the nature and conduct of art 36 legal reviews. The first article of note, titled 'New Wars, New Weapons? The Obligation of States to Assess the Legality of Means and Methods of Warfare', was co-written by Isabelle Daoust, Robin Coupland and Rikke Ishoey and published in 2002.[29] Despite its title, the article did not address new wars and new weapons in the sense of new methods of armed conflict and weapon technology, including autonomy in weapons. It did, however, raise two important issues. First, it discussed the relevance of the Martens clause to the art 36 obligation.[30] It identifies the role of the Martens clause[31] in addressing gaps in both treaty or customary international law. This is particularly applicable to the development of new technology weapons, such as autonomous weapons, which often outpaces the creation of new international law. However, the suggestion that the legality of weapons may be determined

25 Ibid.

26 ICRC, 'ICRC Expert Meeting on Weapons Reviews of Weapons and the SIrUS Project' (2001) 83(842) *International Review of the Red Cross* 539, 539–42 <https://international-review.icrc.org/sites/default/files/S156077550010584Xa.pdf>.

27 Ibid.

28 Ibid 539.

29 I Daoust, R Coupland and R Ishoey, 'New Wars, New Weapons? The Obligation of States to Assess the Legality of Means and Methods of Warfare' (2002) 84 (846) *International Review of the Red Cross* 245, 345–62.

30 Ibid 351.

31 AP 1 (n 18) art 1(2) states, 'In cases not covered by this Protocol or by other international agreements, civilians and combatants remain under the protection and authority of the principles of international law derived from established custom, from the principles of humanity and from the dictates of public conscience'.

based on the Martens clause is not widely accepted. This book argues that the legal review of AWS may require consideration of issues beyond the application of legal rules and principles and so acknowledges the role of the Martens clause. While the 'principles of humanity and dictates of public conscience' do not create legal obligations, they permit national legal reviews to consider other considerations reflected in state policy, for example state policy on human control over the application of force in armed conflict. Second, the article identified the importance of multidisciplinary input into legal reviews. While this issue was identified during the ICRC's meeting of experts in 2001, it correctly emphasised the requirement to include expert advice to fully consider military, technical, health-related and environmental questions during the legal review.[32] There may be the requirement for multidisciplinary input for the legal review of AWS to include not only technical input from computer engineers and AI scientists but also advice from ethicists to assist in the application of moral and ethical considerations.

In 2003, the ICRC published a second article in their *International Review of the Red Cross* on the conduct of legal reviews. In contrast to the academic style of Daoust, Coupland and Ishoey (2002), it was written by Lieutenant-Colonel Justin McClelland, a legal officer in the British Army Legal Service, who provided a practitioner's perspective on legal reviews. His article was titled 'The Review of Weapons in Accordance with Article 36 of Additional Protocol I', and is significant because it identifies the relationship between the legal review process and the state's capability acquisition process.[33] This was important as, for the first time, it articulated how an art 36 legal review is able to inform government decisions during the development and acquisition of weapons. The article is also noteworthy as it developed the discussion by Daoust, Coupland and Ishoey on the different review methodologies adopted by states; for example, the committee method and the individual reviewer methods.[34] McClelland's article is also notable for its analysis of the scope of the art 36 legal review obligation and definition of key art 36 phrases such as 'new weapon, means or method of warfare' and describing, in practical terms, the legal criteria that should be applied during the legal review.[35]

32 See Daoust, Coupland and Ishoey (n 29); A Backstrom and I Henderson, 'New Capabilities in Warfare: An Overview of Contemporary Technological Developments and the Associated Legal and Engineering Issues in Article 36 Weapons Reviews' (2012) 94 (886) *International Review of the Red Cross* 483.

33 Justin McClelland, 'The Weapons Review of Weapons under Article 36 of Additional Protocol 1' (2003) 850 *International Review of the Red Cross* 397, 401.

34 Daoust, Coupland and Ishoey (n 29).

35 McClelland (n 33) 406–13.

McClelland's article also provided an important practitioner's perspective on key elements of the legal review, including the analysis of the prohibition on weapons that cause superfluous injury and unnecessary suffering.[36] McClelland suggests that, in determining whether a weapon causes superfluous injury or unnecessary suffering, there are qualitative and quantitative considerations.[37] He argues the former refers to the level of suffering caused to an individual, whereas the latter describes the scale of suffering. While he correctly argues that these levels of suffering are measured against the military advantage to be gained from using the weapon, he does not describe how the levels are objectively measured. Additionally, he does not address the second limb of art 35(2) prohibiting methods of warfare of a nature to cause superfluous injury or unnecessary suffering.[38]

McClelland's article expands the understanding of the art 36 phrase, 'new weapon, means or method of warfare'. Noting that this phrase is closely related to the art 35 phrase 'methods and means of warfare', McClelland explains that a weapon 'connotes an offensive capability that can apply to a military object or enemy combatant'.[39] This is consistent with the ICRC Commentary, which states, 'The words "methods and means" include weapons in the widest sense, as well as the way in which they are used'.[40] This approach treats the word 'weapons' as synonymous with the phrase 'means of warfare'. However, McClelland expands on the ICRC's narrower interpretation, suggesting that 'the concept refers to military equipment that is not a weapon per se but nonetheless has an impact on the offensive capability of the force to which it belongs'.[41] This is an important point as it recognises that a weapon may operate as a system that contains components that, while not directly causing harm or damage, are integral to the operation of the weapon system.

McClelland's article is widely cited and remains relevant to the legal review of conventional weapons. It does not, however, consider the application or status of the Martens clause or the legal review obligation in the context of new technology weapons. It reflects a traditional legal review process, which is appropriate for legal review of conventional, human-controlled weapons. There is, however, no consideration of how autonomy in weapons may affect the conduct of a legal review process.

---

36 Ibid 407.
37 Ibid.
38 Ibid.
39 Ibid 404.
40 ICRC Commentary (n 13) [1402].
41 McClelland (n 33) 405.

In 2006, Hays Parks, a well-known and respected international law practitioner with over three decades of experience conducting legal reviews for the United States military, published a comprehensive article titled 'Conventional Weapons and Legal Reviews'.[42] The article emphasises the distinction between the law regulating the legality weapons *vis-a-vis* the law regulating the use of otherwise lawful weapons. This distinction is drawn from the ICRC's Commentary on the scope of art 36, particularly that a state 'is not required to foresee or analyse all possible misuses of a weapon'. This book argues that the ICRC's interpretation of the art 36 scope is too narrow in relation to AWS that perform functions that are governed by IHL e.g. distinguishing between lawful and unlawful targets.

Hays Parks' article reflects his experience conducting legal reviews and provides an extensive analysis of the US legal review process and the legal criteria employed. It includes the legal tests applied during the legal review and examples of analysis.

In describing the general content of a legal review, Hays Parks' article identifies, but does not develop, an important issue concerning the scope of art 36. He explains that 'the obligations for legal review in art 36 are limited to steps up to and including acquisition'.[43] He adds that '[e]mployment of the weapon in a manner consistent with the law of war is a battlefield commander's responsibility'.[44] While these two statements are not developed during the article, they illustrate two important issues addressed by this book.

First, the article's suggestion that the art 36 legal review obligation is complete once a weapon has been acquired may be argued as inconsistent with the requirement to review an existing weapon that has been the subject of a modification.[45] Hays Parks identifies in his article that a 'product improvement programme for a pistol, rifle or carbine previously reviewed does not require an extensive memorandum of review'.[46] However, he does not expressly identify this as a review of a weapon post-acquisition. The important issue highlighted here is that the article indicates that the art 36 legal review obligation is linear and limited in duration. This view is consistent with both McClelland (2003) and Daoust, Coupland and Ishoey (2002). In contrast, this book argues that, for AWS, the art 36 legal review obligation must extend beyond the acquisition to

42 W Hays Parks, 'Conventional Weapons and Weapons Reviews' (2005) 8 *Yearbook of International Humanitarian Law* 55, 55–142.

43 Ibid 129.

44 Ibid.

45 ICRC Guide (n 1) 10.

46 Hays Parks (n 42) 110–11.

include the early design and in-service life of the weapon. This is to ensure the weapon's ongoing compliance with the reviewing state's legal and ethical obligations. This is particularly the case for weapons with AI capable of learning.

The second important issue raised by Hayes Parks is the dichotomy between the law regulating the legality of a weapon per se and the law regulating the use of a weapon on the battlefield. He correctly states that the responsibility for the latter rests with the military commander.[47] This dichotomy underpins a key presumption applied during a legal review of a conventional, human-controlled weapon, that an otherwise lawful weapon (as determined by a legal review) will be used lawfully on the battlefield. This presumption enables the legal reviewer to focus on these aspects of the weapon's normal or expected use that are relevant to the general prohibitions codified in art 35 of AP 1. This presumption is referred to in this book as the 'presumption of lawful use', and it is argued in Chapter 6 that this presumption is not applicable to any AWS functionality that engages a reviewing state's IHL obligations. This is because IHL accountability mechanisms that would otherwise apply to military commanders and weapon users do not apply to an AWS itself. Interestingly, Hays Parks identifies a corresponding 'presumption of legality' that military commanders need not be concerned about the legality of a weapon or ammunition issued to them.[48]

Hays Parks' article coincided with the release of the ICRC's Guide[49] and an ICRC seminar held in Jongny-sur-Vevey, Switzerland, held to encourage more states to implement their legal review obligations. The ICRC's underlying aim in publishing their guide was to assist states in establishing and improving national procedures for determining the legality of new weapons, means and methods of warfare. The ICRC Guide is divided into two parts. The first part is intended to clarify the scope of the art 36 obligations and outlines the types of weapons that are subject to a legal review, the international law rules these weapons must be assessed against, and evidence that may be required to complete a legal review. The second part addresses state legal review mechanisms and procedures to assist AP 1 states yet to establish formal legal review processes. This includes identifying the appropriate national authority for conducting legal reviews, the stages of the state procurement process at which reviews should occur and the procedures for decision-making and record-keeping.

47 Ibid 129.
48 Ibid 106.
49 ICRC Guide (n 1).

As a guide, this is a valuable, practical contribution to the study and application of art 36 of AP 1. It drew on contemporary – although limited[50] – state practice and the earlier academic publications described above. The guide is broadly focused as it is directed at dual audiences. First, it identifies and addresses issues that practitioners responsible for conducting an art 36 legal review will need to consider. It attempts to assist them by outlining the approaches and considerations necessary for the legal review of new weapons, means or methods of warfare. The second audience is members of governments who will ultimately establish an internal mechanism for the legal review of new weapons.

While the ICRC Guide addresses both audiences well, it is not without criticism. Hays Parks argues that the ICRC Guide's discussion concerning health-related considerations and environment-related considerations 'marginalises military necessity, a fundamental element in any legal review'.[51] He also challenges the ICRC's assessment of the customary international law status of certain weapons, namely bullets that flatten or expand easily in the human body and exploding bullets.[52] These points, supported by others,[53] emphasise the internal nature of legal reviews and the potential for differing interpretations of international law obligations.

The ICRC Guide fulfils its intended aim well and remains a useful document; however, it contains several limitations. First, the ICRC Guide is directed at the legal review of conventional weapons. As such, it does not address the challenges associated with the legal review of new technology weapons, including AWS and cyber weapons. While the ICRC Guide acknowledges 'the rapid development of weapons', it does not attempt to address potential legal review challenges raised by the development of new technology weapons.[54] In this regard, it limits its practical application to the legal review of existing conventional weapons or modifications to those weapons. Second, numerous challenges are not addressed in the ICRC Guide:

a) *Scope of the art 36 legal review obligation.* The ICRC Guide correctly states that the 'material scope of the article 36 legal review is therefore very broad'[55] and lists the range of weapons and circumstances

50 Ibid fn 8 identifies eight states known to have national weapons reviews: Australia, Belgium, the Netherlands, Norway, Sweden, the US, the UK and Germany.

51 Hays Parks (n 42) 136.

52 Ibid.

53 D Turns, 'Weapons in the ICRC Study on Customary International Humanitarian Law' (2006) 11(2) *Journal of Conflict and Security Law* 201, 201–37.

54 This is the subject of the updated ICRC Guide which us due to be released in 2024.

55 ICRC Guide (n 1) 8.

in which a weapon would fall within the art 36 legal review obligation. Unfortunately, noting that the art 36 phrase 'new weapon, means or method of warfare' is undefined in international law, it does not expand on its meaning beyond its own Commentary on AP 1. In particular, the ICRC Commentary on AP 1 states that 'methods and means' includes 'weapons in the widest sense, as well as the way in which they are used'.[56] This narrow explanation suggests that the phrase 'weapon, means or method of warfare' describes different aspects of a single weapon or device. It does not explore whether the art 36 legal review obligation can arise in the context of a means or method of warfare in isolation of a weapon. This is a narrow interpretation and does not provide practical assistance in the context of new technology weapons. For example:

i) *AI as a means of warfare.* This book argues that an AWS' AI system designed to inform human decisions concerning the use of force may be categorised by a reviewing state as a means of warfare, separately from a weapon system it is associated with. In this regard, the art 36 legal review obligation may attach to an AI system independently of, and in addition to, a weapon. An example may be an AI system designed to que an AWS operator on to potential targets. In this respect, an AI system may be subject to a legal review by itself but also as a component of a weapon system.

ii) *AI as a method of warfare.* The ICRC Commentary on AP 1 suggests that the method of warfare is directly linked to a weapon in that it describes how the weapon is used. While this proposition is not challenged, it does not address whether the art 36 legal review obligation arises in the context of a method of warfare that is not directly linked to a weapon. IHL recognises methods of warfare that are not directly associated with weapon use (e.g., starvation and naval blockade). Such methods of warfare are not generally considered the subject of a legal review.[57] This is reflected in the use of the terminology 'legal review'. However, the development of new military capabilities, such as autonomous or cyber weapons that challenge traditional definitions of weapons but enable the use of force in armed conflict may require consideration by a legal review.

b) *When in doubt, seek legal advice.* The ICRC Guide follows its examples of the material scope of the legal review with a recommendation to seek legal advice from the legal review authority as to whether the device or

56 ICRC Commentary (n 13) [1402].

57 Based on the author's experience conducting art 36 reviews in the Australian Defence Force.

system proposed for study, development or acquisition is a weapon. This is appropriate but provides little by way of practical guidance for the legal adviser receiving such a request. The answer to such a question will require consideration of a range of factors, including state policy. If there is no policy, such as a legal review directive addressing the scope of the legal review, there is a risk of inconsistent advice. An important issue is which 'study or development' triggers the art 36 legal review obligation. This book argues that state-sponsored research and development organisation activities, such as Australia's TASDCRC or the US's Defence Advanced Research Projects Agency ('DARPA'), are within the scope of the legal review obligation.

c) *When does the legal review obligation end?* The ICRC Guide does not provide guidance on the temporal extent of the art 36 legal review obligation. A plain reading of the phrase 'study, development, acquisition or adoption' provides an indication that the legal review is required during one or more stages of a weapon entering into service of the reviewing state. While it is not indicated in either the ICRC's Guide or the Commentary to AP 1, the art 36 obligation is satisfied if the weapon successfully passes a legal review prior to its use in armed conflict. The ICRC Guide does, however, suggest that there is a requirement to reconsider the ongoing validity of a legal review if, following its introduction into service, there is a modification that alters its function or the reviewing state subsequently joins a new international treaty that may affect the legality of the weapon.[58] The ICRC Guide does not, however, consider the requirement for an ongoing legal review to ensure that any changes to its methods of operation, for example, because it is enhanced by an AI neural network, which is capable of machine learning, or to ensure that the data used to train and test an AWS, are appropriate for a new operating environment. This book argues the need for an ongoing legal 'governance' requirement for AWS throughout their in-service life cycle to ensure their ongoing compliance with IHL and international law.

d) *Scope and application of the Martens clause.* The ICRC Guide correctly highlights the relevance of the Martens clause to the legal review. It advises that during a legal review, 'Consideration should be given to whether the weapon accords with the principles of humanity and the dictates of public conscience' without providing further explanation of what these phrases mean in practice.[59] Moreover, the ICRC Guide

58 ICRC Guide (n 1) 9.

59 Ibid 15.

suggests that the Martens clause is a legal standard relevant to determining the legality of a weapon.[60] This view is not broadly accepted by academics[61] or states.[62] While this book does not argue that the Martens clause represents a separate legal standard beyond the existing principles of international law, it does regard the Martens clause as a mechanism enabling the reviewing state to consider broader, non-legal issues beyond specific or general weapon law prohibitions and restrictions including issues related to national policy. These issues are particularly prevalent where states develop a framework for the ethical use of AI.

e) *Empirical data to be considered.* The ICRC Guide provides practical advice on the data required to enable the conduct of a legal review. The data relevant to the nature and use of a weapon includes the technical description of the weapon, its technical performance, health-related considerations relating to the types of injuries caused and environmental factors. Such data remain relevant to the legal review of an AWS but do not capture the development and operation of an AWS. This book argues that the expanded approach to the legal review of an AWS will consist of two areas of legal analysis. The first relates to the weapon itself, and the empirical data required will follow closely the guidance provided by the ICRC in their guide. The second line of review will focus on the AWS functions that are governed by IHL targeting rules and principles. A proposed 'functional review' of AWS autonomous functions governed by IHL is discussed in Chapter 8.

f) *Test and evaluation.* The need to verify an AWS's ability to perform its functions in compliance with the state's legal and ethical requirements will require a thorough process of test and evaluation. The ICRC Guide does not discuss the requirement for or nature of testing data to inform a legal review. Testing may be undertaken by the defence project procuring the AWS capability or independently by the weapon manufacturer or selling state to inform the legal review. A test and evaluation process will focus on those aspects of the AI's functions that engage IHL rules and principles and is intended to identify circumstances in which

---

60 Ibid: 'A weapon which is not covered by existing rules of international humanitarian law would be considered contrary to the Martens clause if it is determined per se to contravene the principles of humanity or the dictates of public conscience.'

61 C Greenwood, 'The Law of Weaponry at the Start of the New Millennium' in Michael N Schmitt and Leslie C Green (eds), *The Law of Armed Conflict: Into the New Millennium* (U.S. Naval War College, 1999).

62 Australian Government, *The Australian Article 36 Review Process*, UN Doc CCW/GGE.2/2018/WP.6 (30 August 2018) fn 20 ('Australian Article 36 Review Process').

compliance is reduced. This book argues in Chapter 7 that a test and evaluation process should involve use cases and test scenarios that are consistent with the weapon's normal or expected use and anticipated operating environments.

g) *Review of methods of warfare.* The ICRC Guide emphasises the requirement for a legal review to consider the anticipated use of a weapon. However, this consideration is confined to the subject weapon's normal or expected use and only in relation to those aspects of use that concern the harm to civilians resulting from indiscriminate use and harm to combatants by causing suffering that is unnecessary in relation to the military advantage anticipated from the use of the weapon. The ICRC Guide does not consider the need for a legal review analysis to examine other IHL rules regulating methods of warfare as they are the responsibility of the weapon user, who is personally accountable for the lawful use of the weapon. This book argues in Chapter 6 that, where an AWS' functions are governed by IHL rules regulating its method of warfare, they should be analysed by the legal review.

The ICRC period concludes with the publication of their guide. The focus of this period was achieving greater state compliance with the art 36 obligation by clarifying the scope and method of conducting legal reviews.

Since 2018, the ICRC has undertaken a review of their guide. The purpose of this review was to include guidance on more contemporary issues relating to the legality of weapons, including the challenges raised by the development of new technology weapons.[63] The updated version of the ICRC Guide it is expected to be released in 2024.[64]

2 The LAWS Period (2012–2017)

With one notable exception, academic discourse concerning the legal review process waned following the release of the ICRC Guide. However, in 2009 Dr William Boothby published his book *Weapons and the Law of Armed Conflict*.[65] This important text, updated in 2016,[66] provides a detailed description and analysis of international law regulating weapons. It is an invaluable resource

63 Based on information provided to the author by the ICRC in November 2018.

64 Based on information provided to the author by the ICRC in November 2022.

65 W Boothby, *Weapons and the Law of Armed Conflict* (Cambridge University, 2009).

66 W Boothby, *Weapons and the Law of Armed Conflict* (Cambridge University Press, 2nd ed, 2016).

for lawyers and laypersons seeking to understand the history, scope and interpretations of international law concerning weapons. It includes a summary of the legal review obligation consistent with academic discourse during the ICRC period.

In 2012, international concern about the development of AWS raised the issue of legal reviews. Fuelled by predictions that Hollywood-inspired terminator robots would soon become a reality, non-government organisations, including the Campaign to Stop Killer Robots[67] and the International Committee for Robot Arms Control,[68] commenced campaigns seeking to encourage states to pre-emptively ban AWS (referred to 'LAWS').[69] This commenced a second period of academic debate concerning the legal review obligation and its role in the development of LAWS.

The significance of legal reviews in ensuring the legality of weapons used in armed conflict received increased international attention during the 'LAWS period'. In 2013, states party to the CCW agreed to convene informal Meetings of Experts at the UN in Geneva. This was followed in 2017 by an agreement to establish a mandate for a Group of Governmental Experts to 'assess questions related to emerging technologies in the area of lethal autonomous weapon systems'.[70]

The ICRC continued to play an active role during the LAWS period; however, their focus was more consistent with their traditional role of advocating for the application of IHL to protect the victims of armed conflict. Their contribution to the debate included a proposed definition of what constitutes an autonomous weapons system amid the ongoing debate concerning the definition of LAWS. State and other non-government organisations played a role in advancing the academic debate concerning the legal review obligation in relation to LAWS.

During this period, SIPRI became particularly active in advocating for the conduct of legal reviews and has produced several reports concerning art 36. This was partly in response to the CCW recognition of the importance of art 36 as an international law obligation.

67 See Stop Killer Robots (Website) <https://www.stopkillerrobots.org/>.

68 See International Committee for Robot Arms Control (Website) <https://www.icrac.net/>.

69 Losing Humanity (n 11).

70 United Nations, *Background of LAWS in the CCC* (Web Page) <https://www.un.org/disarmament/the-convention-on-certain-conventional-weapons/background-on-laws-in-the-ccw/>.

In November 2015, SIPRI published the report titled 'Implementing Article 36 Legal reviews in the Light of Increasing Autonomy in Weapon Systems' (the '2015 Report').[71] The report presents the authors' key takeaways from a legal review seminar hosted in Stockholm by SIPRI on 29 and 30 September 2015. It provides an overview of the challenges that arise for legal review processes as the level of autonomy in weapon systems increases and, unlike academic literature during the ICRC period, focuses specifically on the legal review of weapons with autonomy and cyber weapons.

In outlining the scope of the art 36 legal review obligation, the 2015 Report relies on and reinforces existing commentary and interpretations for the art 36 obligation.[72] While the 2015 Report is concerned with the legal review of increasingly AWS, it does not challenge these early views expressed during the ICRC period.

The 2015 Report does, however, include some insightful observations that suggest a need for states to reassess their approaches to the legal review of AWS. First, in describing 'Review Criteria', the 2015 Report observes that:

> In addition, with regard to autonomous weapon systems, reviews should take into account whether the system can comply with other rules relating to the conduct of hostilities (e.g., distinction, proportionality and precaution).[73]

This observation is significant as it reflects an early awareness of the need to reconsider the traditional scope of a legal review to include those IHL rules regulating methods of warfare. This represents an early academic discussion of the need to consider a broader range of issues than those considered during a traditional legal review. This is the basis of the proposal to add a 'functional review' of the AWS functions that engage IHL rules discussed in Chapter 7.

The 2015 Report also expands on the discussion of the Martens clause and its relevance to the legal review process. While raising the relevance of international human rights law it does not go further to consider the need for a state to include other non-legal issues in the context of the Martens cause such as state policies on human control over decisions concerning the use of lethal force in armed conflict. The 2015 Report does refer to considering state policy in the

71 V Boulanin, 'Implementing Article 36 Weapons Reviews in the Light of Increasing Autonomy in Weapon Systems' (November 2015) *SIPRI Insights on Peace and Security* 2015/1 ('2015 Report').

72 Ibid 4.

73 Ibid 5.

conduct of a legal review but does not do so in the context of the Martens clause.[74]

The 2015 Report concludes by providing a practical 'checklist for the review of weapons that include automated or autonomous features'.[75] The list includes questions relating to fully autonomous systems. For example:

(b) If the weapon can select and fire at a target autonomously, can it comply with the principles of distinction, proportionality and precaution in attack?[76]

As identified by Boothby,[77] such questions identify a need for the legal review to consider IHL rules concerning methods of warfare outside those contained in arts 35 and 51(4) of AP I. They assume, however, that an autonomous weapon will have full autonomy in relation to the use of force and do not address the possibility of human control over AWS. The 2015 Report also does not expand on how a state may address issues concerning compliance with the principles of distinction, proportionality and precautions in attack.

The 2015 Report emphasises the importance of testing and evaluation processes and notes that it is a 'central challenge for the review of weapons with automated and autonomous systems'.[78] The 2015 Report then provides a checklist of test and evaluation objectives, including:

(a) the weapon system has been adequately programmed to respect the requirements of international law;
(b) the system performs as anticipated and intended in normal conditions – that is, is capable, effective, reliable and suitable for the task assigned;
(c) the intended effect of the weapon does not cause indiscriminate damage, unnecessary suffering or superfluous injury, or have long term, widespread or severe impact on the natural environment;
(d) the weapon includes safety or anti-tamper mechanisms that will minimize the probability or consequences of unintended loss of control due to system failure or cyber-attack;
(e) the probability of system failure of critical and non-critical functions is at the required or acceptable level;

74 Ibid 9.
75 Ibid 13–15.
76 Ibid 14.
77 Boothby (n 65) 230–33.
78 Boulanin (n 71) 14.

(f) the system will remain under adequate 'meaningful human control' – that is, it is understandable to trained operators, it can provide traceable feedback on status, and an operator can activate or deactivate system functions or override decisions; and
(g) the potential consequences of accidental misuse, loss of control, systems failure or cyber-attack are foreseeable.[79]

The 2015 Report also argues the need for a systems approach to the legal review of an AWS by reviewing the weapon's hardware, principally its sensors, separately to its software. This is an important point in the context of AI systems that may be designed to operate with a range of weapons systems. The separation of the traditional legal review process from the AI system and its programming is discussed in Chapter 6.

The SIPRI 2015 Report is significant in that it is an early attempt to address the practical issues associated with the legal review of autonomous and cyber weapons. It illustrates the importance of the legal review process and reinforces much of the academic literature and commentary concerning the legal review process. The report is also significant in that it identifies the need for the legal review process to consider artificial decision-making either in the context of fully autonomous decisions or autonomy in support of human decisions. Notably, it also identifies the necessity for a legal review to assess the legality of autonomous decisions concerning the use of force and its legality in relation to the IHL rules and principles comprising distinction, proportionality and precautions in attack collectively known as 'targeting law'. This issue is a critical aspect of the legal review obligation with regard to AWS and is a significant departure from the traditional legal review process.

However, the 2015 Report does not challenge the traditional interpretations of art 36. These views, developed during the ICRC period, relate to the scope of the legal review obligation and interpretation of the phrase 'means of warfare'. This is illustrated in the key recommendations made by legal review practitioners who attended the legal review seminar:

a) start the review process as early as possible in the procurement process, and if possible, incorporate the legal reviews into the acquisition process at key decision points;
b) take a multidisciplinary approach, seeking input from various fields of expertise (legal, technical, operational and medical); and

79 Ibid.

c) examine empirical evidence provided by the manufacturer and intended end user, and if necessary, conduct tests and evaluations to assess the weapon's performance and the possible risks associated with its use.[80]

The first recommendation of SIPRI applies the traditional view that the legal review process is tied to the state acquisition process and does not consider the need for additional legal review steps, including informing research and development prior to a capability entering the acquisition process and after it has been introduced into service. While the second recommendation correctly emphasises the need for multidisciplinary input into the legal review, it does not identify the need for experts from broader fields, including computer scientists to ensure the AI's development reflects the state's legal obligations; cognitive scientists to help design human–machine interfaces; ethicists to consider the nature of human control over decisions to use force. Moreover, it does not recognise that a state may utilise the legal review process to consider issues beyond the legality of weapons. For example, a legal review may consider a weapon's compliance with state domestic policy, which, in the absence of specific legal regulations, provides direction on issues not expressly regulated by IHL, such as the requirement for, and nature of, human control over the use of autonomous weapons, standards of compliance with legal rules and the degrees of trust and transparency needed to deploy a system into uncontrolled and adversarial environments.

In September 2017, SIPRI hosted a further conference to 'discuss the importance of, and challenges associated with, reviewing the legality of weapons, means and methods of warfare that are based on three emerging fields of technology: cyberwarfare technologies, artificial intelligence and robotics and human enhancement'.[81] The report recording the outcomes of this conference was titled 'Article 36: Dealing with the Challenges Posed by Emerging Technologies' ('2017 Report') and was published in December 2017. It recorded the key outcomes of discussions involving 75 experts from government and civil society.

The SIPRI 2017 Report includes the recommendation to build upon elements of best practice for the conduct of legal reviews.[82] In making this

80 Ibid 6.

81 V Boulanin and M Verbruggen, 'Article 36: Dealing with the Challenges Posed by Emerging Technologies' (December 2017), *Stockholm International Peace and Research Institute* ('SIPRI 2017 Report'), iii.

82 Ibid viii.

recommendation, it cites many of the ICRC's publications to define the key art 36 terms and affirms the ICRC Commentary's interpretations of the phrase 'in some or all circumstances'.[83] The experts in attendance from government and civil society did not appear to challenge the traditional ICRC interpretations and guidance in the context of autonomous or other new technology weapons.

In the context of defining autonomy, the 2017 Report importantly emphasises that autonomy is a relative notion.[84] In doing so, it highlights the requirement to consider the extent to which humans are involved in the task carried out by the autonomous system. This is an important recognition that expands upon earlier binary perspectives of autonomy. The 2017 Report recognises that the spectrum of autonomy includes weapons that are enhanced by AI to team with humans.

This second SIPRI report correctly focuses its attention on considering IHL rules relevant to targeting or 'targeting law' in the context of a legal review.[85] This emphasis is important as it diverges from the traditional legal review approach, which limits its assessment of weapon use to those prohibitions contained in arts 35 and 51(4) of AP I codifying the general prohibitions against unnecessary suffering and superfluous injury and indiscriminate effects. While the report states that 'no existing weapon system has sufficient level of situational awareness to autonomously evaluate military advantage or expected collateral damage against military advantage', it questions whether this will ever be technically possible.[86] This view leads to a discussion of the use of autonomy in decision support.

The 2017 Report argues that the use of autonomy in decision support raises different questions for consideration by a legal review.[87] It suggests that the emphasis is less on compliance with targeting law and more on reliability and consideration of questions, including:

a) What type of information is the system feeding to the human operator, and how reliable is that information?
b) Is the system's behaviour comprehensible to trained operators?
c) What are the technical limitations of the system, and how do these affect the use of the weapon by the human operator?[88]

---

83 ICRC Commentary (n 13) [1469].
84 Boulanin and Verbruggen (n 81) 17.
85 Ibid 18.
86 Ibid 21.
87 Ibid 21.
88 Ibid.

These questions raise the important issues of testing, evaluation and verification of software, human cognitive factors relating to the interface between the AI system and the human operator and operator training. These factors are not common in a traditional legal review of a conventional weapon but are increasingly important in the context of human–machine teaming. This book argues that, even though a human may ultimately be the decision-maker, the legal review must still address AI systems' ability to operate in compliance with targeting law by considering the legality of any recommendations that relate to targeting. This is to ensure that the information provided to the operator by the system can be relied upon. This is especially so where the AI functionality includes preventing unlawful human decisions where it identifies an error.

The 2017 Report has 'additional considerations'which interestingly include the situation where a weapon is captured by the enemy, a malfunction results in unintended harm or the system is subject to a cyber-attack.[89] This is not based on a recognised legal rule or principle, as weapons law does not directly regulate these issues. Any weapon can fall into the hands of the enemy; however, this possibility does not raise IHL compliance issues. These additional considerations are relevant considerations for the art 36 review of both conventional and AWS; however, the latter may present greater risks, legal and operational, to the military and therefore require closer consideration during the conduct of a legal review.

Ultimately, SIPRI's 2017 Report makes a valuable contribution to the discussion concerning the art 36 legal review of AWS but does not extend knowledge beyond identifying what law an autonomous system should be capable of complying with. It does not extend the discussion by describing how a legal review may, in practice, undertake an assessment of the legality of an autonomous system. It does not attempt to describe a best practice; rather, it emphasises the importance of art 36 legal reviews and describes the challenges identified by a range of experts. The 2017 Report concludes by identifying ongoing challenges to art 36 legal review of autonomous systems. These include the increased complexity and cost of the legal review process, the sustainability of a legal review for an autonomous weapon capable of machine learning and, finally, identifying the appropriate standard of acceptance for an autonomous system to pass a legal review. These issues are explored further in Chapters 7 and 8.

---

89 Ibid 22.

3 The CCW GGE Period (2018 to Present)

The SIPRI reports coincided with the start of the formal UN GGE debate under the auspices of the CCW.[90] Commencing in 2014, the CCW debate demonstrated the extent of international concern for the prospect of autonomous weapons and sought to clarify the application of existing international law and whether there is a need for an international treaty pre-emptively banning their use in armed conflict. The debate is protracted and appears unable to reach a consensus on the need for additional laws. Throughout the debate, states and civil society have identified the importance of legal reviews and emphasised the importance of its role as a mechanism for states to assess the legality of AWS.

States and civil society share different views on the efficacy of legal reviews. Several states have submitted informal position papers during the GGE addressing legal reviews as part of their contribution to the debate. The range of views on the role of art 36 legal reviews in the context of autonomous weapons is broad. For example, some argue that legal reviews will not solve the problem (of AWS) and suggest that legal reviews were designed for a very different type of weapon.[91] Others argue that 'new evaluation and testing procedures may need to be conceptualized and developed'[92] and that the prospect of machine learning weapons 'would be problematic from a legal review perspective because the weapon would change its characteristics over time, effectively requiring a continued legal review'.[93]

In 2018, Australia submitted a position paper to the second meeting of the Group of Government Experts titled 'The Australian Article 36 Review Process'.[94] Australia's 2018 GGE position paper provided an overview of its approach to its legal review obligation and described its process for the conduct of legal reviews. Consistent with McClelland, Australia's legal reviews are aligned with the capability acquisition process within the Department of Defence.[95] Unfortunately, despite the paper being presented in the context of

---

90 *Convention on Prohibitions or Restrictions on the Use of Certain Conventional Weapons Which May be Deemed to be Excessively Injurious or to Have Indiscriminate Effects* (10 October 1980) and Amendment to Article 1 (21 December 2001) 1342 UNTS 137 ('*CCW*').

91 Mines Action Canada Statement, CCW Meeting of Experts on LAWS, *Challenges to International Humanitarian Law* (April 2016) 1.

92 Switzerland, CCW Meeting of Experts on LAWS, *Challenges to International Humanitarian Law* (April 2016).

93 Gilles Giacca, *Notes of CCW Meeting of Experts on LAWS: Challenges to International Humanitarian Law* (April 2016) 4.

94 Australian Article 36 Review Process (n 62).

95 Ibid 4.

the CCW debate on LAWS, Australia's position paper did not take the opportunity to describe how it would apply its art 36 process to autonomous weapons beyond briefly indicating its ability to 'implement any necessary reforms required for the review of emerging technologies such as autonomous weapons systems'.[96] Australia's position paper was more an expression of its compliance with the art 36 legal review obligation than a meaningful contribution to the discussion of how legal reviews can contribute to ensuring the legality of LAWS.

In contrast, Argentina's 2018 delegation to the GGE submitted a working paper concerning the art 36 legal review of new technology weapons. It was titled 'Strengthening of the Review Mechanism of a New Weapon, Means or Methods of Warfare',[97] and, unlike Australia's working paper, addressed the challenges of increasingly technological weapons to the legal review process. The paper made an honest assessment that, despite the art 36 legal review obligation being four decades old, 'the implementation at national level of Article 36 remains still weak and ambiguous'.[98] The paper distinguishes between states that study and develop new technology weapons and many states who primarily acquire weapons from other states or weapon manufacturers thus distinguishing between weapon-exporting and weapon-importing states..

Argentina's paper argues that an importing state should be able to 'make an implicit delegation of its obligations [under article 36 of AP 1] relying on the review mechanism that should be carried out by the state that developed the weapon in question'.[99] This approach is novel and raises several issues, not least of which is a state's ability to delegate international treaty law obligations. Although the paper does not discuss how to undertake art 36 legal reviews of AWS, Argentina's report does highlight the merits of states exchanging information as contemplated by art 84 of AP 1.[100]

The progress and outcomes of the GGE have, to date, been modest. In August 2018, a draft set of guiding principles was released to enable states to fully consider them prior to the meetings scheduled for 2019. These principles were affirmed, without amendment, in a meeting of states party to the CCW in

96 Ibid.

97 Argentinian Government, *Strengthening of the Review Mechanism of a New Weapon, Means or Methods of Warfare*, UN Doc CCW/GGE.1/2018/WP.2 (4 April 2018), <https://reachingcriticalwill.org/images/documents/Disarmament-fora/ccw/2018/gge/documents/GGE.1-WP2-English.pdf>.

98 Ibid 3.

99 Ibid.

100 AP 1 (n 18) art 84.

November 2019.[101] They are an important milestone as they represent the first tangible consensus-based outcome. Relevant to art 36 reviews, the 11 Guiding Principles state:

> a) IHL continues to apply in full to all weapons systems, including the potential development and use of lethal autonomous weapon systems;
> b) Human responsibility for decisions on the use of weapon systems must be retained since accountability cannot be transferred to machines. This should be considered across the entire life cycle of the weapon system;
> c) Human–machine interaction, which may take various forms and be implemented at various stages of the life cycle of a weapon, should ensure that the potential use of weapons systems based on emerging technologies in the area of lethal autonomous weapon systems is in compliance with applicable international law, in particular IHL. In determining the quality and extend of human–machine interaction, a range of factors should be considered including the operational context, and the characteristics and capabilities of the weapons system as a whole;
> d) Accountability for developing, deploying and using an emerging weapons system in the framework of the CCW must be ensured in accordance with applicable international law, including through the operation of such systems within a reasonable chain of human command and control;
> e) In accordance with States' obligations under international law, in the study, development, acquisition, or adoption of a new weapon, means or method of warfare, determination must be made whether its employment would, in some or all circumstances, be prohibited by international law;
> f) Risk assessments and mitigation measures should be part of the design, development, testing and deployment cycle of emerging technologies in any weapons systems;
> g) Consideration should be given to the use of emerging technologies in the area of lethal autonomous weapon systems in upholding compliance with IHL and other applicable international law obligations.[102]

101 *Final Report of Meeting of the High Contracting Parties to the CCW*, UN Doc CCW/MSP/2019/9 (13–15 November 2019) <https://undocs.org/CCW/MSP/2019/9>.

102 Ibid.

These guiding principles are a tangible outcome of more than six years of UN meetings and international debate. They also suggest that a likely outcome of the CCW consideration of LAWS is non-binding soft-law declarations addressing specific issues, including the need for human control over the use of force and the importance of human accountability.

In recent years, that has been a proliferation of academic discourse on the legal review of AWS. Notably, on 21 March 2019, Dustin Lewis published a blog article titled 'Legal Reviews of Weapons, Means and Methods of Warfare Involving Artificial Intelligence: 16 Elements to Consider'.[103] Lewis identified 16 elements of interest in the legal review of AWS, including legal agency, explainability, reconstruction ability, value decisions and normative judgements.[104] These elements are unique to AWS and are not identified in earlier literature. This reflects a need to reconsider the content of a traditional legal review to address AWS-specific issues. Lewis's blog post was closely followed by Netta Goussac's blog post titled 'Safety Net or Tangled Web: Legal Reviews of AI in Weapons and Warfighting'.[105] Her article poses a series of rhetorical questions to highlight the legal and ethical challenges faced by states conducting legal reviews of AWS. She identifies important issues, including the need to consider AI-enabled decision tools in legal reviews where they form part of a weapon system (the 'means of warfare') or the way in which the system is used (the 'methods of warfare').[106] The article emphasises the need for states to agree upon a common understanding of the degree of human control required to assess an AWS as lawful.[107] Netta Goussac's article also identifies the need for new approaches to the legal review of AWS as '[t]raditional testing regimes will be unsuitable for weapons that incorporate AI in their critical functions'.[108] These themes were progressed by Lauren Sanders and myself in subsequent

103 D Lewis, 'Legal Reviews of Weapons, Means and Methods of Warfare Involving Artificial Intelligence: 16 Elements to Consider', *International Committee of the Red Cross Humanitarian Law & Policy Blog* (Blog Post, 21 March 2019) <https://blogs.icrc.org/law-and-policy/2019/03/21/legal-reviews-weapons-means-methods-warfare-artificial-intelligence-16-elements-consider/>.

104 Ibid.

105 N Goussac, 'Safety Net or Tangled Web: Weapons Reviews of AI in Weapons and War-Fighting', *International Committee of the Red Cross Humanitarian Law & Policy Blog* (Blog Post, 18 April 2019) <https://blogs.icrc.org/law-and-policy/2019/04/18/safety-net-tangled-web-legal-reviews-ai-weapons-war-fighting>.

106 Ibid.

107 Ibid.

108 Ibid.

blogs.[109] These posts, while not authoritative, reflect a need to consider the challenges a state may encounter when undertaking a legal review.

The topic of AWS legal reviews was further analysed in several publications. In May 2021, the NATO Cooperative Cyber Defence Centre of Excellence (CCD-COE) published a new text, edited by Associate Professor Rain Liivoja and Ms Ann Väljataga, titled *Autonomous Cyber Capabilities Under International Law*.[110] The text explored concepts and frameworks, international legal obligations and international legal responsibility particular to autonomous cyber capabilities. Relevantly, Alex Tattersall and I authored a chapter describing the issues and conduct on the legal review of an autonomous cyber weapon. This chapter argued the need for a legal review of an AWS to undertake a 'use review' to consider those functions governed by IHL rules regulating methods of warfare. The need for an analysis of IHL targeting rules is developed further in Chapter 7 of this book.

In December 2021, Dr Natalia Jevglevskaja published her book *International Law and Legal review: Emerging Military Technology under the Laws of Armed Conflict*.[111] The text provides an updated, contemporary, in-depth, academic exploration of the obligation of states party to AP 1 to determine whether their intended use of weapons in armed conflict is consistent with their obligations under international law. It represents the first comprehensive text entirely dedicated to art 36 and its application to new technology weapons. It attempts to build upon the ICRC Guide but does suggest how many of the challenges presented by the legal review of AWS may be addressed.[112] The book is written against the background of increasing state investment in new weapons, means and methods of warfare.[113] It provides a valuable resource for both states with legal review systems and those seeking to establish one. These challenges include identifying which AWS fall within the scope of the art 36 legal

---

109 L Sanders and D Copeland, 'Developing an Approach to the Legal Review of Autonomous Weapon Systems', *International Law Association Reporter* (27 November 2020) <https://ilareporter.org.au/2020/11/developing-an-approach-to-the-legal-review-of-autonomous-weapon-systems-lauren-sanders-and-damian-copeland/>; Sanders and Copeland 0(n 3); Copeland and Sanders (n 4).

110 R Liivoja and A Väljataga (eds), *Autonomous Cyber Capabilities Under International Law* (NATO CCDOE Publications, 2021) 256 <https://ccdcoe.org/uploads/2021/05/Autonomous_Cyber_Capabilities_210525.pdf>.

111 Jevglevskaja (n 7).

112 ICRC Guide (n 1).

113 P Wezeman, A Kuimova and S Wezeman, *Trends in International Arms Transfers, 2021* (SIPRI, March 2022) <https://www.sipri.org/publications/2022/sipri-fact-sheets/trends-international-arms-transfers-2021>.

review obligation,[114] the need to consider targeting law within the legal review methodology[115] and the relevance of the Martens clause in the legal review of AWS.[116]

Finally, from 28–30 March 2023 the Australian Department of Defence's Directorate of Operations and International Law hosted the first Expert Meeting on the legal review of AWS in Sydney, Australia. The meeting identified and discussed challenges associated with the legal review of an AWS. The aims of the meetings included establishing a mechanism for the voluntary exchange of best practice and identify elements of possible good practice. Annexed to the report titled, *Enhancing the Legal Review of Autonomous Weapon Systems,* is a list of 30 elements of good practice identified during the meeting.[117] These elements were refined during a second expert meeting held 16 -18 April 2024 and will be published in the second half of 2024.

In addition, an online legal review portal was announced during the second expert meeting. The online portal, to be published as a cooperative project between the Asia Pacific Intitute of Law and Security and the United Nations Office of Disarmament Affairs, is designed to provide states, industry and academics with a resource of publicly available information regarding state practice and academic discourse on legal reviews.[118]

In conclusion, this literature review identified three broad periods of academic discourse regarding the art 36 legal review obligation and its application to AWS. It is only during the most recent period that there has been an increased focus on the legal review of AWS. The trajectory of these analyses clearly accepts the task of determining the legality of AWS is far more complex than it is for conventional human-controlled weapons. However, while the CCW GGE period has seen an increase in literature, there remains little practical guidance or evidence of national process or best practice. It is at this point that this book seeks to add to the scholarly debate by not only identifying why the traditional legal review process is insufficient to determine the legality of AWS but to propose an expanded approach to enable a state to make such a determination.

114 Ibid 211–17.

115 Ibid 218–21.

116 Ibid 222–6.

117 N Goussac, Jevglevskaja, N, Liivoja, R, and Sanders, L, (2023). *Enhancing the Legal Review of Autonomous Weapon Systems: Report of an Expert Meeting.* Brisbane, QLD Australia: Law and the Future of War Research Group, TC Beirne School of Law, The University of Queensland <https://espace.library.uq.edu.au/view/UQ:2bbfd31>.

118 Asia-Pacific Institute for Law and Security, (2024) *Portal on the Legal Review of Weapons* (Website) <https://apils.org/>.

Before analysing the legal review obligation and process, it is important to understand how international law regulates weapons. This is essential knowledge for those completing weapon reviews and an important foundation for the later arguments regarding the sufficiency of the traditional legal review process. The next chapter will therefore survey the body of Public International Law as it applies to weapons. This will not only reveal the gaps in international law as it applies to AWS but provide an understanding of the content of a legal review.

CHAPTER 3

How Does International Law Regulate AWS?

> If the new and frightful weapons of destruction which are now at the disposal of nations seem destined to abridge the duration of future wars, it appears likely, on the other hand, that future battles will only become more and more murderous.
>
> HENRY DUNANT, *Memory of Solferino*, 1862[1]

∵

The preceding survey of scholarly work and international debate alludes to the challenges raised by the art 36 obligation to undertake a legal review of an AWS. Before discussing these challenges, it is necessary to understand how international law has developed to govern a state's possession and use of weapons, including AWS. This will demonstrate the nature and *ad hoc* development of international norms governing weapons or 'weapons law' and how they are challenged by autonomous functionality in weapons. This chapter also provides the foundation for later arguments concerning the adequacy of the 'traditional legal review method' by describing the law that is applied to an AWS during a legal review.

It would be misleading to think that weapons law is confined to the rules that apply in times of armed conflict (i.e., IHL). For this reason, Section 2 will outline the broader objectives of international weapons law, including arms control, disarmament and export control. This is important to this book because it reflects the multiple objectives of international law regulation of weapons. This is followed by a historic survey of the development of weapons law (Section 3) before Section 4 directs attention to the specific and general weapons law norms. An understanding of these norms is important as they form part of the legal analysis during a legal review. Section 5 examines the role of the Martens clause during a legal review and whether autonomy in weapons functions necessitates an expanded approach incorporating national policy

1 H Dunant, *A Memory of Solferino* (ICRC Geneva, 2002), <https://www.icrc.org/sites/default/files/external/doc/en/assets/files/publications/icrc-002-0361.pdf>.

 DOI:10.1163/9789004707047_005

designed to address ethical and moral concerns. This is important as existing international law does not address many of the challenges presented by AWS. The answer to questions such as the requirements for human control, reliability, accountability and explainability are likely to be addressed by national AWS policies such as responsible AI in the military frameworks.

1 The Objectives of Weapons Law

Generally, weapons law rules seek to regulate a state's possession or use of weapons. This is intended to address a range of political and humanitarian objectives both in times of peace and during armed conflict. Before describing the specific sources of weapons law, it is instructive to survey the range of political and humanitarian objectives. First, arms control treaties, such as the *Ottawa Convention*,[2] prohibit the development, production, acquisition, possession, stockpiling or transfer of certain weapons defined by the relevant treaty. Arms control treaties are recognised as 'mutually agreed upon restraints or controls (usually between states) on the development, production, stockpiling, proliferation, deployment and use of troops, small arms, conventional weapons and weapons of mass destruction'.[3] Arms control treaties are intended to reduce a state's capacity to engage in armed conflict and, if this is not possible, to reduce its consequences.[4] Similarly, disarmament, counter-proliferation or non-proliferation treaties seek to reduce or eliminate certain categories of weapons. For example, the *Treaty on the Non-Proliferation of Nuclear Weapons* aims to 'prevent the spread of nuclear weapons and weapons technology, to promote cooperation in the peaceful uses of nuclear energy'.[5] Such treaties are either unilateral or reciprocal in nature.[6] Non-proliferation treaties apply not only to weapons of mass destruction (including nuclear, radiological, chemical and biological weapons) but also to conventional weapons.[7] These are complemented by arms trade treaties[8] and export control

2 *The Convention on the Prohibition of the Use, Stockpiling, Production and Transfer of Anti-Personnel Mines and on Their Destruction*, opened for signature on December 3, 1997 (entered into force on March 1, 1999) ('Ottawa Convention').

3 NATO, *Arms Control, Disarmament and Non-proliferation in NATO* (6 April 2022).

4 Ibid 277.

5 *Treaty on the Non-Proliferation of Nuclear Weapons*, opened for signature on 1968 (entered into force 1970) <https://www.un.org/disarmament/wmd/nuclear/npt/>.

6 NATO (n 3).

7 Ibid.

8 *Arms Trade Treaty*, opened for signature 3 June 2013 (entered into force 24 December 2014).

regimes[9] designed to reduce the proliferation of weapons through the export of military and dual-use goods and technology. Finally, IHL treaties, including customary IHL norms,[10] are humanitarian in character and act to constrain means and methods of warfare to limit their effects on the victims of armed conflict. They are concerned with, *inter alia*, the lawful use of weapons. Each discrete area of international weapons law seeks to achieve different, albeit complementary, political objectives. Where the treaty binds the reviewing state, they must be considered during a legal review.

In contrast to the vast array of weapon types in state arsenals, the list of weapons that are subject to specific weapons law treaties is short. To illustrate the weapons that are subject to specific treaty regulation, the table annexed to this chapter summarises existing specific weapons law treaties. Several observations can be drawn from the subject of these treaties:

a) First, the development of weapons law treaties regulating specific weapons is *ad hoc*. Their creation follows significant development or use of weapons, such as during or after the World Wars, and are generally the product of clear political, humanitarian and security motivations.[11]

b) Second, at the time of writing, there are no specific international law treaties regulating autonomy in weapons or autonomy as a class of weapons. This does not mean that existing weapons treaties are not relevant to determining the legality of AWS. Autonomy is a feature of a weapon's functionality, which is distinct from the weapon type or the weapon effect. Any weapon, including existing weapons regulated by weapons law, may be enhanced or modified with AI to become an AWS. A weapon is not rendered unlawful per se based on autonomous functionality alone. Approximately 30 states party to the CCW have publicly supported a ban on fully autonomous weapons.[12] None of these states are militarily significant states.[13] This is consistent with the view that

---

9 *Wassenaar Arrangement on Export Controls for Conventional Arms and Dual-Use Goods and Technologies* <https://www.wassenaar.org/>.

10 ICRC, *Customary International Humanitarian Law Database* (Website) <https://ihl-databases.icrc.org/customary-ihl/eng/docs/v1_rule> ('ICRC Database').

11 H Nasu and R McLaughlin (eds), *New Technologies and the Law of Armed Conflict* (TMC Asser Press, 2014) 4–5.

12 Human Rights Watch, in *Killer Robots: Growing Support for a Ban*, cite the following countries as calling for a ban on LAWS: Algeria, Argentina, Austria, Bolivia, Brazil, Chile, China (use only), Colombia, Costa Rica, Cuba, Djibouti, Ecuador, El Salvador, Egypt, Ghana, Guatemala, the Holy See, Iraq, Jordan, Mexico, Morocco, Namibia, Nicaragua, Pakistan, Panama, Peru, the State of Palestine, Uganda, Venezuela and Zimbabwe: <https://www.hrw.org/news/2020/08/10/killer-robots-growing-support-ban>.

13 Ibid.

> a relationship exists between the strategic effect of a weapon and the prospect of weapon being the subject of international regulation.[14]

As art 36 expressly requires states party to AP I to determine whether a weapon is 'prohibited by this Protocol or *by any other rule of international law applicable*',[15] it is necessary for those conducting the legal review to understand the sources and development of international weapons law as it applies to their state. Intuitively, this requires an understanding of not only a state's international law obligations but also how they are applied in the context of specific weapon technologies.

2 Sources and Development of Weapons Law

Before examining the specific content of weapons law, it is useful to understand its sources and trace its historic development. Article 38 of the Statute of the International Court of Justice describes the sources of international law as:

> a) international conventions, whether general or particular, establishing rules expressly recognized by the contesting States;
> b) international custom, as evidence of a general practice accepted as law [for example to prohibition on weapons that cause superfluous injury or unnecessary suffering];
> c) the general principles of law recognized by civilized nations [for example the IHL principle of distinction requiring weapons capable of attacking military objectives]; and
> d) subject to the provisions of Article 59, judicial decisions and the teachings of the most highly qualified publicists of the various nations, as subsidiary means for the determination of rules of law.[16]

Weapons law is derived predominately from the first three of these sources of law. The ability of these sources of law to keep pace with advances in weapon technology is the subject of regular debate. Many weapons law norms are of general application and, therefore, are technology agnostic. The ICRC's former president Jakob Kellenberger, in his official statement at the 60th anniversary

14 D Copeland, 'Legal Review of New Technology Weapons' in Nasu and McLaughlin (n 11) 52.

15 *Protocol Additional to the Geneva Conventions of 12 August 1949, and relating to the Protection of Victims of International Armed Conflicts (Protocol I)*, opened for signature 8 June 1977, 1125 UNTS 3 (entered into force 7 December 1978) ('*AP I*').

16 United Nations, *Charter of the United Nations*, 1945, 1 UNTS XVI, art 38(1).

of the Geneva Conventions, emphasised that new rules were not required to respond to the changing nature of armed conflict. He did, however, concede that the ICRC had found 'gaps or weaknesses in the existing legal framework' so that the law needed 'further development or clarification'.[17] Nasu and McLaughlin observe:

> the elasticity of the general principles is not limitless, and there can be no question that whilst the law of armed conflict continues to lag behind technological development, the need for instances of greater specificity, and technology sensitivity in law-making, application and interpretation, exists.[18]

This is especially true for the application of IHL principles during the legal review of AWS. Greenwood observes that:

> these principles are capable of being applied to weapons of the kind which was beyond contemplation when those principles were first developed. The flexibility of the general principles thus makes them of broader application than the specific provisions which are all too easily overtaken by new technology.[19]

Undoubtedly, as the development of new technology weapons continues, there will be a greater emphasis on state and academic discourse to clarify the application of existing law to new means and methods of warfare. Boothby observes that 'while the law may sometimes appear outdated and irrelevant, it can also be argued that the law of weaponry is dynamic, agile and flexible, and most certainly not belittled in an age of rapid technical advance'.[20] Also, absent state motivation for new laws, soft law will play an increasingly important role in interpreting the application of existing norms to new technologies.[21] This may influence national policy guidance intended to clarify the application of

17 J Kellenberger, *Learning from the Past to Face the Future* (Statement, 2009), <http://www.icrc.org/eng/resources/documents/Statement/geneva-conventions-Statement-president-120809.htm>.

18 Nasu and McLaughlin (n 11) 6.

19 C Greenwood, 'The Law of Weaponry at the Start of the New Millennium' in Michael N Schmitt and Leslie C Green (eds), *The Law of Armed Conflict: Into the New Millennium* (U.S. Naval War College, 1999), 221.

20 W Boothby, *Weapons and the Law of Armed Conflict* (Cambridge University, 2009), 370.

21 Nasu and McLaughlin (n 11) 6.

weapons law rules to autonomous weapons. This will be considered in more depth in Chapter 7.

2.1 *Geneva Law and Hague Law*

To understand the starting point from which international law regulates AWS, it is useful to situate the relevant law within the broad body of international law. IHL regulates the conduct of armed conflict (*jus in bello*) and contrasts with the international law rules governing the resort to the use of force (*jus ad bellum*) and following armed conflict (*jus post bello*).[22] IHL is traditionally regarded as having two pillars of humanitarian concern, each named after the cities in which the laws were predominately created: first, Geneva Law, which has developed to protect the victims of armed conflicts,[23] and second, Hague Law, which seeks to mitigate and circumscribe the cruelty of war for humanitarian purposes.[24] Subsequent normative developments, including the drafting of the 1977 Additional Protocols to the Geneva Conventions of 1949, have reduced this historical distinction and effectively merged the bodies of law.[25]

Geneva Law arose from the humanitarian concern for the protection of sick and wounded combatants. The inspiration for this law is traced to a battlefield in Northern Italy during the Italian war of unification.[26] On 24 June 1859, a Swiss activist named Mr Henry Dunant came across the aftermath of a battle at Solferino, which left 6,000 soldiers dead and 40,000 wounded. The wounded were left on the battlefield to suffer and die from their battle wounds. Mr Dunant recorded his experience in *Un Souvenir de Solferino*[27] and urged both the creation of the Red Cross and the gathering of nations in Geneva for an international conference to agree on how to alleviate the suffering of sick and wounded combatants in armed conflict.[28] This First Geneva Convention was subsequently clarified and expanded at the Hague Peace Conferences

---

22 A Roberts and R Guelff (eds), *Documents on the Laws of War* (Oxford University Press, 3rd ed, 2000) 1.

23 JS Pictet, 'The New Geneva Conventions for the Protection of War Victims' (1951) 45(3) *The American Journal of International Law* 462, 462–75.

24 *Legality of the Threat or Use of Nuclear Weapons (Advisory Opinion)* [1996] ICJ Rep 226 [260] ('Nuclear Weapons Case').

25 M Schmitt, 'Military Necessity and Humanity in International Humanitarian Law: Preserving the Delicate Balance' (2010) 50(4) *Virginia Journal of International Law* 795, 810.

26 ICRC (Website) <https://www.icrc.org/eng/resources/documents/misc/57jnvr.htm>.

27 Dunant (n 1).

28 *First Geneva Convention for the Amelioration of the Condition of the Wounded in Armies in the Field* (entered into force 22 August 1864).

of 1899 and 1907 and eventually replaced in 1929. It is the predecessor to the Geneva Conventions of 1949 and their Additional Protocols.[29]

Similarly, Hague Law was inspired by the increasingly destructive nature of weapons and, in particular, their effects on combatants. The forerunners to 'Hague Law' were the 1856 Declaration of Paris[30] and the 1868 St. Petersburg Declaration.[31] The Paris Declaration addressed means and methods of naval warfare, while the St. Petersburg Declaration responded to the refinement of a Russian bullet, originally capable of exploding on impact with a hard surface, to explode and shatter on contact with a soft surface such as animals or a human body. The use of such bullets against troops was regarded by Russia's imperial war minister as improper and led to his recommendation to Tsar Alexander II that the bullet be renounced. States were invited to an International Military Commission in St. Petersburg to consider its regulation.

The St. Petersburg Declaration is noteworthy not only as it was the first modern international treaty prohibiting the use of a specific munition in warfare but also because it created the precedent for regulating means of warfare.[32] It was also the first international treaty to articulate a humanitarian basis for restricting the use of certain weapons. The general prohibition against weapons of a nature to cause 'unnecessary suffering' (discussed in Section 4) owes its origin in the Declaration's preamble, which denounced 'arms which uselessly aggravate the sufferings of disabled men, or render their death inevitable'.[33] Most relevantly, the Declaration foreshadowed the requirement for a state to consider the legality of weapons by stating that:

> The Contracting or Acceding Parties reserve to themselves to come hereafter to an understanding whenever a precise proposition shall be drawn up in view of future improvements which science may affect in the armament of troops, in order to maintain the principles which, they have established, and to conciliate the necessities of war with the laws of humanity.[34]

---

29 Dunant (n 1); J Garner, *International Law and the World War* (Longmans, Green and Co, 1920) 1(17) et seq.

30 *Declaration Respecting Maritime Law* (entered into force 16 April 1856).

31 *Declaration Renouncing the Use, in Time of War, of Explosive Projectiles under 400 Grammes Weight*, opened for signature 29 November 1868 (entered into force 11 December 1868) ('St. Petersburg Declaration').

32 Roberts and Guelff (n 22) 53–4.

33 St. Petersburg Declaration (n 31).

34 Ibid.

The creation of the St. Petersburg Declaration demonstrates the reactive nature of weapons law normative development. In many cases, international law regulating weapons has followed rather than preceded the development of new weapon technology.

3 Specific and General Weapons Law

At the time of writing, weapons law does not directly address autonomy as a weapon characteristic. Of course, specific and general weapons law rules apply to AWS in the same way they apply to all forms of weaponry. For example, the *Chemical Weapons Convention* would specifically prohibit any AWS from utilising prohibited chemicals to achieve its effect. Similarly, AWS designed to cause superfluous injury would be prohibited. The application of IHL norms to AWS was conclusively resolved by states party to the CCW who agreed, by consensus during the 2019 GGE on LAWS, to a set of Guiding Principles that include:

> a) IHL continues to apply in full to all weapons systems, including the potential development and use of lethal autonomous weapon systems;[35]

Before turning to the analysis of specific weapons law norms, it is important to note that AWS are complex weapon systems that are likely to comprise multiple interdependent components, including a platform, sensors, communications equipment, operating systems and a device that causes the intended effect (e.g., damage to objects or injury/death to combatants).[36]

The following section surveys both the specific and general weapons law prohibitions. This is designed to provide an understanding of how weapons law regulates specific weapons and weapons that cause prohibited effects. This will also demonstrate the *ad hoc* nature of weapons law and existing regulatory gaps. Greenwood alludes to these gaps by observing 'the remarkable progress which has been made in the development of weaponry and the methods of

35 *Guiding Principles affirmed by the Group of Governmental Experts on Emerging Technologies in the Area of Lethal Autonomous Weapons System*, Annex III to the Final Report of the Meeting of the High Contracting Parties to the Convention on Prohibitions or Restrictions on the Use of Certain Conventional Weapons Which May be Deemed to be Excessively Injurious or to Have Indiscriminate Effects, UN Doc CCW/MSP/2019/9 (13 December 2019) ('UN GGE Guiding Principles').

36 D Mauri, *Autonomous Weapons Systems and the Protection of the Human Person: An International Law Analysis* (Edward Elgar Publishing, 2022), 123–4.

warfare during the 20th century has been unmatched by development in the law'.[37] The survey will provide insight into the content of the legal review process and the challenges faced by a legal reviewer of new technology weapons such as those with autonomous capacity. The absence of specific treaty law will necessitate state interpretation of existing provisions. The ICJ stated in the Nuclear Weapons Case that a key advantage of specific regulation is the clarity of restrictions or prohibitions. The Court concluded that those prohibitions should be clearly stated in the law rather than created by deduction.[38]

Finally, this section will discuss how weapons law addresses humanitarian concerns with specific weapon types or weapons that cause certain effects. It assumes humans will operate, control and be responsible for the use of weapons and so does not address many of the concerns raised by autonomy in weapons.

3.1 *Specific Weapons Law Prohibitions*

Following from the St. Petersburg Declaration, modern weapons law has developed predominately through international treaties. Dinstein argues that the 'sole safe means of ensuring that a specific weapon will be interdicted is to say so unequivocally in a binding multilateral treaty'.[39] The creation of treaty-based weapons law development has, however, been inconsistent. Citing the use of gas during the First World War and the resulting 1925 Geneva Gas Protocol,[40] Turns notes that 'treaties prohibiting weapons are almost invariably a reaction to abuse in the last conflict'.[41] While some may disagree with this generalisation, there are two clear characteristics of weapons law:

1) Not all new weapons, means and methods of warfare have become the subject of specific weapons law. Notable exceptions include flechette[42] and depleted uranium[43] munitions.

---

37 Greenwood (n 19) 185.

38 *Legality of the Threat or Use of Nuclear Weapons (Advisory Opinion)* [1996] ICJ Rep 226 [260] ('Nuclear Weapons Case'), [226].

39 Y Dinstein, *The Conduct of Hostilities under the Law of International Armed Conflict* (Cambridge University Press, 2nd ed, 2010) 67.

40 *Protocol for the Prohibition of the Use in War of Asphyxiating, Poisonous or Other Gases, and of Bacteriological Methods of Warfare*, opened for signature 17 June 1925 (entered into force 8 February 1928) ('1925 Gas Protocol').

41 D Turns, 'Weapons in the ICRC Study on Customary International Humanitarian Law' (2006) 11(2) *Journal of Conflict and Security Law* 201, 204.

42 Flechette rounds are small, steel, anti-personnel projectiles like arrows or darts. They may be fired individually or more commonly in large numbers from shotguns or artillery.

43 Depleted uranium munitions rounds are designed to penetrate enemy equipment such as vehicles and tanks using high kinetic energy. They typically ignite on impact igniting fuel or munitions. See (website) <https://www.epa.gov/radtown/depleted-uranium>.

2) A fundamental characteristic of weapons law is a humanitarian concern for the effect of weapons on combatants.[44]

For these reasons, there are a range of weapons, means or methods of warfare that are the subject of specific prohibitions or restrictions. These include poison and poisoned weapons; dropping explosives and projectiles from balloons,[45] asphyxiating gas and chemicals,[46] expanding bullets,[47] biological weapons,[48] mines and booby traps,[49] non-detectable fragments,[50] incendiary weapons,[51] blinding lasers,[52] anti-personnel mines[53] and cluster munitions.[54]

---

44 M Schmitt, 'Military Necessity and Humanity in International Humanitarian Law: Preserving the Delicate Balance' (2010) 50(4) *Virginia Journal of International Law* 795, 803.

45 1899 *Hague Declaration (IV,1), to Prohibit, for the Term of Five Years, the Launching of Projectiles and Explosives from Balloons, and Other Methods of Similar Nature*, opened for signature 29 July 1899 (entered into force 4 September 1900) (revised by the 1907 Hague Declaration).

46 1899 *Hague Declaration 2 Concerning Asphyxiating Gases* (29 July 1899), revised by the 1907 *Hague Convention (IV) Respecting the Laws and Customs of War on Land*, opened for signature 18 October 1907 (entered into force 26 January 1910) ('1907 Hague Convention IV'); 1925 Gas Protocol (n 193); the *Convention on the Prohibition of the Development, Production, Stockpiling and Use of Chemical Weapons and on their Destruction* (13 January 1993) ('CWC'); *Rome Statute of the International Criminal Court*, opened for signature 17 July 1988, 2187 UNTS 90 (entered into force 1 July 2002) art xvii ('Rome Statute').

47 1899 *Hague Declaration 3 Concerning the Prohibition of Using Bullets which Expand or Flatten Easily in the Human Body* (29 July 1899).

48 *Convention on the Prohibition of the Development, Production and Stockpiling of Bacteriological (Biological) and Toxin Weapons and on Their Destruction*, opened for signature 10 April 1972, 1015 UNTS 163 (entered into force 26 March 1975).

49 *Protocol on Prohibitions or Restrictions on the Use of Mines, Booby-Traps and Other Devices as Amended on 3 May 1996 (Protocol II, as Amended on 3 May 1996) Annexed to the Convention on Prohibitions or Restrictions on the Use of Certain Conventional Weapons Which May be Deemed to be Excessively Injurious or to Have Indiscriminate Effects*, opened for signature 3 May 1996, 2048 UNTS 93 (entered into force 3 December 1998).

50 *Protocol I on Non-Detectable Fragments*, opened for signature 10 April 1981 (entered into force 2 December 1983).

51 *Protocol III on Prohibitions or Restrictions on the Use of Incendiary Weapons*, opened for signature 10 April 1981 (entered into force 2 December 1983).

52 *Protocol IV on Blinding Laser Weapons*, opened for signature 13 October 1995, 2024 UNTS 163 (entered into force 30 July 1998).

53 *Convention on the Prohibition of the Use, Stockpiling, Production and Transfer of Anti-Personnel Mines and on Their Destruction*, signed 18 September 1997, 2056 UNTS 211 (entered into force 1 March 1999) ('*Ottawa Convention*').

54 *Convention on Cluster Munitions*, opened for signature 30 May 2008, 2688 UNTS 39 (entered into force 1 August 2010) ('*Convention on Cluster Munitions*').

3.1.1 Pre-WW1 IHL Treaties

There appear to be two periods that account for most of the treaties that form the body of weapons law. The period covers the latter half of the 19th century and prior to the outbreak of the First World War (WW1). This was a comparatively productive period that saw significant progress through the success of peace conferences convened at the Hague in 1899 and 1907. All weapons law treaties created in this period applied only to international armed conflict as international law did not generally address internal armed conflict until after the Second World War (WW2).[55]

A distinguishing feature of treaties during this period was their pragmatic nature. States intentionally limited their treaty obligation to armed conflict between state parties but not when an opposing state employed the prohibited weapon in contravention of the treaty obligation or when a non-state party joined the conflict. An example is found in the 1899 Hague Declaration II on the Laws and Customs of War on Land and 1907 *Hague Convention (IV) Respecting the Laws and Customs of War on Land* that did not apply 'except between contracting Powers, and then only if all the belligerents are parties to the Convention'. The pre-WW1 treaties pragmatically allowed states to prohibit their use in certain circumstances but did not create a military disparity as compared to non-state parties. Following the conclusion of WW1, the 1925 Geneva Gas Protocol did not contain a no first use clause; however, many states became party 'subject to the reservation that it is binding only in relation to other States bound by it and shall cease to be binding if an enemy or its allies fail to respect its prohibitions'.[56]

This pragmatic approach to weapons regulation has not continued into more recent weapons law treaties, which contain more comprehensive regulation reflecting the trajectory of modern arms control treaties.

3.1.2 Post-WW2 Treaties

The second subcategory of IHL weapons treaties is those that were developed following the conclusion of the WW2. Despite significant humanitarian

---

55 While Common art 3 to the Geneva Conventions of 1949 recognised the 'armed conflict not of an international character occurring in the territory of one of the High Contracting Parties', it did not contain provisions relating specifically to weapons. International law did not regulate the use of weapons in non-international armed conflict until Protocol II to the *CCW* (n 5) was amended in 1996.

56 Roberts and Guelff (n 22) 165. For example, France made a reservation on ratification of the 1925 Gas Protocol (n 191) that, 'The said Protocol shall *ipso facto* cease to be binding on the Government of the French Republic in regard to any enemy State whose armed forces or whose Allies fail to respect the prohibitions laid down in the Protocol'.

concerns during WW2 (e.g., the extensive use of incendiary weapons in urban areas), the Geneva Conventions of 1949 did not address the use of weapons.

A principal source of IHL treaty law during this period was the 1980 *Convention on Prohibitions or Restrictions on the Use of Certain Conventional Weapons Which May be Deemed to be Excessively Injurious or to Have Indiscriminate Effects* (CCW).[57] The CCW was developed as a diplomatic vehicle to enable the regulation of conventional weapons and complements the general weapons law provisions found in AP 1. In contrast to the pre-WW1 treaties, the restrictions and prohibitions found in the CCW protocols apply even in an armed conflict with a non-state party.[58] While the CCW is an important modern development in weapons law, it is not without its critics. Hays Parks notes that 'had any weapon in question been deemed by governments to be "excessively injurious or to have indiscriminate effects" per se, as the resolution title suggests, its use would already be prohibited, making new treaty provisions unnecessary'.[59]

States remain central to the regulation of weapons. The creation of the 1997 Ottawa Convention banning anti-personnel land mines and the 2008 Oslo Convention banning cluster munitions has demonstrated the increasingly important contribution of civil society and non-government organisations. This influence continues and plays a prominent role in the ongoing UN debate regarding the regulation of AWS.

3.1.3 Specific Treaty Prohibitions Now Considered to Be Customary International Law

Many specific weapons law treaties are recognised as declaratory of customary international law.[60] For example, the rules contained in the 1907 Hague Declaration IV are recognised as customary in nature.[61]

In 2005, the ICRC published its Study on Customary International Humanitarian Law ('ICRC Study') and identified several specific customary

57 *Convention on Prohibitions or Restrictions on the Use of Certain Conventional Weapons Which May be Deemed to be Excessively Injurious or to Have Indiscriminate Effects* (10 October 1980) and Amendment to Article 1 (21 December 2001) 1342 UNTS 137 ('CCW').

58 Ibid art 7(1) states, 'When one of the parties to a conflict is not bound by an annexed Protocol, the parties bound by this Convention and that annexed Protocols shall remain bound'.

59 W Hays Parks, 'Conventional Weapons and Weapons Reviews' (2005) 8 *Yearbook of International Humanitarian Law* 55–142, 75.

60 Dinstein (n 39) 61.

61 Nuclear Weapons Case (n 38) [75], [80].

international law rules relative to weapons.[62] These include prohibitions or limitations on poison or poisoned weapons (Rule 72, p. 251), biological weapons (Rule 73, p. 256), chemical weapons (Rule 74, p. 259), riot control agents as a means or method of warfare (Rule 75, p. 263), herbicides (Rule 76, p. 265), bullets that expand or flatten in the body (Rule 77, p. 268), bullets that explode in the body (Rule 78, p. 272), booby traps (Rule 78, p. 275), landmines (Rule 80, p. 278), incendiary weapons (Rules 84, 85, pp. 287–9) and laser weapons (Rule 86, p. 292).

While extensive, the accuracy of the ICRC Study is subject to debate.[63] Turns argues that, of the 16 customary rules identified by the ICRC as dealing with specific weapons, only those rules concerning poison weapons, expanding bullets and exploding bullets are 'incontestably covered by customary international law'.[64] Despite its significance and utility, it is unlikely that the ICRC Study is regarded by all states as a determinative statement of the existence of customary international humanitarian law rules relevant to means and methods of warfare.[65] States not party to a specific weapons law treaty from which the customary rules are derived must determine their position on the status of specific customary international humanitarian law prohibition.

3.2 *General Weapons Law Prohibitions*

In contrast to specific weapons law treaties, general weapons law prohibitions are concerned with certain weapon effects rather than specific weapon classes or categories. These effects include superfluous injury or unnecessary suffering, or indiscriminate effects. The International Court of Justice succinctly described the general weapon prohibitions in their 1996 advisory opinion on the threat or use of nuclear weapons:

> humanitarian law, at a very early stage, prohibited certain types of weapons either because of their indiscriminate effect on combatants and civilians or because of the unnecessary suffering caused to combatants, that is to say, a harm greater than that unavoidable to achieve legitimate military objectives. If an envisaged use of weapons would not meet the

62 JM Henckaerts and L Doswald-Becks, *Customary International Humanitarian Law* (Cambridge University Press, 2005) ('ICRC CIL Study').

63 Turns (n 41) refers to the ICRC Study as a 'blunderbuss: indiscriminate and firing in all directions, hitting some of its targets but arguably damaging a great deal else besides', 203.

64 Ibid 205.

65 See, eg, JB Bellinger and WJ Hayes, 'A US Government Response to the International Committee of the Red Cross Study on Customary International Humanitarian Law' (2007) 89 *International Review of the Red Cross* 443.

> requirements of humanitarian law, a threat to engage in such use would also be contrary to that law.[66]

The following subsections explore these general prohibitions in turn.

3.2.1 Superfluous Injury or Unnecessary Suffering

This general prohibition against weapons calculated to cause superfluous injury or unnecessary suffering is concerned with the weapons that cause excessive harm to combatants that is not justified by military necessity. The St. Petersburg Declaration recognised that weapons that 'uselessly aggravate the suffering of disabled men or render their death inevitable'[67] are contrary to 'laws of humanity'.[68] The drafters of the St. Petersburg Declaration suggest that the point at which the 'necessities of war ought to yield to the requirements of humanity' expressed the delicate balance between the IHL principles of military necessity and humanity. In doing so, the St. Petersburg Declaration provided a measure for the limitation on weapons that 'uselessly aggravated the sufferings of disabled men or render their death inevitable'. Identifying this balance to determine when a weapon exceeds a legitimate military objective is an important element of a legal review.

Greenwood describes this delicate balance by stating:

> [It] prohibits outright any weapon (or means of warfare) which is of a nature to cause unnecessary suffering. In addition, where a particular weapon has a legitimate use but is also capable of being used in a way which will, in the circumstances, cause unnecessary suffering (and all weapons can be so used), the principle prohibits the latter use (or method of warfare) even though it does not give rise to an outright ban on the weapon itself.[69]

3.2.1.1 *Inconsistent Language: a Need for Clarity*

The IHL rule prohibiting weapons of a nature to cause superfluous injury or unnecessary suffering is the subject of academic debate. Some scholars argue that the prohibition is unclear, vague and barren of practical results,[70]

---

66 Nuclear Weapons Case (n 38) [78].

67 Ibid.

68 Ibid.

69 Greenwood (n 19) 194.

70 A Cassese, 'Weapons Causing Unnecessary Suffering: Are They Prohibited?' (1975) 58 *Rivista di Diritto Internazionale* 12, 35.

while others suggest that the vagueness of the rule is a virtue.[71] The embryonic principle of unnecessary suffering, first articulated in the St. Petersburg Declaration, was adopted as an express rule in the regulations annexed to the 1899 Hague Convention II and its 1907 counterpart.[72] Controversy arose primarily from the difference in the English language interpretation of the original French text 'propre a causer des maux superflus' in the 1899 Convention and repeated in the 1907 Convention. The English translation of art 23(e) of the 1899 Convention states that 'it is especially prohibited ... to employ arms, projectiles or material *of a nature to cause superfluous injury*'.[73]

In contrast, art 23(e) of the 1907 Convention states, 'It is especially forbidden ... to employ arms, projectiles or material *calculated to cause unnecessary suffering*'.[74]

The inconsistency in translation between the 1899 and 1907 phrases has generated academic discussion.[75] The question is whether there is a legal significance between the different interpretations. Some suggest the former refers to immediate, physical damage, whereas 'superfluous injury' refers to permanent damage or disfigurement.[76] Greenwood argues that:

> the concept of 'injury' or 'suffering' includes the totality of a victim's injury, and that a distinction between physical and psychological injuries would be artificial, as well as having no basis in past practice concerning weaponry.[77]

While the different adjectives are attributed to variations in the English translation of the original, identical official French language texts in 1899 and

---

71 R Liivoja, 'Protecting Warfighters from Superfluous Injury and Unnecessary Suffering' in Matt Killingsworth (ed), *Who Do the Laws of War Protect? Civility, Barbarity and the Evolution of International Humanitarian Law* (Cambridge University Press) 21.

72 *Convention (II) with Respect to the Laws and Customs of War on Land and its Annex*, opened for signature 29 July 1899 (entered into force 4 September 1900) ('1899 Hague Convention II'); 1907 Hague Declaration IV (n 46).

73 Ibid art 23(g).

74 1907 Hague Convention IV (n 46).

75 See Liivoja (n 71).

76 M Bothe, KJ Partsch and WA Solf, *New Rules for Victims of Armed Conflicts: Commentary on the Two 1977 Protocols Additional to the Geneva Conventions of 1949* (Martinus Nijhoff Publishers, 1982) 196.

77 Greenwood (n 19) 196.

1907,[78] the variation generated discussions on the appropriate interpretation of the prohibition.

Ultimately, the modern expression of this principle, found in art 35(2) of AP 1, resolved some of this interpretive uncertainty. It did so by adopting both the 1899 and 1907 formulations to create the dual term 'superfluous injury or unnecessary suffering'. It also discarded the subjective 'calculated to cause' language in preference of the objective 'of a nature. 'Calculated to cause' suggests a deliberate intention to design a weapon that inevitably causes unnecessary suffering. This 'design intent' focus contrasts with an 'effects-based' analysis suggested by the phrase 'of a nature to cause'.[79]

Article 35(2) of AP 1 does not attempt to resolve the dual terminology and states, 'It is prohibited to employ weapons, projectiles and material and methods of warfare of a nature to cause superfluous injury or unnecessary suffering'.[80]

This modern formulation of this IHL prohibition is not without its critics. Hays Parks argues that the contents of the phrase 'calculated to cause' is a 'clearer expression of the intent of governments to focus on design and intended purpose rather than every remote possibility of injury'.[81] Boothby supports this view, suggesting that the term 'of a nature' refers to 'what invariably happens when it is used'.[82] This preference for the 'calculated to cause' design purpose approach is echoed in the US Law of War Manual.[83] However, these views do not appear to be representative of a broader state practice.

Article 35(2) of AP 1 extends the prohibition beyond the customary international law prohibition, reflected in the Hague Regulations, to include the way the weapon is used. This intention is clear in the art 35(2) language prohibiting 'weapons, projectiles, material and <u>methods of warfare</u>'. This, for the first time, regulates both weapon effects and specific methods of weapon use. Such an approach requires a legal reviewer to consider the prohibition against superfluous injury or unnecessary suffering in two ways, first in terms of the nature of the weapon, projectile or material and second in relation to specific uses of the subject weapon, projectile or material. The relevant question is whether

78 S Haines, 'The Developing Law of Weapons: Humanity, Distinction, and Precautions in Attack' in Andrew Clapham and Paola Gaeta (eds), *The Oxford Handbook of International Law in Armed Conflict* (Oxford University Press, 2018) 11.

79 Liivoja (n 71) 16.

80 AP 1 (n 15) art 35(2).

81 Hays Parks (n 59) 86–7.

82 Boothby (20) 58.

83 US Department of Defense, *Law of War Manual* (Office of General Counsel, June 2015, revised December 2016) ('US Law of War Manual'), paragraph 6.6.1.

the weapon or any specific uses are 'of a nature' to cause superfluous injury or unnecessary suffering.

The art 35(2) distinction between 'weapons, projectiles and material' and 'methods of warfare' that are of a nature to cause superfluous injury or unnecessary suffering is a fine one. A legal review will consider the prohibition against 'weapons, projectiles and material' by the reference to the normal or expected use. If such use inevitably results in injury or suffering to combatants that is not justified by military necessity, the weapons, projectiles and material is determined to be prohibited per se. This is addressed further in the subsequent paragraphs.

A legal review must also consider the second element of art 35(2), which considers other uses outside the normal or expected use. If certain uses are of a nature to cause superfluous injury or unnecessary suffering, those uses are prohibited. For example, if an anti-material munition previously determined as lawful in its normal or expected use (e.g., attacking enemy vehicles) was used against combatants, it may cause significant harm to the person, which is not justified by military necessity. This is especially so where another weapon (e.g., a rifle) would achieve the same military advantage without causing the same injury or suffering to the combatant.

If the potentially unlawful use was categorised as a 'misuse', distinguished by an individual's actions rather than the normal or expected use, the legal review would not consider it in detail. However, if the use was categorised as a normal or expected use, the question of how it would be determined that such a method of warfare was of a nature to cause superfluous injury or unnecessary suffering must be asked. This issue is addressed in more detail below.

3.2.1.2 *Application of the Superfluous Injury or Unnecessary Suffering Rule in Practice*

In practice, assessing whether a weapon causes superfluous injury or unnecessary suffering is a difficult task. There is no internationally agreed approach to determining whether a weapon is prohibited by art 35(2) of AP I and little publicly available information on how reviewing states undertake this determination.

As a preliminary matter, it is important to re-emphasise two points. First, the prohibition against superfluous injury or unnecessary suffering is aimed at alleviating the suffering of combatants.[84] While it is often noted that an objective of IHL is to 'reduce unnecessary suffering and injury to both civilians

84 Nuclear Weapons Case (n 38) [78]; Schmitt (n 44) 809.

and combatants',[85] the IHL rule in art 35(2) of AP 1 is not directed towards protecting civilians who are specifically protected from direct attack by the IHL rule of distinction[86] and excessive incidental injury or death by the rule of proportionality.[87]

Second, any suffering or injury caused by a particular weapon must be balanced against the military advantage anticipated from its use. It is only when the suffering is unnecessary or injury superfluous that the prohibition arises. The difficult question is where the balance between military necessity and humanity lies. Hays Parks describes the test as:

> a balancing test [which] is applied between the force dictated by military necessity to achieve a legitimate objective vis-a-vis injury that may be considered superfluous to the achievement of the stated or intended objective (in other words, whether the suffering caused is out of proportion to the military advantage to be gained).[88]

There are, however, differing views on how this principle is applied in practice. The ICJ, in the Nuclear Weapons Case, defined unnecessary suffering as 'harm greater than that unavoidable to achieve legitimate military objectives'.[89] It is generally accepted that suffering that has no military purpose violates this principle. Ultimately, the ICJ concluded that this principle has a fundamental humanitarian character that applies to all kinds of weapons, past, present and future.[90] This principle underpins the development of many weapons treaties, including the bans on anti-personnel mines,[91] blinding lasers[92] and cluster munitions.[93] Each of these weapon systems was designed to cause permanent harm to their victims, both combatants and innocent civilians, and suggest that the permanence of an injury is relevant to determining whether it causes unnecessary suffering or superfluous injury.

---

85 See Norwegian Defence Force *Manual of the Law of Armed Conflict* (Chief of Defence, English Language Ed, 2018) 6; Greenwood (n 19) 191.

86 AP 1 (n 15) art 48.

87 Ibid art 57(2)(a)(iii).

88 Hays Parks (n 59) 58.

89 Nuclear Weapons Case (n 38) [78].

90 Ibid.

91 Ottawa Convention (n 53).

92 CCW (n 57) Protocol V.

93 *Convention on Cluster Munitions*, opened for signature 30 May 2008, 2688 UNTS 39 (entered into force 1 August 2010).

There remains a degree of imprecision in the specific legal threshold beyond which suffering is determined to be unnecessary. It is widely acknowledged that the test is difficult to apply. Hays Parks emphasises that the weapon effect cannot be considered in isolation from the military context. He suggests that the degree of unnecessary suffering must be 'clearly disproportionate to the intended objective(s) for development of the weapon (that is, the suffering must outweigh substantially the military necessity for the weapon). The fact that a weapon causes injury or death does not lead to the conclusion that the weapon causes superfluous injury, or is illegal per se'.[94]

It is recognised that the principle of military necessity permits the killing or wounding of an enemy combatant in battle.[95] Suffering is an inevitable consequence of armed conflict, and the prohibition against unnecessary suffering or superfluous injury does not prohibit the infliction of serious injury.[96] Dinstein argues that 'the effects of the use of certain weapons may be appalling, but this is not, in and of itself, enough to render the weapons illegal'.[97] It appears that the threshold beyond which suffering is considered unnecessary is not precisely determined. The US Department of Defence has articulated the following test for unnecessary suffering:

> The prohibition of unnecessary suffering constitutes acknowledgement that necessary suffering to combatants is lawful and may include severe injury or loss of life. There is no agreed international definition for unnecessary suffering. A weapon or munition would be deemed to cause unnecessary suffering only if it inevitably or in its normal use has a particular effect and the injury caused is considered by governments as disproportionate to the military necessary for it, that is, the military advantage to be gained from its use. This balancing test cannot be conducted in isolation. A weapons or munition's effects must be weighed in light of comparable, lawful weapons or munitions in use on the modern battlefield. A weapon is not unlawful merely because if may cause severe suffering or injury. The appropriate determination is whether a weapon or munition's employment for its normal or expected use would be prohibited in some or all circumstances.

94 W Hays Parks, 'Joint Service Combat Shotgun Program' (1997) 10 *Army Law Review* 16, 18.

95 Ibid.

96 Ibid 68.

97 Dinstein (n 39) 64–65.

> The correct criterion is whether the employment of a weapon for its normal or expected use inevitably would cause injury or suffering *manifestly disproportionate* to its military effectiveness.[98]

It appears that the threshold for concluding that a weapon is of a nature to cause unnecessary suffering or superfluous injury is high. The injury caused must be clearly or manifestly disproportionate to the military advantage gained. Bothe, Partsch and Solf suggest that the test is whether:

> the suffering is needless, superfluous, or manifestly disproportionate to the military advantage reasonably expected from the use of the weapon. On the humanitarian side of the equation against which military advantage is to be balanced are such factors as the painfulness or severity of wounds, mortality rates, and the incidence of permanent damage or disfigurement and the feasibility of treatment under field conditions. Neither element of the equation can be taken in isolation. All such comparative judgments logically lead to an inquiry into how much suffering various weapons cause and whether available alternate weapons can achieve the same military advantage effectively but cause less suffering. The comparison of, and balancing between, suffering and military effectiveness is difficult in practice because neither side of the equation is easy to quantify. Inevitably, the assessment will be subjective even when sufficient agreed factual data are available on wound effects and military effectiveness.[99]

The determination of whether a weapon causes unnecessary suffering or superfluous injury is made in the context of a weapon's normal or expected use, as known at the time of the legal review.

3.2.1.2.1 Autonomous Methods of Warfare Resulting in Superfluous Injury or Unnecessary Suffering

An issue that has not received significant academic attention is whether a *method* of warfare that is of a nature to cause superfluous injury or unnecessary suffering is prohibited. The prohibition in art 35(2) of AP 1 focuses on weapons that are 'of a nature to cause superfluous injury or unnecessary suffering' and, therefore, whether a weapon is unlawful per se as it causes harm

98 Hays Parks (n 59) fn 25.
99 Bothe, Partsch and Solf (n 76) 196.

that is disproportionate to the military necessity of its use. It does not address the use of otherwise lawful weapons in ways that cause superfluous injury or unnecessary suffering, such as precision targeting of specific parts of the human anatomy (e.g., the eyes, knees or genitals) to cause specific, long-term, debilitating wounds. Such methods of warfare may be practically impossible for human weapon operators; however, future AWS may be technically capable of such methods of warfare. Moreover, an AWS may determine these methods to be the most effective in attacking human targets as the caring for the wounded requires additional manpower.

Such methods of warfare may not be deliberately programmed into an AWS however the AWS may, through machine learning, self-identify this method of attacking human targets. Unlawful methods of warfare could manifest during the weapon test and evaluation or during its operational use. This presents several challenges to the reviewing state and its military commanders. This includes the need for ongoing legal review of AWS to ensure that such risks are mitigated.

Having considered the general prohibition against weapons of a nature to cause superfluous injury or unnecessary suffering, the next weapons law rule of general application is that which prohibits weapons that are by nature indiscriminate.

3.2.2 Indiscriminate Effects

A fundamental principle of IHL is distinction. This principle is given effect by the general weapons law prohibition against weapons that are by nature indiscriminate.[100] To be considered discriminate, a weapon must be capable of being directed at a specific military objective and, therefore, distinguishing between (a) lawful targets (combatants, military objectives, members of an organised armed group and civilians taking a direct part in hostilities) and (b) unlawful targets (combatants *hors de combat*, non-combatants (e.g. medical and religious personnel), civilians and civilian objects).[101] Second, an otherwise discriminate weapon must not be used indiscriminately.[102]

The first component of the discrimination rule concerns the technical capability of the weapon to be aimed at and strike an intended target. The second aspect focuses on whether the intended target is lawful. Identifying lawful targets requires application of laws regulating methods of warfare that define the categories of persons and objects protected by IHL. The rules concerning the

---

100 ICRC Database (n 10) Rule 71 'Weapons that are by Nature Indiscriminate'.

101 AP I (n 15) art 35(4)(b).

102 Ibid art 35(4)(a).

use of a weapon are generally determined concurrently with the weapon's use in armed conflict and are regarded as separate legal considerations to determining whether a weapon is unlawful per se.

Together with the prohibition against weapons causing superfluous injury or unnecessary suffering, the distinction rule is described by the ICJ as one of the 'cardinal principles of international humanitarian law'.[103] Consistent with the ICJ, the ICRC identifies the principle of distinction as a norm of customary international law.[104] It is less clear whether the general prohibition against indiscriminate weapons existed as a norm of customary international law prior to the negotiation of AP 1. Some scholars have questioned the existence of a customary international law rule prohibiting indiscriminate weapons prior to the creation of AP 1.[105]

Despite its normative status, the principle of distinction was not codified until the ratification of AP 1, which states at art 48:

> In order to ensure respect for and protection of the civilian population and civilian objects, the Parties to the conflict shall at all times distinguish between the civilian population and combatants and between civilian objects and military objectives and accordingly shall direct their operations only against military objectives.[106]

In addition to the general prohibition, the rule of distinction is given practical effect by art 51(4) of AP 1, which prohibits indiscriminate attacks, defined as attacks:

> a) which are not directed at a specific military objective;
> b) which employ a method or means of combat which cannot be directed at a specific military objective; or
> c) which employ a method or means of combat the effects of which cannot be limited as required by this Protocol; and consequently, in each such case, are of a nature to strike military objectives and civilians and civilian objects without distinction.[107]

An indiscriminate weapon is one that cannot be aimed at lawful targets and so is likely to hit both civilians and civilian objects as well combatants and

103 Nuclear Weapons Case (n 38) [78].
104 ICRC CIHL Database (n 62).
105 Boothby (n 20) 75.
106 AP 1 (n 15) art 48.
107 Ibid art 51(4).

military objectives. Articles 51(4)(b) and (c) prohibit an attack using indiscriminate weapons.[108] There is a fine distinction to be made between a weapon that is indiscriminate 'by nature' and the indiscriminate use of a lawful, discriminate weapon.[109] Hays Parks emphasises that any weapon may be employed in an indiscriminate manner: 'An indiscriminate attack employing an otherwise lawful weapon or weapon system would not make either unlawful'.[110]

The prohibition against indiscriminate weapons is concerned with whether a weapon is designed to be capable of being directed against military objectives. The circumstances in which the weapon is intended to be used is relevant. A legal review analysis of whether a weapon is indiscriminate is based on the normal or expected use of the weapon. For example, a weapon that is insufficiently accurate to discriminate between combatants and civilians in an urban environment may have military utility in an open environment where there are no civilians or civilian objects. Most unguided field artillery is illustrative of this point. In such cases, the legal review of the weapon and military manual for the use of the weapon should emphasise this limitation on the lawful use of the weapon. These operational limitations would be incorporated into the rules of engagement or weapon operating procedures.[111]

A legal review will determine a particular weapon is unlawful per se where testing demonstrates that it is unable to be aimed at a specific target or its effect is unable to be controlled. It will not, however, consider specific use cases to determine whether such uses are indiscriminate. There is no specific formulation for determining whether a weapon is indiscriminate. It is recognised as a high standard as even an unguided weapon with wide area effects may be used discriminately in certain circumstances. For example, the US GBU-43 Massive Ordinance Air Blast, otherwise known as the 'Mother of all Bombs', contains more than 8 kgs of explosives, equivalent to 10 tonnes of TNT, and has a blast radius of 1.6 km.[112] If this is used to attack an enemy target within a civilian population, its use would be indiscriminate. Alternately, the same weapon may be used discriminately in a remote area absent civilians or

---

108 M Schmitt, 'Precision Attack and International Humanitarian Law' (2005) 87 *International Review of the Red Cross* 445, 454.

109 Dinstein (n 39) 62; Boothby (n 20) 78–9; Hays Parks (n 59) 59.

110 Hays Parks (n 59) 59.

111 ICRC, *A Guide to the Weapons Review of New Weapons, Means and Methods of Warfare: Measures to Implement Article 36 of Additional Protocol I of 1977* (2006) ('*ICRC Guide*'), 15.

112 US GBU-43 Massive Ordinance Air Blast (website) <https://www.defense.gov/Multimedia/Photos/igphoto/2001732840/>.

civilian objects. Indeed, few weapons are illegal per se because they are indiscriminate in nature.[113]

The dichotomy between the weapons law determination of the legality of a weapon per se and the targeting law assessment of the lawfulness of a particular weapon use will become less clear in the context of AWS, where the AWS will perform functions governed by targeting laws. A reviewing state will bear significant legal risk if it limits its legal review analysis of an AWS to arts 51(4)(b) and (c) of AP 1 and allows the determination of art 51(4)(a) to remain an issue of targeting law addressed only at the point of the weapon's operational use.

4 Martens Clause

The Martens clause is named for its author, Fyodor Fyodorovich Martens, a member of the Russian delegation to the 1899 Hague Peace Conference, who drafted the following (original English translation) as an expedient compromise to a potential diplomatic impasse regarding the status of civilians taking up arms against an occupying military force:[114]

> Until a more complete code of the laws of war have been issued, the High Contracting parties deem it expedient to declare that, in cases not included in the Regulations adopted by them, the inhabitants and belligerents remain under the protection and rule of the principles of the law of nations, as they result from the usages established among civilised peoples, from the laws of humanity, and the dictates of the public conscience.[115]

The Martens clause first appeared in the Preamble to Hague Convention II of 1899, containing the Regulations on the Laws and Customs of War on Land.[116] Despite the Martens clause's initial narrow context, its relevance broadened as it became cited more widely. The Martens clause has remained an important part of IHL for over a century.

The contemporary Martens clause is found in art 1(2) of API, which states:

113 K Anderson, D Reisner and M Waxman, 'Adapting the Law of Armed Conflict to Autonomous Weapon Systems' (2014) 90 *International Law Studies* 386, 400.

114 I Henderson, *The Contemporary Law of Targeting* (Martinus Nijhoff Publishers, 2009) 28.

115 Ibid 28–9.

116 1907 Hague Convention IV (n 46).

(2) In cases not covered by this Protocol or by other international agreements, civilians and combatants remain under the protection and authority of the principles of international law derived from established custom, from the principles of humanity and from the dictates of the public conscience.

The AP 1 text differs slightly from the 1899 original. In both versions, the clause refers clearly to customary international law and to dictates of public conscience; however, the original 'laws of humanity' was replaced with the 'principles of humanity'. In the context of weapons, the principles of humanity are interpreted as prohibiting means and methods that are not necessary to attain a definite military advantage.[117] This is consistent with the IHL principle of military necessity, which permits combatants to take measures necessary for securing submission of an enemy at the earliest moment but prohibits the destruction of property as an end in itself.[118] In contrast, the meaning of 'dictates of public conscience' is less clear. Sparrow suggests that the relevant 'public' is the global public and that the dictates of public conscience may be identified through public polls and expert opinion of 'esteemed justices, community leaders and learned professors' obtained through public deliberation.[119]

Turning to the legal status of the Martens clause, there are a range of views.[120] In the Nuclear Weapons Case, the ICJ noted that the Martens clause 'has proven an effective means of addressing the rapid evolution of military technology'.[121] The ICRC argues the Martens clause acts a 'safety net for humanity' and 'prevents the assumption that anything that is not explicitly prohibited by relevant treaties is therefore permitted'.[122] However, states, scholars and non-government organisations disagree on whether the clause should be applied narrowly, as an aid to interpreting existing laws, or expansively, creating new sources of law. Greenwood argues for the narrow interpretation that the Martens clause 'makes it clear that the general principles embodied in

117 R Ticehurst, 'The Martens Clause and the Laws of Armed Conflict' (1997) 317 *International Review of the Red Cross* 125, 125–34.

118 Australian Government, ADF, Australian Defence Doctrine Publication 06.4 *Law of Armed Conflict* (11 May 2006) [2–2]–[2.6].

119 R Sparrow, 'Ethics as a Source of Law: The Martens Clause and Autonomous Weapons', *ICRC Humanitarian Law and Policy* (Blog Post, 14 November 2017) <https://blogs.icrc.org/law-and-policy/2017/11/14/ethics-source-law-martens-clause-autonomous-weapons/>.

120 Ticehurst (n 117).

121 Nuclear Weapons Case (n 38) [78].

122 ICRC, *Ethics and Autonomous Weapon Systems: An Ethical Basis for Human Control?* (3 April 2018) 5–6, <https://www.icrc.org/en/document/ethics-and-autonomous-weapon-systems-ethical-basis-human-control>.

customary law still apply and that the use of a weapon contrary to those principles is unlawful'.[123] Cassese regards the interpretation of the laws of armed conflict as including not only treaties and customs but also the principles of international law derived from the principles of humanity and dictates of public conscience.[124] In 1948, the US Military Tribunal sitting in Nuremberg described the Martens clause in the *Krupp* case as:

> much more than a pious declaration. It is a general clause, making the usages established among civilized nations, the laws of humanity and the dictates of public conscience into the legal yardstick to be applied if and when the specific provisions of the Convention and the Regulations annexed to it do not cover specific cases occurring in warfare, or concomitant to warfare.[125]

The alternative view, supported by groups seeking a pre-emptive ban on lethal autonomous weapon systems, is that the principles of humanity and the dictates of public conscience are independent sources of legal obligation. According to this interpretation, if a weapon is not prohibited by a treaty or customary law, it may still be unlawful if it contravenes the principles of humanity or the dictates of public conscience. This was strongly argued in the Human Rights Watch (HRW) 2012 report titled *Losing Humanity: The Case Against Killer Robots*.[126] In their report, HRW argued that 'fully autonomous weapons would likely contravene the Martens clause, which prohibits weapons that run counter to the 'dictates of public conscience'.[127] However, this argument has not gained much support. As Greenwood points out, there is no evidence of a weapon being treated as unlawful solely on account of the Martens clause.[128] There is little academic support for the view that the 'principles of humanity' and the 'dictates of public conscience' are separate standards for determining the legality of weapons.[129]

123 Greenwood (n 19) 206.

124 Ibid 192–3.

125 '*United States of America v Krupp von Bohen and Halbak*' in Hershc Lauterpacht (ed), *Annual Digest and Reports of Public International Law Cases: Being a Selection from the Decisions of International Courts and Tribunals and Military Courts during the Year 1948* (1953) 622.

126 International Human Rights Clinic and Human Rights Watch, *Losing Humanity: The Case Against Killer Robots* (IHRC and HRW, 2012), 24 ('Losing Humanity'). <https://www.hrw.org/report/2012/11/19/losing-humanity/case-against-killer-robots>.

127 Ibid 4.

128 Greenwood (n 98) 206.

129 Ibid.

In the Nuclear Weapons Case, the ICJ found the Martens clause to be a norm of customary international law and, therefore, applicable to all states.[130] Unfortunately, the ICJ's decision did not clarify which interpretation of the Marten clause is preferred. In confirming the Martens clause's continuing existence and applicability, the ICJ stated that the Martens clause 'has proved to be an effective means of addressing the rapid evolution of military technology',[131] and it was applicable to 'all forms of warfare and to all kinds of weapons, those of the past, those of the present and those of the future'.[132]

4.1 *Are Ethics Relevant to the Legal Review of AWS?*

While the Martens cause is not regarded as a legal standard for determining the legality of weapons, does this mean that the principles of humanity and dictates of public conscious are not relevant to the legal review of an AWS? In its oral statement to the ICJ during the Nuclear Weapons Case, Australia noted that neither humanity nor the dictates of public conscious are static concepts. Determining the fundamental principles of humanity necessitates consideration 'of developments … including political, technical and social developments, as well as developments in the law'.[133] IHL rules and principles are built upon basic values of humanity shared by all civilisations.[134] As argued earlier, the Martens clause confirms the importance of the principles of international law as derived from the principles of humanity and the dictates of public conscience.[135] In 2015, the ICRC observed that the development of AWS raised fundamental questions (e.g., concerning the role of humans in the use of force) that cannot be left solely to national legal reviews.[136] There are some issues that are not clearly addressed by IHL that states may address through national policy. The legal review process determines whether a new weapon, means or method of warfare complies with a state's legal obligations. Legal reviews may,

130 Nuclear Weapons Case (n 177) [84].
131 Ibid [78].
132 Ibid.
133 G Evans, 'Oral Statement of the Government of Australian', *Legality of the Threat or Use of Nuclear Weapons (Advisory Opinion)* [1996] ICJ Pleadings [15].
134 Permanent Mission of Austria to the United Nations in Geneva, *Contribution of Austria to the Chair's Request for Guiding Principles on Emerging Technologies in the Area of LAWS* (1 September 2020) 3 <https://documents.unoda.org/wp-content/uploads/2020/09/20200901-Austria.pdf>.
135 AP I (n 7) art 1(2).
136 Article 36, *Article 36 Reviews and Addressing Lethal Autonomous Weapon Systems* (Briefing Paper, April 2016) 2 <https://article36.org/wp-content/uploads/2016/04/LAWS-and-A36.pdf>.

however, inform national policy designed to address the fundamental questions raised by AWS, including their responsible, safe and ethical use. Concerns arising from state use of AI are amplified by recent examples of unethical AI, including biased predictions of criminal recidivism[137] and welfare debt.[138] Many of the arguments against AWS are based on ethical concerns, including the prospect of 'delegating life-and-death decisions to a machine'.[139]

4.2 *Martens Clause as an Avenue for Considering Soft Law and National Governance Frameworks during a Legal Review*

The Martens clause may play an increasingly important role in the analysis of a weapon during a legal review. Australia has publicly stated that it applies the Martens clause in the conduct of legal reviews.[140] The Martens clause may assist a state in interpreting its existing international law obligations to address AWS-related ethical and moral challenges. Such interpretations may be informed by soft law[141] and national or international AI governance frameworks that address a range of non-legal but important considerations, including the delegation of targeting decision-making to machines, standards of compliance, data bias, the need for explainable and predictable AI and accountability mechanisms.

4.2.1 Soft Law

Non-binding international instruments, or so-called 'soft law', play an important role in international law. A government may support a non-binding agreement or make political statements in international or domestic forums to show support for a particular issue without being legally bound by treaty

137 See for example the US Correctional Offender Management Profiling for Alternative Sanction ('COMPAS'), which was designed to assess a defendant's risk of recidivism however was found to exhibit a noticeable bias against black defendants: <https://www.uclalawreview.org/injustice-ex-machina-predictive-algorithms-in-criminal-sentencing/>.

138 See for example Australia's 2016 automated 'Robodebt' scheme, which incorrectly issued A$1.73 billion in debt notices to over 400,000 welfare recipients: <https://www.abc.net.au/news/2021-06-11/robodebt-condemned-by-federal-court-judge-as-shameful-chapter/100207674>.

139 Losing Humanity (n 126) 4.

140 Australian Government, *The Australian Article 36 Review Process*, UN Doc CCW/GGE.2/2018/WP.6 (30 August 2018), fn 20 ('Australian Article 36 Review Process').

141 'The term soft law is used to denote agreements, principles and declarations that are not legally binding. Soft law instruments are predominantly found in the international sphere. UN General Assembly resolutions are an example of soft law': European Centre for Constitutional and Human Rights Website, Glossary <https://www.ecchr.eu/en/glossary/hard-law-soft-law/>.

obligations. This is increasingly common in IHL where there is an absence of a treaty instrument and uncertainty in relation to new norms.

Non-binding agreements are therefore an influential tool to assist states and practitioners alike to interpret and apply existing IHL rules to new challenges.[142] In contrast to the treaty-making process, they are a comparatively quick process. Some recent examples of soft law include the San Remo Manual,[143] the Harvard Manual[144] and the Tallinn Manuals.[145] In practice, these publications are non-binding documents, prepared by academics to assist states to interpretate their IHL obligations, including those relating to new weapons, means or method of warfare. Soft law is useful to help inform legal reviewers of how IHL can regulate new weapon technologies such as AWS.

AWS related soft law may be developed to assist in AWS legal review. Numerous delegations to the GGE on LAWS have called for states to share best practice in the legal review of AWS.[146] One of the most significant outputs of the GGE on LAWS to date is the Guiding Principles, which are a form of non-binding instrument that will influence state behaviour.[147] They provide an important basis for states to affirm the application of existing IHL norms to AWS and the basis for identifying 'best practice'. These non-binding agreements may be represented in national policy and reflected in the range of considerations relevant to the legal review of AWS.

142 E Crawford, *Non-Binding Norms in International Humanitarian Law* (Oxford University Press, 2021).

143 L Doswald-Beck, *San Remo Manual on International Law Applicable to Armed Conflicts at Sea* (Cambridge University Press, 1995) ('San Remo Manual').

144 Program on Humanitarian Policy and Conflict Research at Harvard University, *HPRC Manual on International Law Applicable to Air and Missile Warfare* (Program on Humanitarian Policy and Conflict Research, 2010) ('Harvard Manual').

145 M Schmitt (ed), *Tallinn Manual 2.0 on the International Law Applicable to Cyber Operations* (Cambridge University Press, 2nd ed, 2017) ('Tallinn Manual 2.0').

146 Argentina, *Questionnaire on the Legal Review Mechanisms of New Weapons, Means and Methods of Warfare*, GGE on LAWS, UN Doc CCW/GGE.1/2019/WP.6 (29 March 2019) ('Argentina Questionnaire').

147 *Guiding Principles affirmed by the Group of Governmental Experts on Emerging Technologies in the Area of Lethal Autonomous Weapons System*, Annex III to the Final Report of the Meeting of the High Contracting Parties to the Convention on Prohibitions or Restrictions on the Use of Certain Conventional Weapons Which May be Deemed to be Excessively Injurious or to Have Indiscriminate Effects, UN Doc CCW/MSP/2019/9 (13 December 2019) ('UN GGE Guiding Principles').

4.2.2 AI Governance Frameworks

In addition to soft law, states may enact or interpret their national obligations influenced by international standards for the governance of AI. National governance frameworks specifically addressing the use of AI in the military has recently been the subject of international meetings such as the Responsible use of Artificial Intelligence in the Military Domain (REAIM) co-hosted by the Governments of the Netherlands and the Republic of South Korea.[148]

REAIM was preceded by a number of national initiatives to regulate the use of AI. For example, in 2019, Australia's Federal Department of Industry, Science, Energy and Resources has led the Australian development of an ethical framework by publishing *Australia's Artificial Intelligence Ethics Framework*.[149] This framework describes eight voluntary AI Ethics Principles to be applied during each phase of an AI system's life cycle. These principles are intended to reduce the risk of negative effects of AI and ensure its use is supported by good governance standards. The principles are:

a) *Human, societal and environmental wellbeing*: AI systems should benefit individuals, society and the environment.
b) *Human-centred values:* AI systems should respect human rights, diversity, and the autonomy of individuals.
c) *Fairness:* AI systems should be inclusive and accessible and should not involve or result in unfair discrimination against individuals, communities, or groups.
d) *Privacy protection and security:* AI systems should respect and uphold privacy rights and data protection and ensure the security of data.
e) *Reliability and safety:* AI systems should reliably operate in accordance with their intended purpose.
f) *Transparency and explainability:* There should be transparency and responsible disclosure so people can understand when they are being significantly affected by AI and can find out when an AI system is engaging with them.

148 Government of the Netherlands and Government of the Republic of Korea, *Responsible use of AI in the Military domain* ('REAIM') the Hague, 15–16 February 2023 (Web Page) <https://www.government.nl/ministries/ministry-of-foreign-affairs/news/2023/02/16/reaim-2023-call-to-action>.

149 Department of Industry, Science, Energy and Resources, *Australia's Artificial Intelligence Ethics Framework*, Commonwealth of Australia (Web Page) <https://www.industry.gov.au/data-and-publications/australias-artificial-intelligence-ethics-framework>.

g) *Contestability:* When an AI system significantly affects a person, community, group or environment, there should be a timely process to allow people to challenge the use or outcomes of the AI system.
h) *Accountability:* People responsible for the different phases of the AI life cycle should be identifiable and accountable for the outcomes of the AI systems, and human oversight of AI systems should be enabled.[150]

These voluntary principles present unique compliance challenges for military AI applications. The question is whether there is a need for AI governance frameworks designed specifically for the military. In 2021, the North Atlantic Treaty Organisation (NATO) adopted an Artificial Intelligence Strategy consisting of 'mutually reinforcing principles' as a foundation for establishing best practices for the military use of AI by its member states and allies.[151] The principles consist of:

a) *Lawfulness:* AI applications will be developed and used in accordance with national and international law, including IHL and human rights law, as applicable.
b) *Responsibility and Accountability:* AI applications will be developed and used with appropriate levels of judgement and care; clear human responsibility shall apply to ensure accountability.
c) *Explainability and Traceability:* AI applications will be appropriately understandable and transparent, including through the use of review methodologies, sources, and procedures. This includes verification, assessment and validation mechanisms at either a NATO and/or national level.
d) *Reliability:* AI applications will have explicit, well-defined use cases. The safety, security and robustness of such capabilities will be subject to testing and assurance within those use cases across their entire life cycle, including through established NATO and/or national certification procedures.
e) *Governability:* AI applications will be developed and used according to their intended functions and will allow for appropriate human–machine interaction; the ability to detect and avoid unintended consequences; and the ability to take steps, such as disengagement or deactivation of systems, when such systems demonstrate unintended behaviour.

150 Ibid.

151 Z Stanley-Lockman and E Christie, *An AI Strategy for NATO* (Web Page, 25 October 2021) <https://www.nato.int/docu/review/articles/2021/10/25/an-artificial-intelligence-strategy-for-nato/index.html>.

f) *Bias Mitigation:* Proactive steps will be taken to minimise any unintended bias in the development and use of AI applications and in datasets.

States, including the US,[152] Canada,[153] Australia,[154] France[155] and the UK,[156] have developed policies outlining their approach to ethical AI in the military context. These are complemented by work within state alliances such as NATO,[157] supranational bodies such as the Organisation for Economic Co-Operation and Development (OECD)[158] and private enterprises such as Google.[159] The introductory sentence in the CCW GGE on LAWS Guiding Principles is as follows:

> It was affirmed that international law, in particular the United Nations Charter and International Humanitarian Law (IHL), as well as relevant ethical perspectives, should guide the continued work of the Group.[160]

State policies identify a similar range of ethical AI principles, including being responsible, equitable, traceable, reliable, governable, controlled and lawful.[161]

---

152 Office of the Deputy Secretary of Defense, *Implementing Responsible Artificial Intelligence in the Department of Defense* (Washington, DC, 26 May 2021).

153 Department of National Defence of Canada, *The Department of National Defence and Canadian Armed Forces Data Strategy* (3 December 2019).

154 SK Devitt et al, *A Method for Ethical AI in Defence* (DSTG-TR-3786, Defence Science and Technology Group, February 2021) ('MEAID') <https://tasdcrc.com.au/a-method-for-ethical-ai-in-defence/>; SK Devitt and D Copeland, 'Australia's Approach to AI Governance in Security and Defence' in M Raska, Z Stanley-Lockman and R Bitzinger (eds), *AI Governance for National Security and Defence: Assessing Military AI Strategic Perspectives* (Routledge, 2022).

155 C Villani, *Towards a French and European Strategy* (French Government, 2018) 113–14.

156 United Kingdom Government, *Guidance: Ethics, Transparency and Accountability Framework for Automated Decision-Making* (13 March 2021) <https://shorturl.at/GQNqj>. United Kingdom Government, Ministry of Defence, *Ambitious, Safe, Responsible: Our Approach to the Delivery of AI-enabled Capability in Defence* (June 2022).

157 Edward Hunter Christie, *Artificial Intelligence at NATO: Dynamic Adoption, Responsible Use* (Web Page, 24 November 2020) <https://www.nato.int/docu/review/articles/2020/11/24/artificial-intelligence-at-nato-dynamic-adoption-responsible-use/index.html>.

158 OECD, *Principles of Artificial Intelligence* (Web Page, May 2019) <https://oecd.ai/en/ai-principles>.

159 Google AI, *Artificial Intelligence at Google: Our Principles* (Web Page) <https://ai.google/principles/>.

160 UN GGE Guiding Principles (n 147).

161 Z Stanley-Lockman, *Responsible and Ethical Military AI: Allies and Allied Perspectives* (Centre for Security and Emerging Technology, August 2021) 48.

The question is whether such principles are relevant to or independent of the art 36 legal review obligation. Ultimately, this is a decision for states to make in their national policy. A state may consider the application of ethical principles during their art 36 legal review process. In one sense, existing laws already reflect ethical principles. For example, the IHL rule of distinction in art 48 of AP 1 reflects the ethical value of avoiding harm to those not taking part in hostilities. In another sense, it has long been recognised that ethics, expressed broadly as 'laws of humanity' or 'dictates of public conscience', are relevant to addressing challenges brought by technical developments in warfare. The International Military Commission responsible for the 1868 St. Petersburg Declaration declared that 'whenever a precise proposition shall be drawn up in view of future improvements which science may affect in the armament of troops, in order to maintain the principles which they have established, and to conciliate the necessities of war with the laws of humanity'.[162]

5 Conclusions

While there are no international law treaty specifically prohibiting or restricting AWS as a class of weapon, international law regulates AWS in several ways. For example, states party to certain arms control treaties are prohibited from developing, producing, acquiring, possessing, stockpiling or transferring AWS that utilise specific weapon types such as chemical or biological weapons, anti-personnel mines or cluster munitions. Similarly, disarmament, counter-proliferation or non-proliferation treaties require states party to reduce or eliminate the categories of weapons such as nuclear AWS. Finally, IHL regulate means and methods of warfare including AWS used in armed conflict. This includes specific treaty law that is recognised as customary international law. Similarly, IHL's rules of general application prohibit AWS that of a nature to cause unnecessary suffering or superfluous injury to combatants, are indiscriminate or cause effects that cannot be limited are prohibited by IHL.

It is clear that international law generally, and weapons law specifically, does not address all the risks raised by AWS. Many concerns arise from ethical and moral considerations and states may seek guidance from other sources including ethical principles and soft law. These sources may inform a state's interpretation of its international law obligations and be articulated in, or reflective of, national policy. These may form an important part of an AWS legal review.

162 St. Petersburg Declaration (n 31).

The challenge for states conducting legal reviews of AWS is to ensure that their national process enables a determination of the legality of an AWS against its international law obligations. Before considering how a state may do this, is it important to understand the sources and scope of the legal review obligation. For states party to AP 1, this requires a understanding of the operative terms of the art 36 text and how they apply to AWS. Accordingly, the next chapter will identify the origins of the legal review obligation before analysing the scope and operative elements of the art 36.

TABLE 3.1 Summary of specific weapons law prohibitions and restrictions

Weapon or munition	Specific treaty and CIL status	Nature of prohibition
Explosive or incendiary bullets	*IHL Treaty*: 1868 St. Petersburg Declaration applicable in IAC. *CIL*: This prohibition is regarded by the ICRC as norm of customary international law applicable in both IAC and NIAC (see CIL Rule 78).	*Specific Prohibition* on the *use* during armed conflict of: 'projectiles of a weight below 400 grammes which is either explosive or charged with fulminating or inflammable substances'. The prohibition reflects the superfluous injury and unnecessary suffering principle.
Expanding bullets	*IHL Treaty*: 1899 Hague Declaration IV, 3 Concerning Expanding Bullets applicable in IAC 1998 Rome Statute, Article 8(2)(b)(xix) *CIL*: This prohibition is regarded by the ICRC as norm of customary international law applicable in both IAC and NIAC (see CIL Rule 77)	*Specific Prohibition* on the *use* during armed conflict of: 'bullets which expand or flatten easily in the human body, such as bullets with a hard envelope which does not entirely cover the core or is pierced with incisions'. The prohibition reflects the superfluous injury and unnecessary suffering principle,

TABLE 3.1 Summary of specific weapons law prohibitions and restrictions (*cont.*)

Weapon or munition	Specific treaty and CIL status	Nature of prohibition
Poison, poisoned weapons	*IHL Treaty*: 1899 Hague Convention II and 1907 Hague Convention IV applicable in IAC. *1998 Rome Statute, art 8(2)(b)(xvii) applicable in IAC.* *CIL*: This prohibition is regarded by the ICRC as norm of customary international law applicable in both IAC and NIAC (see CIL Rule 72).	*Specific Prohibition* on the *use* during armed conflict of: 'The right of belligerents to adopt means of injuring the enemy is not unlimited ... it is especially forbidden: (a) To employ poison or poisoned weapons'. The prohibition addresses both the superfluous injury and unnecessary suffering and the indiscriminate principles,
Asphyxiating gas	*IHL Treaty*: 1899 Hague Declaration IV and 1925 Geneva Gas Protocol *CIL*: This prohibition is regarded by the ICRC as norm of customary international law applicable in both IAC and NIAC.	*Specific Prohibition* on the *use* during armed conflict: a. 1899 Hague Declaration IV, 2: 'to abstain from the use of projectiles the sole object of which is the diffusion of asphyxiating or deleterious gases' b. 1925 Gas Protocol prohibits: 'the use in war of asphyxiating, poisonous or other gases, and of all analogous liquids, materials or devices'. The prohibition addresses the superfluous injury and unnecessary suffering principle.
Non-detectable fragments	*IHL Treaty*: 1980 Protocol I to CCW applicable in IAC and NIAC for states that have ratified the scope extension.	*Specific Prohibition* on the *use* during armed conflict of: 'any weapon the primary effect of which is to injure by fragments which in the human body can escape detection by X-rays'.

TABLE 3.1 Summary of specific weapons law prohibitions and restrictions (*cont.*)

Weapon or munition	Specific treaty and CIL status	Nature of prohibition
	CIL: This prohibition is regarded by the ICRC as norm of customary international law applicable in both IAC and NIAC	The prohibition addresses the superfluous injury and unnecessary suffering principle caused by non-detectable fragments impeding medical treatment to combatants.
Mines, booby traps and other devices	*IHL Treaty*: 1980 Protocol II to CCW applicable in IAC and NIAC for states that have ratified the scope extension. *CIL*: These restrictions are regarded by the ICRC as norm of customary international law applicable in both IAC and NIAC for states not party to the 1997 Ottawa Convention.	*Specific Restrictions* on the *use* during armed conflict: a. anti-personnel land mines (see the specific prohibition on APML prohibited under the 1997 Ottawa Convention) b. the use of anti-vehicle mines is permitted where: (1) they are not designed to be detonated by mine-detectors; and (2) where they have anti-handling devices they are deactivated when the mine deactivates; and (3) they are cleared, removed, destroyed, or appropriately maintained after cessation of hostilities. c. the use of booby traps is restricted to ensure they are used discriminately, only directed against combatant and feasible precautions are taken to ensure civilians do not become victims. Booby traps may not be used near populated areas unless placed in close vicinity of a military objective and measures taken to protect civilians (e.g., signs, warnings) The restrictions are primary concerned with the protection to civilians.

TABLE 3.1 Summary of specific weapons law prohibitions and restrictions (*cont.*)

Weapon or munition	Specific treaty and CIL status	Nature of prohibition
Incendiary weapons	*IHL Treaty*: 1980 Protocol III to CCW applicable in IAC and NIAC for states that have ratified the scope extension. *CIL*: These restrictions are regarded by the ICRC as norm of customary international law applicable in both IAC and NIAC.	*Specific Restrictions* on the *use* of incendiary weapons during armed conflict: a. prohibited to attack civilian population, civilians or civilian objects; b. prohibited to attack by air-delivered incendiary weapon any military objective located within a concentration of civilians; c. prohibited to attack by incendiary weapons other than air-delivered incendiary weapon any military objective located within a concentration of civilians except where the military objective and the concentration of civilians are clearly separated and then only if feasible precautions are taken to minimise loss of civilian life and damage to civilian objects. The restrictions are primary concerned with the protection to civilians.
Blinding laser weapons	*IHL Treaty*: 1995 Protocol IV to CCW applicable in IAC and NIAC for states that have ratified the scope extension *CIL*: This prohibition is regarded by the ICRC as norm of customary international law applicable in both IAC and NIAC.	*Specific Prohibition* on the *use* in armed conflict and *transfer* of: 'laser weapons specifically designed, as their sole combat function or as one of their combat functions, to cause permanent blindness to unenhanced vision, that is to the naked eye or to the eye with corrective eyesight devices'.

TABLE 3.1 Summary of specific weapons law prohibitions and restrictions (*cont.*)

Weapon or munition	Specific treaty and CIL status	Nature of prohibition
		The prohibition addresses the superfluous injury and unnecessary suffering principle caused by permanent blindness to combatants and the social costs of caring for large numbers of blinded veterans post conflict.
Anti-personnel land mines	*Arms Control Treaty*: 1997 Ottawa Convention applicable in all circumstances.	*Specific Prohibition* on the *use, development, production, acquisition, Stockpiling, transfer* of: 'anti-personnel mines' designed to explode by the presence, proximity or contact of a person and that will incapacitate, injure or kill one or more persons'. The prohibition addresses the superfluous injury and unnecessary suffering principle caused to both combatants and civilians and the social costs of the ongoing threat post conflict.
Biological/ bacteriological weapons	*Arms Control Treaty*: 1972 Biological Weapons Convention applicable in all circumstances. *CIL*: This prohibition is regarded by the ICRC as norm of customary international law applicable in both IAC and NIAC.	*Specific Prohibition* on the *development, production, stockpiling, or otherwise acquisition or retention* of: a. 'microbial or other biological agents or toxins whatever the origin or method of production, of types and in quantities that have not justification for prophylactic, protective or other peaceful purposes; and b. Weapons, equipment or means of delivery designed to use such agents or toxins for hostile purposes or in armed conflict.'

TABLE 3.1 Summary of specific weapons law prohibitions and restrictions (*cont.*)

Weapon or munition	Specific treaty and CIL status	Nature of prohibition
		While the text of the treaty does not expressly prohibit the 'use' of biological/ bacteriological weapons, states party confirmed that art 1 effectively prohibits use.
Chemical weapons	*Arms Control Treaty*: 1993 Chemical Weapons Convention. *CIL*: This prohibition is regarded by the ICRC as norm of customary international law applicable in both IAC and NIAC.	*Specific Prohibition* on the *use, development, production, otherwise acquisition, stockpiling or retention* of chemical weapons including undertaking never under any circumstance to: a. 'engaging in any military preparations to use chemical weapons' and b. 'assist, encourage or induce, in any way, anyone to engage in any activity prohibited to a state Party by the Convention.'
Cluster munitions	*Arms Control Treaty:* 2008 Cluster Munitions Convention	*Specific Prohibition* on the *use, development, production, otherwise acquisition, stockpiling, retention or transfer* of cluster munitions, including a. assisting, encouraging or inducing anyone to engage in any activity prohibited to a state party.

Note: CIL, customary international law; IAC, international armed conflict; NIAC, non-international armed conflict.

CHAPTER 4

Sources and Scope of the Legal Review Obligation and Application to AWS

Having identified how international law regulates a state's possession and use of AWS, this chapter considers how a state may ensure compliance with its international law obligations through national legal review processes. It begins by identifying the origins, sources and scope of the legal review obligation itself. Before it is possible to consider whether the traditional legal review obligation is sufficient to determine the legality of AWS, it is necessary to understand the nature of the legal review obligation, the traditional interpretations of the law and how they may be applied to an AWS.

This chapter commences with a survey of the origins of the legal review obligation and the scope and content of the two primary sources, namely the general obligation upon states of good faith in complying with international law and the express art 36 of AP 1 obligation.[1] This is followed by a comparison of these sources and their application to AWS. The focus of this chapter is consequently upon the analysis of the individual operative elements of art 36 that determine what, when and how a legal review is conducted. In doing so, this chapter challenges several of these traditional interpretations of the art 36 terms as they apply to AWS. These interpretations inform the scope of a legal review and so it is necessary to consider whether the use of autonomy in weapons requires re-interpretation of the art 36 obligation.

1 Origins of the Legal Review Obligation

As noted in Chapter 3, the notion that states should consider the legality of weapons used in armed conflict was first given modern expression in the 1868 St. Petersburg Declaration.[2] While the St. Petersburg Declaration did not in

1 *Protocol Additional to the Geneva Conventions of 12 August 1949, and relating to the Protection of Victims of International Armed Conflicts (Protocol I)*, opened for signature 8 June 1977, 1125 UNTS 3 (entered into force 7 December 1978) ('AP 1').

2 *Declaration Renouncing the Use, in Time of War, of Explosive Projectiles under 400 Grammes Weight*, opened for signature 29 November 1868 (entered into force 11 December 1868) ('St. Petersburg Declaration').

© DAMIAN COPELAND, 2025 | DOI:10.1163/9789004707047_006

itself create an express obligation on states' part to review weapons,[3] the drafters clearly contemplated the need for states to consider the legality of future weapons by including:

> The Contracting or Acceding Parties reserve to themselves to come hereafter to an understanding whenever a precise proposition shall be drawn up in view of future improvements which science may affect in the armament of troops, in order to maintain the principles which, they have established, and to conciliate the necessities of war with the laws of humanity.[4]

The Hague Peace Conferences, building upon the humanitarian sentiments expressed in the St. Petersburg Declaration, strengthened the view that states should impose limits on means and methods of warfare through international law. The emerging obligation to ensure the legality of weapons was reinforced by art 1 of the 1899 Hague Declaration II with Respect to the Laws and Customs of War, as it requires states party to issue instructions to their armed forces that conform to the rules annexed to the Convention.[5] While art 1 does not expressly require legal reviews, it may be read in light of rules, such as art 23(e) of Hague Declaration IV,[6] to require states to ensure the legality of their weapons.[7]

The status of art 36 of AP 1 as reflective of customary international law has been the subject of academic debate.[8] Arguments supporting customary status are diminished by the lack of state legal review practice, with only 20 of the 174 states party to AP 1 known to undertake formal legal reviews.[9] This may have contributed to the omission from the ICRC's Study of Customary International Humanitarian Law of the legal review obligation. Jevglevskaja concludes, correctly in my view, that art 36 of AP 1 has not crystallised into customary law.[10]

---

3 N Jevglevskaja, *International Law and Weapons Review: Emerging Military Technology under the Laws of Armed Conflict* (Cambridge University Press, 2021) 34.

4 Ibid.

5 1907 *Hague Convention (IV) Respecting the Laws and Customs of War on Land*, opened for signature 18 October 1907 (entered into force 26 January 1910) ('1907 Hague Convention IV'), art 1.

6 Ibid art 23(e), prohibiting the employment of 'arms, projectiles or material of a nature to cause superfluous injury'.

7 W Hays Parks, 'Conventional Weapons and Weapons Reviews' (2005) 8 *Yearbook of International Humanitarian Law* 55, 55–142, 57.

8 N Jevglevskaja, 'Weapons Review Obligation Under Customary International Law' (2018) 94 *International Laws Studies* 186, 210.

9 ICRC, *A Guide to the Weapons Review of New Weapons, Means and Methods of Warfare: Measures to Implement Article 36 of Additional Protocol I of 1977* (2006) ('ICRC Guide') 5.

10 Jevglevskaja (n 8) 209.

1.1 *Obligation of Good Faith*

The international law principle of *pacta sunt servanda* reflects a general duty upon states to comply with their treaty obligations. This obligation of good faith is expressed as a 'universal rule' in the Preamble to the 1969 *Vienna Convention on the Law of Treaties* and in art 26 in the following terms:

> Every treaty in force is binding upon the parties to it and must be performed by them in good faith.[11]

Hays Parks argues this obligation includes 'a duty to ensure military weapons and munitions comply with Hague Convention IV and obligations contained in other treaties'.[12] This implies a need for states to take steps to comply with the object and purpose of their treaty obligations. In the case of weapons law treaties, this includes considering the legality of the weapon in advance of its employment in armed conflict. Boothby concludes that:

> All states, being therefore bound by the customary elements of weapons law, are obliged to ensure that, in acquiring new weapons, they comply with those rules. This is at least in the author's view the logical implication of the stipulation in article 3 to the Hague Convention IV, 1907, that states are responsible for all acts of the armed forces.[13]

During the Diplomatic Conference responsible for the drafting of AP I, the head of the Swedish Delegation, Dr Hans Blix, observed:

> [e]ven without an article of this kind [article 36], it is incumbent upon a State to determine whether the means or methods of warfare it might employ are legal. The article serves to underline this duty.[14]

The ICRC arrived at a similar conclusion in their 2006 Guide:

> The faithful and responsible application of its international law obligations would require a State to ensure that the new weapons, means

---

11 *Vienna Convention on the Law of Treaties*, opened for signature 23 May 1969, 155 UNTS 331 (entered into force 27 January 1980) art 26.

12 Hays Parks (n 7) 57.

13 W Boothby, *Weapons and the Law of Armed Conflict* (Cambridge University, 2009) 341.

14 H Blix, 'Means and Methods of Combat' in UNESCO (ed), *International Dimensions of Humanitarian Law* (Henry Dunant Institute, 1988) 135, 140.

> and methods of warfare it develops or acquires will not violate these obligations.[15]

There is a strong argument for states, at the minimum, to act in good faith to ensure their possession and use of weapons is consistent with their treaty and customary international law obligations. If this is accepted, the question that follows is what is the scope and content of this obligation?

1.1.1 Scope and Content of the Good Faith Obligation

There is a paucity of uniform state practice to identify the scope of the good faith obligation. Only a handful of states have publicly outlined their formal legal review processes.[16] Of those states, many are signatories to the AP I and, therefore, source their legal review obligation from treaty law. Notably, the US identifies the obligation of good faith as a legal basis for its legal review program. Hays Parks, provided insight into why the US undertakes legal reviews by stating:

> as a party to law of war treaties prohibiting the use of certain weapons or munitions, the United States has agreed to certain obligations which it must implement in good faith.[17]

The minimum scope of the good faith review obligation is an analysis of a weapon or munition against the state's international law obligations prior to their use in armed conflict. Accordingly, to comply states are merely required to determine if their possession and use of a weapon complies with their customary and treaty international law obligations prior to their use in armed conflict. There is no evidence that weapons acquired for other purposes (e.g., domestic counter-terrorist operations) are subject to this obligation. A state may assess the legality of weapons acquired for such domestic military uses in accordance with national laws.

There is no clear answer to the question of when the good faith review obligation arises. The length, cost and complexity of most modern weapons procurement processes would encourage a legal review early in the procurement process to avoid procuring a weapon that is unable to be used lawfully

---

15 ICRC Guide (n 9) 4.

16 Y Sandoz, C Swinarski and B Zimmerman (eds), *Commentary on the Additional Protocols of 8 June 1977 to the Geneva Conventions of 12 August 1949* (ICRC and Martinus Nijhoff, Geneva, 1987) ('ICRC Commentary') fn 19 to [1474].

17 Hays Parks (n 7) 105.

in armed conflict. It would, therefore, fall to the reviewing state to develop a policy framework that describes when a legal review is to be undertaken. For example, US Directive 3000.09 *Autonomy in Weapon Systems* contains 'Guidelines for Review of Certain Autonomous or Semi-Autonomous Weapon Systems', which require a legal review 'before a decision to enter formal development is made'.[18]

The content of the good faith legal review obligation is also unclear. The content will include weapons and munitions; however, as weapon technology becomes more sophisticated, the requirement to review weapon systems and weapon platforms will require states to determine a policy position to address these issues. Weapons are increasingly systems based, meaning that a legal review may need to consider those components of the weapon that, while not causing the weapon effect, are relevant to the weapon's target identification system. This issue is important to the legal review of AWS, which will include components such as the weapon itself, sensors, communications and operating systems.

States are at liberty to define the scope of their national legal review process and fill the legal gap with their own policy frameworks. This is exactly what several non-states party to the AP I have done. Notably, the US Department of Defense has published internal regulations mandating the conduct of legal reviews within each of its military services (Army, Air Force, Marines and Navy).[19] Meier describes the content of the US legal review as:

> The legal review should consider three questions to determine whether the acquisition or procurement of a weapon system is prohibited. The first question answered is whether there is a specific rule of law, whether as a treaty obligation or viewed as customary international law, prohibiting or restricting the use of the weapon. Second, if there are not specific prohibition or restriction, then the review should determine whether the

18 US Department of Defense, Directive Number 3000.09 *Autonomy in Weapon Systems* (21 November 2012, updated Jan 25, 2023) enclosure 3 ('US Directive 3000.09') <https://media.defense.gov/2023/Jan/25/2003149928/-1/-1/0/DOD-DIRECTIVE-3000.09-AUTONOMY-IN-WEAPON-SYSTEMS.PDF>.

19 For example, US Army Regulation 27–53 *Legal Review of Weapons and Weapon Systems* (September 23, 2019); US Department of the Navy, Instruction 5000.2E *Implementation and Operation of the Defense Acquisition System and the Joint Capabilities Integration and Development System* (1 September 2011); Department of the Air Force, Instruction 51–402 *Weapons Reviews of Weapons and Cyber Capabilities* (27 July 2011).

> weapon's intended use is calculated to cause superfluous injury. Finally, the third question is whether the weapon is inherently indiscriminate.[20]

The good faith legal review obligation requires, as a minimum, the legal review prior to its use in armed conflict, ensuring that the use of the weapon is consistent with the customary rules of international law relevant to weapons and any treaty obligations binding the reviewing state. An analysis of this nature does not appear onerous; however, limited state practice suggests that it is not a priority for many states. This may be attributed to a range of non-legal factors, including the potential cost of the legal review process and the desire to develop or procure a weapon in secrecy for reasons of national security.[21] Boothby emphasises this point by arguing:

> [A] proper legal review of a new weapon will, of necessity, discuss its construction, design, control mechanisms, destructive characteristics, intended circumstances of use and intended military effect in some detail. A potential adversary getting hold of such details may be assisted thereby to counter the weapon, so there are likely to be strong military and security reasons for keeping the review confidential.[22]

The scope of the good faith legal review obligation differs from the art 36 obligation in its express nature. While the art 36 AP I obligation is comparatively prescriptive, the good faith obligation is arguably narrower. Take, for example, the art 36 terms 'weapons, means and methods of warfare'. While this phrase is not authoritatively defined by international law, it requires states to adopt their own national interpretations. It is uncertain whether the good faith obligation extends to reviewing the 'means and methods of warfare'; that is, components of a weapon system and how a weapon is used.

Despite the earlier focus on the nature of weapons,[23] a legal review cannot be limited to physical characteristics. A weapon must be assessed in relation to its design and intended use. This is especially true of AWS utilising AI to

---

20 MW Meier 'Lethal Autonomous Weapons Systems (LAWS): Conducting a Comprehensive Weapons Review (2016) *Temple International and Comparative Law Journal*, 30:1, 119–132, 126.

21 ICRC Commentary (n 16) [1463]–[1464].

22 Boothby (n 13) 343.

23 For example, weapons of '*a nature to cause superfluous injury or unnecessary suffering*': 1907 Hague Convention IV (n 198) art 23(a) and its modern representation in AP I (n 1) art 35(2).

make decisions independent of humans. This is because any lawful weapon may be used unlawfully. Therefore, it is necessary for a legal review to consider the expected use of the weapon to determine whether some or all the planned usage risks offending the state's international law obligations.

In her book *International Law and Legal review*, Natalia Jevglevskaja explores whether, at the time it came into force, art 36 was a reaffirmation of a similar provision found elsewhere in IHL. She did this by surveying the content of the international law instruments regulating weapons that were in effect in 1977 and ultimately concluded that none of these instruments included an obligation that resembles art 36.[24]

1.1.2 Application of the Good Faith Obligation to AWS

The obligation of good faith is premised on the existence of an international law obligation binding the reviewing state. It is therefore a process of analysing each international law obligation against the weapon to determine its legality. The obligation appears to be concerned with the legality of a weapon per se and not with the lawful use of a weapon in armed conflict.

The absence of international law specifically regulating AWS or autonomy in weapons does not reduce the good faith obligation to determine the legality of AWS. International law may still apply to an AWS system. For example, an AWS that employs banned chemicals is prohibited by the Chemical Weapons Convention.[25]

One may conclude that the obligation of good faith requires states to ensure that their possession and use of AWS are consistent with their international treaty law obligations and customary international law. To this extent, while this obligation resembles that found in AP 1, albeit in less clear terms. This was, no doubt, a motivation for drafters of AP 1 to consider the need for an express legal review obligation.

We now turn to the express legal review obligation upon states party to AP 1, which provides clarity as to the obligation but raises a range of issues of interpretation and practical application.

1.2 *Treaty Law – Article 36 of AP 1*

The need for an express legal review obligation was a critical issue addressed during the drafting of the Additional Protocols to the Geneva Conventions. It is no coincidence that art 36 follows the 'basic rules' contained in art 35, which

---

24 Jevglevskaja (n 3) 33–4.

25 *Convention on the Prohibition of the Development, Production, Stockpiling and Use of Chemical Weapons and on their Destruction* (13 January 1993) ('CWC').

include the rule that a state's right to choose methods and means of warfare is not unlimited.[26] Article 36 operationalises these basic rules and states:

> In the study, development, acquisition or adoption of a new weapon, means or method of warfare, a High Contracting Party is under an obligation to determine whether its employment would, in some or all circumstances, be prohibited by this Protocol or by any other rule of international law applicable to the High Contracting Party.[27]

Jevglevskaja accurately observes:

> Article 36 does not prohibit any specific weapon per se but seeks to ensure that, as a result of the review procedure, certain weapons will not be used at all or the conditions of their employment will be constrained in accordance with AP 1 or other rules of international law applicable to the reviewing State.[28]

Her view is consistent with the ICRC's Commentary to AP 1, which states:

> The determination of legality required of States by this article is not intended to create a subjective standard. Determination by any State that the employment of a weapon is prohibited or permitted is not binding internationally, but it is hoped that the obligation to make such a determination will ensure that means or methods of warfare will not be adopted without the issue of legality being explored with care.[29]

Similarly, the ICRC Guide states that the purpose of art 36 is to:

> prevent the use of weapons that would violate international law in all circumstances and to impose restrictions on the use of weapons that would violate international law in some circumstances, by determining their lawfulness before they are developed, acquired or otherwise incorporated into a state's arsenal.[30]

---

26 AP 1 (n 1) art 35(1): 'In any armed conflict, the right of the Parties to the conflict to choose methods and means of warfare is not unlimited'.

27 Ibid art 36.

28 Jevglevskaja (n 3) 18.

29 ICRC Commentary (n 16) [1469].

30 ICRC Guide (n 9) 4.

Drawing on these interpretations, one may conclude that both the good faith and art 36 legal review obligations require a state to consider the legality of a weapon prior to its employment in armed conflict. However, the art 36 text extends this requirement to include 'study, development, acquisition or adoption'. This step may occur well before a weapon's use in armed conflict. These terms are not defined in AP 1, however, they reflect the common stages in which a state may acquire a weapon. This also reflects the practical reality of a state's weapon development or acquisition process in that it makes economic sense to identify as early as possible in that process whether the use of a weapon will, in some or all circumstances, offend the state's weapon law obligations.

Article 36 uses the phrase 'weapons, means or method of warfare' as an indication of the scope of the treaty obligation. Neither the phrase nor its individual terms are defined; however, it may be read as a clarification upon the good faith obligation. Notably, 'methods of warfare' can be read to require a legal review to consider more than the physical nature or characteristics of the weapon. As will be discussed in Chapter 6, a weapon review of an AWS must address the fact that a lawful weapon can be used in an unlawful way.

1.2.1 Scope and Content of the Art 36 Obligation

The scope of the art 36 obligation is not defined by international law. Consistent with the international law principle of sovereignty,[31] reviewing states are permitted to determine how they will fulfil their legal review obligation on a national basis. Identifying the scope of the legal review obligation is an important precondition as it determines the types of weapons to be reviewed, what aspects of the weapon are to be reviewed and when a legal review will be undertaken.

There is no independent international body overseeing or regulating the conduct of state legal reviews. The prospect of creating a special body responsible for drawing up a list of prohibited weapons or methods of warfare was considered by delegates during the drafting of AP 1.[32] There was, however, no consensus on this point as some delegations regarded the proposal as implying disarmament, which was outside the scope of the conference.[33] Accordingly,

31 H Steinberger, 'Sovereignty' in Max Planck Institute for Comparative Public Law and International Law, *Encyclopaedia for Public International Law* (Vol 10, North Holland, 1987) 414: 'Sovereignty in the sense of contemporary Public International Law denotes the basic international legal status of a state that is not subject, within its territorial jurisdiction, to the governmental, executive, legislative, or judicial jurisdiction of a foreign state or to foreign law other than Public International Law'.

32 ICRC Commentary (n 16) [1463]–[1464].

33 Ibid.

the status quo for states bound only by a good faith obligation to review weapons is unlikely to change in the foreseeable future. States will remain at liberty to apply their own diligence in the legal review of new autonomous weapons. The most recent call for international oversight of state legal reviews was made by Japan in their submission to the CCW GGE regarding the operationalisation of the GGE Guiding Principles. Japan recommended the introduction of an implementation mechanism of legal review into the annual report of the CCW as a confidence-building measure.[34]

The express language of art 36 provides state parties with far greater insight into the scope of their legal review obligation. The drafters clearly intended to equip states with an express obligation to legally review weapons without mandating a specific methodology.[35] The article's operative elements allude to the nature and scope of the legal review obligation without specifying how each of the signposts is to be met or the standard that is required. This is consistent with the principle of state sovereignty in that it allows a state to maintain control over its military capability and, thus, its ability to defend itself against an aggressor state.

2 Analysing the Article 36 Operative Terms

It is instructive to analyse the operative terms of the art 36 text and consider how they might apply to AWS. In conducting this analysis, this section illustrates how the traditional interpretations may limit the legal review of AWS.

As noted previously, while art 36 provides an express legal review obligation, it does not dictate the method or impose a common standard for determining the legality of weapons. Therefore, states party to AP 1 must establish national procedures for the legal review of all weapons.[36] Art 36 deliberately omits procedural requirements to give states latitude to determine their internal procedures for complying with this obligation, including when and how

34 Comments by Japan, *Commentary on the Operationalization of the Guiding Principles Affirmed by the Group of Government Experts on Emerging Technologies in the Area of Lethal Autonomous Weapons Systems at National Level* (28 August 2020) <https://documents.unoda.org/wp-content/uploads/2020/09/20200828-Japan.pdf>.

35 Boothby (n 13) 343.

36 I Daoust, R Coupland and R Ishoey, 'New Wars, New Weapons? The Obligation of States to Assess the Legality of Means and Methods of Warfare' (2002) 84 (846) *International Review of the Red Cross* 245, 345–362, 348.

they will undertake the legal review. Accordingly, the scope of art 36 is best illuminated by analysing the meaning given to its operative terms. These are:

a) 'study, development, acquisition or adoption', which determines *when* the legal review arises,
b) 'new weapon, means or method of warfare', which describe *what* is to be the subject of a legal review,
c) 'in some or all circumstances', which limits the scope of what, and
d) 'prohibited by this Protocol or by any other rule of international law', which describes the *how*.

The following sections analyse each of these terms in turn.

2.1 *'Study, Development, Acquisition or Adoption'*

The temporal trigger for the state to conduct a legal review under art 36 is the 'study, development, acquisition or adoption' of the new weapon, means or method of warfare. The relevant question is therefore when does a state undertake study, development, acquisition or adoption of a weapon? Noting the general rules of treaty interpretation,[37] the ordinary meaning of this phrase provides states with a signpost for when the legal review obligation arises. For example, a state may interpret the words as describing the individual stages in the weapon procurement process, which requires a legal review at each stage. This interpretation is reflected in Sweden's approach to legal reviews.[38] Such an interpretation would require a series of interim reviews that inform decision-making as to further procurement. Alternatively, a state may regard the obligation as singular, requiring a legal review at any individual stage of study, development, acquisition or adoption. I have previously suggested that the use of the conjunctive 'or' suggests the latter interpretation is more likely.[39]

Importantly, the phrase emphasises the requirement for states to consider the legality of a new weapon or method of warfare at the earliest stages of the procurement process. The ICRC Guide emphasises that 'reviews should take place at the stage of the conception/design of the weapon, and thereafter at the stages of its technological development (development of prototypes and testing), and in any case before entering into the production contract'.[40]

---

37 *Vienna Convention on the Law of Treaties* (n 11) art 31(1) provides a general rule of interpretation: '*A treaty shall be interpreted in good faith in accordance with the ordinary meaning to be given to the terms of the treaty in their context and in light of its object and purpose*'.

38 Daoust, Coupland and Ishoey (n 36) 351.

39 D Copeland, 'Legal Review of New Technology Weapons' in H Nasu and R McLaughlin (eds), *New Technologies and the Law of Armed Conflict* (TMC Asser Press, 2014) 47.

40 ICRC Guide (n 9) 23.

It is open to states to determine, as a matter of national policy, whether they conduct a series of progressive reviews or a single, final review. Moreover, a state may decide if a legal review obligation has arisen in a certain circumstance. This is particularly the case with the 'study' of a new weapon, means or method of warfare. Hays Parks argues that the purpose of the study is relevant to identifying whether the art 36 review obligation is enlivened. To reinforce his point, he distinguishes the study of a weapon for identifying weapon capabilities, such as an enemy anti-armour weapon, and the study of a weapon 'with a view to development or acquisition'.[41]

States undertaking research or concept development into new military capabilities are obligated by art 36 to undertake a legal review. This obligation would arguably extend to state research and development agencies that undertake the research on behalf of the state. The nature of the legal review is to be determined by the state; however, it is likely to be interim in nature and broad in application. The trigger for the review obligation during the research or concept stage is whether the item is, in fact, a weapon, means or method of warfare. The obligation to review a weapon during the research or development stage is less clear for states subject only to the good faith legal review obligation and one which is likely to be addressed by national policy.

Article 36 does not expressly state whether the scope of 'study, development, acquisition or adoption' includes state production of weapons for sale and export to other states (rather than for acquisition by the reviewing state). A plain reading of this text does not suggest this is implied and is more likely an issue for determination by national export control policy. The ICRC Guide suggests that 'in practical terms', a state producing weapons for export should review the weapon prior to entering into a sale contract.[42] This does not appear to be consistent with state practice. The Swedish Government does not require weapons sold for export to be the subject of a legal review. From a practical perspective, a legal review generally assesses whether the use of a weapon is lawful in accordance with the production state's legal obligations rather than those of the purchasing state. As a corresponding legal review obligation rests with the acquiring state, Sweden's approach seems sensible. A better answer may be for a weapon-producing state to ensure, as a matter of national legislation or policy, that it does not develop or allow its defence industry to develop weapons that are prohibited by international law. This is consistent with the practice of Belgium and the US.[43]

---

41 Hays Parks (n 7) 113.

42 ICRC Guide (n 9) 23.

43 See ibid fn 80.

The terms 'acquisition or adoption' make it clear that the legal review obligation is not limited to weapons developed by a state and includes weapons or munitions that are purchased.[44] Indeed, many states do not have the ability to develop their own weapon systems; therefore, the vast majority of weapons entering a state's military arsenal will be purchased from a foreign state or defence industry. This reality is one reason identified by the ICRC for the limited state practice or mechanism for legal reviews. The distinction between weapon-producing states compared to weapon-acquiring states is emphasised by Argentina in the context of AWS.[45] However, whether a weapon is produced by the review state, purchased from a foreign state or defence industry or gifted by an allied state is not relevant to the legal review obligation. In each case, the correct analysis is whether a new weapon, means or method is entering into the military service of a state.

2.1.1 Evidence of State Legal Review Practice during the Study and Development of a Weapon

There is little evidence of state legal reviews being undertaken during the study or development stage of a weapon's procurement. There are practical reasons for this. First, as others have identified,[46] the research and development of new weapons is often highly classified and closely guarded by state security mechanisms beyond public knowledge. Second, the express legal obligation upon states to undertake legal reviews is relatively recent. Sweden and the US are recognised as the first states to develop, in the early 1970s and prior to the AP 1, a formal legal review process.[47] Until recently, the development of weapons may be characterised as evolutionary (e.g., with greater lethality and precision) rather than revolutionary. In this regard, state weapon procurement has more often occurred through the adoption or acquisition of new weapons or modifications to existing 'military-off-the-shelf' or 'commercial-off-the-shelf' weapons rather than through new weapon technologies. Consequently, the development of state legal review practice by states party to AP 1 has generally focused on 'acquisition or adoption' rather than 'study or development'.[48] However,

44 Hays Parks (n 7) 114.

45 Argentinian Government, *Strengthening of the Review Mechanism of a New Weapon, Means or Methods of Warfare*, UN Doc CCW/GGE.1/2018/WP.2 (4 April 2018), <https://reachingcriticalwill.org/images/documents/Disarmament-fora/ccw/2018/gge/documents/GGE.1-WP2-English.pdf>.

46 Boothby (n 13) 343; J McClelland, 'The Weapons Review of Weapons under Article 36 of Additional Protocol 1' (2003) 850 *International Review of the Red Cross* 397, 414.

47 ICRC Guide (n 9) 4 fn 6.

48 Jevglevskaja (n 3) 126.

more recently, states are increasingly relying on the defence industry[49] and sponsored research agencies such as DARPA[50] and, more recently, Australia's TASDCRC[51] to lead in the research and development of new technologies.

2.1.2 When Does the Legal Review Obligation Start and Finish?

An increasingly complex question in relation to AWS is when the art 36 legal review obligation arises and when it ceases. The phrase 'study, development, acquisition or adoption' suggests that the legal review obligation arises from the moment a state undertakes study or development, with a view to acquiring or adopting a new weapon or method of warfare.

Some regard the study of technology that, at some point in the future, may become capable of use as a weapon as outside the legal review obligation.[52] Similarly, the government study of weapons (e.g., for intelligence purposes without a view to acquisition) is argued to be beyond the art 36 obligation.[53] A middle ground is that legal reviews should be undertaken when the state procures the new weapon for deployment, but reviews can be done at all stages with different levels of intensity.[54]

2.1.3 Does Research Undertaken by Defence Science and Technology Enliven the Article 36 Legal Review Obligation?

States may sponsor private companies or universities to research military uses of technology. The question is whether they should undertake legal reviews of such research.[55] The initial study of a new weapon often occurs in the context of a state's analysis of its current or future gaps in military capability. This analysis considers a state's strategic security requirements and is informed by

---

49 D Copeland and L Sanders, 'Engaging with the Industry: Integrating IHL into New Technologies in Urban Warfare', *International Committee of the Red Cross: Humanitarian Law and Policy Blog* (Blog Post, 7 October 2021) <https://blogs.icrc.org/law-and-policy/2021/10/07/industry-ihl-new-technologies/>.

50 Defence Advance Research Project Agency, *About Us* (Web Page) <https://www.darpa.mil/about-us/about-darpa>.

51 Defence Advance Research Project Agency, *News* (Web Page) <https://www.darpa.mil/news-events/2020-11-11>.

52 W Boothby, *Conflict Law: The Influence of New Weapons Technology, Human Rights and Emerging Actors* (T.M.C. Asser Press, 2014) 168.

53 Hays Parks (n 7) 113.

54 N Tsagourias and G Biggio, 'The Regulation of Cyber Weapons' in Eric Myer and Thilo Marauhn (eds), *Research Handbook on Arms Control Law* (Edward Elgar Publishing, 2021).

55 M Kotlik, 'Reviewing Legal Weapons Reviews: Is it Possible to Verify Compliance?', *EKIL: Talk!* (Blog Post, 19 March 2020) <https://www.ejiltalk.org/reviewing-legal-weapons-reviews-is-it-possible-to-verify-compliance/>.

a government's defence policies.[56] Such analysis often involves the consideration of a range of military options to address the identified capability gap. Such analysis and subsequent decisions to pursue certain options may be informed by a broad legal review analysis of the weapon options considered for development, acquisition or adoption.

It is open to a state to determine the temporal scope of its legal review obligation and, in doing so, when the legal review obligation arises. The modern approach to the study and development of new weapons, means and methods of warfare raises questions for a reviewing state to consider. This is particularly so where state organisations, such as defence science and technology organisations, undertake programs with universities and the defence industry to encourage research and development of new capabilities.

The US has utilised this approach to the study and development of new military capabilities since 1957 in response to the USSR launch of the Sputnik satellite. Since this time, DARPA has sought to be 'the initiator and not the victim of strategic technological surprises'.[57] DARPA employs 202 government employees who oversee around 250 research and development programs. Recent programs include developing the Air Combat Evolution (ACE), which has contracted five companies to develop algorithms to enable mixed teams of crewed and uncrewed combat aircraft to conduct aerial dogfighting autonomously.[58]

The UK's Defence Science and Technology Laboratory's (DSTL) responsibilities include 'acting as a trusted interface between MOD, wider government, the private sector and academia to provide defence science and technology support to military operations by the UK and her allies'.[59] Notably, DSTL's Defence and Security Accelerator (DASA) program creates regional innovation partners to provide advice to organisations seeking UK Government funding to develop their innovations. A recent example of their work is the development of an autonomous submarine titled the Extra Large Uncrewed Underwater Vehicle

56 See Australian Government, Australian Defence Force, *Defence Capability Manual*, Version 1.1 (4 April 2022) <https://www.defence.gov.au/business-industry/industry-governance/industry-regulations/defence-capability-manual>.

57 Defence Advanced Research Projects Agency, *Creating Technology Breakthroughs and New Capabilities for National Security* (August 2019) 3 <https://www.darpa.mil/attachments/DARPA-2019-framework.pdf>.

58 Defence Advanced Research Projects Agency *Air Combat Evolution* (Web Page) <https://www.darpa.mil/program/air-combat-evolution>.

59 United Kingdom, Defence Science and Technology Laboratory, *About Us* (Web Page) <https://www.gov.uk/government/organisations/defence-science-and-technology-laboratory/about>.

(XLUUV).[60] In support of this project, DASA invited defence industry and academia to submit capability proposals to help the Royal Navy understand the utility of uncrewed underwater vehicle systems.[61]

Australia's Defence Science and Technology Group established the TASDCRC on an initial six-year program to research the ethics and law of trusted autonomous systems. This program seeks to 'research, develop, enhance, demonstrate and evaluate the Defence utility of autonomous systems in future operations'.[62] TASDCRC's aim is to develop the capacity of Australia's defence industry to acquire, deploy and sustain the most advanced autonomous and robotic technology. The TASDCRC website indicates that an 'organisation can apply to be a participant in the TASDCRC to gain access to funding along with new opportunities for collaboration between defence, industry and research organisations'.[63]

DARPA, DSTL and TASDCRC are examples of state programs designed to facilitate the study and development of new military capabilities by financing defence industry and research institutions. These organisations, while government-funded, undertake private research and development. As this work is outside the formal defence weapon acquisition processes, it is sometimes referred to as 'below the line', meaning that it is private and outside the official work of the state or its ministry of defence. The question that follows is whether the research sponsored by such organisations falls within the state's legal review obligation.

The AP I legal review obligation is triggered by the 'study, development, acquisition or adoption'. It is not immediately clear whether the obligation is limited to study and development undertaken by a state or whether state-sponsored or private study or development gives rise to the legal review obligation. There is no publicly available evidence that a new weapon, means or method of warfare studied by state research organs such as DSTL or TASDCRC are subject to a formal, albeit preliminary, legal review. Neither the Australian nor the UK legal review manuals refer to the study and development of new

60 United Kingdom, Defence Science and Technology Laboratory, *Competition for Uncrewed Underwater Vehicle Testbed* (Web Page) <https://www.gov.uk/government/publications/competition-uncrewed-underwater-vehicle-testbed>.

61 Ibid.

62 Trusted Autonomous Systems Defence Cooperative Research Centre, *Queensland Industry Presentation* (Presentation, May 2018) <https://tasdcrc.com.au/wp-content/uploads/2018/05/TAS-DCRC-QLD-Industry-Presentation-May-18-CDIC.pdf>.

63 See TASDCRC (website) <https://tasdcrc.com.au/>.

weapons, means or methods of warfare by their respective defence science and technology organisations.

On a broad reading, state-sponsored study and development by industry and academia may be argued to fall within the art 36 obligation. This is particularly true where the study and development of AWS capability includes functionality that is governed by IHL (e.g., the study of an AI system designed to inform targeting decisions). For this reason, the early study and development of autonomous capabilities require legal review to ensure that weapon's algorithms and programming are developed with these legal obligations in mind. It is less likely that such a broad view applies to non-AP 1 states. In the case of the US, the Department of Defense Directive 5000.01 indicates the requirement for a legal review but does not specify when it is required to commence.[64] Equally, it does not refer to research undertaken by DARPA.

States do not appear to have extended their legal review processes to include research into capabilities by their defence science and technology organisations. There are a range of possible reasons for this. First, the defence science and technology organisations such as DARPA and TASDCRC do not operate within the respective defence acquisition systems. While the focus of their research is guided by their government and defence security priorities, their role is to research emerging capabilities to identify potential military application. Consequently, they conduct research outside the responsibility of the area of defence responsible for legal review. This is reflected in both the US Directive on the Defence Acquisition System and Australia's Defence Capability Manual.[65] In many cases, states align the conduct of their legal reviews to their capability acquisition process that follows any initial research and development. This is also reflective of the fact that not all new technology matures into a capability suitable for acquisition by the military. This requires states to balance the investment in legal review of new technologies at the early stages of research and development. This is particularly the case where dual-use technologies may ultimately be used for purposes that require legal review and also for purposes that do not.

It will be a matter for individual states to interpret art 36 of AP 1 and determine whether they consider their legal review obligation to extend to the

64 US Department of Defense, Directive 5000.01 *The Defense Acquisition System* (12 May 2003) ('US Department of Defense Directive 5000.01') <https://www.esd.whs.mil/Portals/54/Documents/DD/issuances/dodd/500001p.pdf?ver=2020-09-09-160307-310>.

65 US Department of Defence (n 64); Australian Government, ADF, *Defence Capability Manual*, Version 1.1 (4 April 2022).

research and development undertaken by defence science and technology organisations. As reliance upon these organisations to develop new weapons technology increases, there may be an increase in state practice.

2.2 *'[N]ew' Weapon, Means or Method of Warfare*

An important threshold question is whether something is a 'new' weapon, means or method of warfare. The ICRC considers the material scope of art 36 to be very broad.[66] This question is answered by refence to a reviewing state's interpretation of the phrase, 'new weapon, means and method of warfare' which effectively describes the subject and scope of the art 36 review obligation. Accordingly, it is imperative that there is a clear understanding of the meaning of the phrase.[67] The interpretation and application of this phrase require consideration of three issues. First, what is a 'new' weapon for the purpose of art 36? Second, what is a weapon? Finally, what does the phrase 'means or method of warfare' mean and is it different from the term weapon? A state completing a legal review in compliance with art 36 will need to answer these questions through domestic law or national policy. The policy is often addressed through a formal directive or order within the government department responsible for completing legal reviews. These documents will, however, require regular revision to address the issues raised by new technology weapons, in particular, AWS.

2.2.1 When Is an AWS Subject to an Article 36 Legal Review?

There is no internationally agreed definition of an AWS or when an AWS is to be considered a 'new weapon, means or method of warfare'.[68] The UK was among the first to release a national definition of AWS in the context of uncrewed drones:

> An autonomous system is capable of understanding higher-level intent and direction. From this understanding and its perception of its environment, such a system is able to take appropriate action to bring about a

66 ICRC Guide (n 9) 9.

67 D Blake and J Imburgia, '"Bloodless Weapons"? The Need to Conduct Weapons reviews of Certain Capabilities and the Implications of Defining them as "Weapons"' (2010) 66 *The Air Force Law Review* 157, 166.

68 M Biontino, *Summary of Technical Issues, CCW Expert Meeting Lethal Autonomous Weapons Systems* (13–16 May 2014) <https://docs-library.unoda.org/Convention_on_Certain_Conventional_Weapons_-_Informal_Meeting_of_Experts_(2014)/Germany_LAWS_Technical_Summary_2014.pdf>.

> desired state. It is capable of deciding a course of action, from a number of alternatives, without depending on human oversight and control, although these may still be present. Although the overall activity of an autonomous unmanned aircraft will be predictable, individual actions may not be.[69]

The UK definition focusses on the level of artificial understanding of human intent and environment and appears to set a high threshold. Alternatively, the US definition focuses on the performance of targeting functions including the selection and engagement of targets:

> A weapon system that, once activated, can select and engage targets without further intervention by a human operator. This includes human-supervised autonomous weapon systems that are designed to allow human operators to override operation of the weapon system, but can select and engage targets without further human input after activation.[70]

The ICRC's definition also focusses on targeting functions referred to as 'critical functions':

> [a]ny weapon system with autonomy in its critical functions. That is, a weapon system that can select (i.e., search for or detect, identify, track, select) and attack (i.e., use force against, neutralize, damage or destroy) targets without human intervention.[71]

These definitions allude to the issues that states are most concerned with. Logically, the absence of human input or supervision is a defining characteristic of autonomy that distinguishes fully autonomous capability from semi-autonomous or automatic capabilities. Autonomy in the performance of targeting functions is also central to these definitions.

Since 2018, the CCW Group of Government Experts has sought to identify the

---

69 United Kingdom Government, Ministry of Defence, Joint Doctrine Publication 0-30.2 *Unmanned Aircraft Systems* (August 2017) 13. <https://assets.publishing.service.gov.uk/government/uploads/system/uploads/attachment_data/file/673940/doctrine_uk_uas_jdp_0_30_2.pdf>.

70 US Directive 3000.09 (n 18) 13–14.

71 ICRC, *Report on the ICRC Expert Meeting on Autonomous Weapon Systems: Technical, Military, Legal and Humanitarian Aspects*, 26–28 March 2014, Geneva (9 May 2014) https://www.icrc.org/en/document/report-icrc-meeting-autonomous-weapon-systems-26-28-march-2014.

> [c]haracterisation of the systems under consideration in order to promote a common understanding on concepts and characteristics relevant to the objectives and purpose of the Convention.

Their 2018 Report highlights that during the meeting of experts, some delegations argued that a working definition of lethal autonomous weapons was essential whereas other delegations did not consider the absence of a definition as an impediment to progress within the CCW.

The CCW's 2018 Report indicates that technical characterisations in terms of physical performance, endurance and targeting acquisition and engagement were also considered relevant to a common understanding. Additional technical characteristics, such as the ability to machine learn, were also identified. However, the report notes that technical characteristics are susceptible to advances in technology, which may quickly lead to uncertainty.

2.2.2 Is a Definition of AWS Necessary for the Purpose of a Legal Review?

Definitions play an important role in international law. From a weapons law perspective, definitions are significant for two reasons. First, treaty law definitions determine which weapons are the subject of a specific prohibition or restriction and which are not. The drafters of the very first example of modern international weapons law, the St. Petersburg Declaration,[72] defined the scope of the prohibition to exploding or fulminating weapons by limiting the weight of the prohibited munitions to those under 400 grams. The technical nature of the definition sought to avoid the application of the prohibition to larger, heavier field artillery shells, which, at the time, represented a significant element of a state's military power.

Second, definitions are important for the purpose of state legal reviews. AP 1 does not define weapons, means or methods of warfare, so states seeking to implement a legal review process to comply with art 36 will create their own policy-based definition. The definition will assist the state's legal reviewer to determine which objects are subject to the state legal review obligation and which are not.

It is likely that a state's policy-based definition of 'weapon, means and method of warfare' for the purpose of a legal review will be broader than treaty-based definitions of a specific weapon. The treaty-based definition of a weapon and the legal review definition of a weapon are distinguished for

72 St. Petersburg Declaration (n 2).

several reasons. First, the treaty-based definition is sourced from international law, negotiated between states on a multilateral basis. The definition is negotiated to ensure a common understanding of the scope of the treaty. In contrast, the policy-based definition is generally broad to allow greated flexibility to determine the scope of their legal review obligation. While the treaty-based definition will be common to states party, the legal review definition will be particular to the individual state and used only for internal processes. Second, the purpose of the two types of definitions differ. The treaty definition is negotiated to precisely describe the application of the prohibition or restriction to a specific weapon. This is also done to avoid the unintentional application of the treaty to other weapons. This limitation is often achieved through a technical description of the weapon or its effects. This approach was used in the St. Petersburg Declaration's reference to munitions under 400 grams to avoid including larger artillery munitions in the prohibition. More recently, the 2008 Cluster Munitions Convention[73] defined a cluster munition as a weapon designed to 'to dispense explosive sub-munitions' and stated that each of the sub-munitions must weigh less than 20 kg.[74]

National definitions of a weapon, means or method of warfare are necessary to allow states to exercise some latitude in fulfilling their legal review obligation. It is possible that states will need to consider a revised or new definition to address autonomy in weapons. If a military capability is not considered to be a 'weapon, means or method of warfare', then a state party to AP 1 is not obligated to complete a legal review.

2.2.3 Is a National AWS Definition Sufficient?

In the absence of a treaty-based definition of AWS, is it necessary for states to develop national definitions of 'weapon, means or method of warfare' that address autonomy in weapons? A national policy-based definition may describe the weapon as a whole or refer to specific characteristics of a weapon system. As mentioned, states generally apply a broad policy-based definition of a weapon for the purpose of identifying which military capabilities the state is required to subject to a legal review. In some cases, it may be that a definition is made deliberately wide to provide the reviewing state with sufficient flexibility in its decision-making. It is for practical reasons that a state legal review policy will generally apply a broader definition of a weapon than that found in a specific treaty law definition.

---

73 *Convention on Cluster Munitions*, opened for signature 30 May 2008, 2688 UNTS 39 (entered into force 1 August 2010).

74 Ibid art 2.

A question that states may consider in creating a national definition is whether there is a need to include some or all the components or systems of a particular weapon. For example, do those components that enable autonomous functions that do not directly engage IHL rules (e.g., navigation or system monitoring) require legal review? If a weapon system has distinguishable components, is it possible for states to consider individual component parts of a weapon for the purpose of the legal review?

Existing precision weapons may undergo an AI enhancement by adding or replacing systems with AI-based systems that perform specific aspects of the weapon's 'normal or expected use'. This could include monitoring the weapon sensors, identifying and tracking potential targets and, depending on the extent of autonomous parameters, either engaging the target independently or cueing the weapon onto a possible target for human decision-making. Similarly, a weapon platform such as a drone used to deliver a weapon may have its navigation system or piloting functions enhanced by AI to enable certain tasks to be performed autonomously.

Autonomous weapon systems are likely to be built as systems of systems. The munition and the means of its delivery may be only one of several systems that enable the autonomous operation of the weapon system. The munition and its means of delivery is likely to be an existing weapon that is operated by humans and non-AI systems. A system's architecture may be necessary to enable a broad range of data inputs from internal and external sensors and other external data from networked systems.

The question of whether some or all of the particular AI systems components are subject to the legal review will be answered by state policy. Currently, many platform-based weapons, such as those launched from ships or aircraft, are the subject of a legal review independently of the platform from which they are launched. This is not regarded as controversial. Similarly, existing weapon systems that are modified or adapted for uses that are different from those that were originally reviewed are routinely the subject of further legal review. For example, the US Phalanx C-IWS, initially developed to provide naval warships with protection from anti-ship missiles,[75] was later modified for land use. This C-RAM is a defensive system designed to protect land forces from incoming rockets, artillery and mortar rounds.[76]

---

75 Raytheon Missiles and Defence, *Phalanx Close In Weapon System* (Web Page) <https://www.raytheonmissilesanddefense.com/capabilities/products/phalanx-close-in-weapon-system>.

76 US Army, *C-RAM* (Web Page) <https://asc.army.mil/web/portfolio-item/ms-c-ram_lpws/>.

2.2.4 What Is a 'New' Weapon for the Purpose of Article 36?

The use of the adjective 'new' in the art 36 phrase 'new weapons, means or method of warfare' suggests that the legal review obligation applies prospectively rather than retroactively.[77] McClelland contends the question of whether a weapon is subject to a legal review is determined by two factors. The first is by reference to the state intending to use a weapon for the first time, even if it has been in use in other states for some time. The former would be new for the purpose of art 36. The second is whether the weapons may be considered new by reference to when a state ratifies AP 1. Those weapons already in service at the time of ratification would not be considered new and may not be the subject of legal reviews.[78]

The ICRC Commentary to AP 1 states that:

> Without necessarily being 'new' in a technical sense, these arms are new for the State which is intending to acquire them after becoming a Party to the Protocol. Thus, their introduction is subject to the evaluation provided for in Article 36.[79]

The ICRC Guide reinforces this and defines the material scope of a legal review to include 'a weapon which a State is intending to acquire for the first time, without necessarily being 'new' in a technical sense'.[80]

The ICRC Guide suggests that the obligation only exists for future weapons as opposed to weapons already in a state's inventory. Hays Parks agrees with the view that the art 36 obligation is prospective rather than retrospective but suggests that '[w]here new, credible evidence is received raising doubts as to the legality of an existing weapon or munition, a legal review would be necessary or at least prudent'.[81] This approach was adopted by the ADF, which determined in its original directive on the legal review of new weapons that only weapons 'studied, developed, adopted or acquired after 1 June 2005' would be the subject of legal review.[82]

The issue of retrospective review also arises in the context of a modification to a weapon already acquired by the reviewing state. The question of

77 Hays Parks (n 7) 114.

78 McClelland (n 46) 404.

79 ICRC Commentary (n 16) [1472].

80 ICRC Guide (n 9) 9–10.

81 Hays Parks (n 7) 114.

82 Australian Government, ADF, Defence Instruction (DI) Operations 44–1 *Weapons Review of New Weapons* (2 June 2005) ('DI OPS 44–1') 1.

whether a modification would render the weapon 'new' is an important one. Modifications are commonplace in modern weapons where technology permits the enhancement of existing capabilities that reduce the need for costly research and development. For example, unguided munitions may be fitted with guidance systems to increase their accuracy. The ICRC Guide lightly addresses this issue by including in their summary of the scope of art 36, 'an existing weapon that has already passed a legal review but that is subsequently modified'.[83] McClelland distinguishes between a modification to a weapon's capability and a structural modification. He argues that the latter, such as a reduction to the weapon's weight to allow easier mobility that does not affect capability, is not 'new' within the meaning of the term in art 36.[84]

Accordingly, a state may regard a weapon to be 'new' for the purpose of art 36 in the following circumstances:

(a) a newly developed weapon capability.
(b) a weapon, while not newly developed, is newly acquired or procured by the reviewing state.
(c) an existing weapon that is modified following its introduction into service.
(d) an existing weapon for which a new method of use is identified.
(e) a weapon affected by the reviewing state, following the art 36 legal review, entering a new treaty obligation prohibiting or restricting a weapon.

2.2.5 When Is an AWS 'New' for the Purpose of Article 36?

The question of when a weapon is 'new' is likely to arise where a state enhances an existing weapon system, one that has previously been the subject of legal review, with AI to enable the performance of some or all of its functions autonomously i.e., to become an AWS. For example, the sensor capabilities and software of a human guided munition may be enhanced to enable the missile to sense, detect, select and attack certain military objectives autonomously. These modifications to a weapon already in possession of a state will undoubtedly fall within the scope of the art 36 legal review as a 'new' or material modification to an existing weapon. However, whether it can rely on an earlier legal review and merely review the AI modification and its effect on the legality of the weapon and its use will be a question of national policy.

83 ICRC Guide (n 9) 10.
84 McClelland (n 46) 404.

The issue of modification will become more challenging for state legal review policy where the modification occurs in digital form only. If a weapon's software is enhanced by AI to remove a human from some or all of the decision-making loop, this will likely fall within the scope of 'new' for the purpose of a legal review. To illustrate this point, we can consider a weapon such as the US C-RAM self-defence system. The weapon is a static, land-based system designed to 'automatically destroy incoming artillery, rockets and mortar rounds' in flight before they strike their ground-based targets.[85] If the C-RAM software is modified to expand the range of military objectives it will seek, detect and attack beyond rockets, artillery and mortars to include enemy fighter aircraft, similar to the US Phalanx system,[86] it would arguably require further a legal review as it is a material change to the weapon's use.

Moreover, if the operating system is capable of machine learning[87] such that it is able to determine its own targets and modify its own behaviour, the legal review obligation is arguably ongoing. This might require the reviewing state to develop an ongoing governance process that may include a mechanism for the weapon system to communicate the change to its capability and request a legal review prior to its operational use. This governance role may require legal advisers deployed to advise military commanders under art 82 to play a role in the ongoing legal review of an AWS. This argument is developed further in this chapter and in Chapter 8.

2.3 *'Weapon, Means or Method of Warfare'*

Finally, as art 36 is found in Part III, Section I of AP 1, titled 'Methods and Means of Warfare', this provides important context for determining the meaning and scope of the phrase in the context of the legal review. Part III, Section I of AP 1 is 'aimed primarily at reaffirming and developing Articles 22, 23 (b) (c) (d) (e) and (f) of the Hague Regulations of 1907'.[88] However, the development of these articles results in some inconsistency in phraseology between the Hague Regulations and AP 1. This is most evident in arts 35 and 36, where the phrases

85 C Heyns, *Report of the Special Rapporteur on Extrajudicial, Summary or Arbitrary Executions*, UN General Assembly, Human Rights Council, A/HRC/23/47 (9 April 2013) 9.

86 Ibid 8.

87 Machine learning is a 'collection of techniques in which a machine learns to perform a specific task without explicit instructions provided by a human – instead relying on patterns, inference and statistical models applied to data.' See G Moy et al, *Technical Report: Recent Advances in Artificial Intelligence and their Impact on Defence* (Defence Science and Technology Group, May 2020) viii ('DSTG Report') <https://www.dst.defence.gov.au/publication/recent-advances-artificial-intelligence-and-their-impact-defence>.

88 ICRC Commentary (n 16) [1380].

'methods and means of warfare', 'weapons, projectiles and material and methods of warfare' and 'means or method of warfare' are used with seemingly the same meaning.

Article 35(1) employs the phrase 'methods and means of warfare' that is also used in the title for both part III and s 1 of Additional Protocol. Article 35(1) restates art 22 of the 1899 and 1907 Hague Conventions, namely, that 'In any armed conflict, the right of the Parties to the conflict to choose methods or means of warfare is not unlimited'.[89]

This phrase is expanded in art 35(2), which re-states art 22(e) of the 1899 and 1907 Hague Convention prohibiting the use of 'arms, projectiles, or material calculated to cause unnecessary suffering'. Article 35(2), however, provides this prohibition with greater clarity by stating, 'It is prohibited to employ weapons, projectiles and material and methods of warfare of a nature to cause superfluous injury or unnecessary suffering'.[90]

The use of the phrase 'methods or means of warfare' in art 35(1) compared to the phrase 'weapons, projectiles and material and methods of warfare' in art 35(2) is not explained.[91]

2.3.1 What Is a 'Weapon, Means or Method of Warfare'?

Despite the centrality of the phrase 'weapon, means or methods of warfare' to the regulation of force in armed conflict, it is not defined by AP 1. Consequently, there are almost as many national definitions as there are states who conduct art 36 legal reviews.[92]

Early legal review practitioners suggested that 'deciding whether an item of equipment is a weapon will be a relatively straightforward process'.[93] However, the task of identifying a 'weapon, means or method of warfare' is becoming less simple as new technology weapons are becoming increasingly 'systems of systems', including sensors, communications technology, mobility platforms, weaponry and AI-based operating systems. The question that must be asked is whether existing interpretations of the phase 'weapon, means or method of warfare' are sufficiently flexible to address new weapon technologies?

89 AP 1 (n 1) art 35(1). This rule was originally in art 22 of the 1899 and 1907 Hague Declarations.

90 Ibid art 35(2).

91 Hays Parks (n 7) 118.

92 Asia-Pacific Institute for Law and Security, (2024) Portal on the Legal Review of Weapons (Website) <https://apils.org/>.

93 McClelland (n 46) 404.

This threshold phrase consists of three individual terms separated by a comma and a conjunctive. This drafting suggests that the terms have separate meaning and may be read together or individually to enliven the legal review obligation. The art 36 phrase 'weapons, means or method of warfare' differs from the similar phrase used in art 35 of AP 1. Article 35 states three basic rules. Each basic rule is contained in a separate paragraph, and each uses similar phraseology to art 36. Article 35 states [emphasis added]:

> (1) In any armed conflict, the right of the Parties to the conflict to choose *methods or means of warfare* is not unlimited.
> (2) It is prohibited to employ *weapons, projectiles and material and methods of warfare* of a nature to cause superfluous injury or unnecessary suffering.
> (3) It is prohibited to employ *methods or means of warfare* which are intended, or may be expected, to cause widespread, long-term and severe damage to the natural environment.[94]

Article 35 uses the phrases 'methods or means of warfare' and 'weapons, projectiles and material and methods of warfare', which are inconsistent with the art 36 phrase 'weapon, means or methods of warfare'. The immediate question is whether the Diplomatic Conference Drafting Committee intended for there to be different meanings. There is no explanation for the drafting inconsistency between arts 35 and art 36 other than an apparent oversight by the Diplomatic Conference Drafting Committee.[95] Given arts 35 and 36 are within the section titled 'Methods and Means of Warfare', there does not appear to be an intended legal difference between the similar phrases in arts 35 and 36.

The phrase 'means or methods of warfare' is commonly understood to mean 'the weapon and how it is used'. McClelland suggests that the terms 'means' and 'methods of warfare' should be read together to include those items of equipment that 'do not constitute a weapon but have an impact on offensive capability of the force to which they belong'.[96] This view is challenged by the potential complexity of an AWS.

Despite the drafting differences, the meaning of the art 35 and 36 phrases must be consistent to enable practical compliance. An instrument, object or equipment assessed by a reviewing state as either a 'weapon', 'means of warfare' or 'method of warfare' is sufficient to enliven the legal review obligation.

---

94 AP 1 (n 1) art 35 (emphasis added).
95 Hays Parks (n 7) 118.
96 McClelland (n 46) 405.

For example, if an object is categorised as a weapon, it is not necessary to determine whether it is also a means or method of warfare. It is informative to consider state practice and academic discourse to identify different approaches to the definition of these terms.

2.3.1.1 *State Definitions of a Weapon or Weapon System*

Evidence of state legal review practice is often found in the form of national directives or instructions. These generally suggest that states who conduct legal reviews focus on the term 'weapon'. In some cases, the definition of weapon extends to 'weapon systems'. In most cases, the definition of a weapon is drafted deliberately broadly[97] and focuses on the use, design purpose and intended effect of the weapon.[98]

In practice, an object will first be assessed to determine if it is a weapon in accordance with the state definition, and only if it is not will it be assessed as either a means or method of warfare. Therefore, the state definition of a weapon plays an important role in the art 36 legal review process.

A survey of state definitions reveals some common elements including:

a) *A description of the use or design purpose of the instrument.* This element generally refers to causing injury or death to enemy personnel and damage to or destruction of objects. For example, Australia's Defence Instruction (General) Operations 44–1 *Legal review of New Weapons* includes in its definition:

> any device, method or circumstance that is intended to be used, and capable of causing, directly or indirectly, death or injury to persons, or destruction of or damage to objects to destroy, injure or defeat an enemy.[99]

This Defence Instruction was updated in May 2020 with the following definition:

> any device, whether tangible or intangible, designed or intended to be used in warfare to cause:

---

97 For example, DI OPS 44–1 (n 82) (superseded by the Weapons review Manual in May 2020) stated that 'any device, method or circumstance' that is intended to be used, and capable of causing, directly or indirectly, death or injury to persons, or destruction of or damage to object to destroy, injure or defeat an enemy'.

98 Boothby (n 13) 39.

99 DI OPS 44–1 (n 82) subsection 3(a).

a. injury to, or death of, persons; or
b. damage to [objects].[100]

Similarly, in the US Army's Regulation 27–53 *Review of the Legality of Weapons under International Law*, the term 'weapon' is described as:

> chemical weapons and all conventional weapons, munitions, material, instruments, mechanisms, or devices which have an intended effect of injuring, destroying, or disabling enemy personnel, materiel, or property.[101]

A focus on the use or design purpose avoids the need to consider objects designed for non-weapon purposes, but capable of being used as a weapon, from being included in the definition of a weapon, thus requiring a legal review. b) *A non-exhaustive list of objects or instruments* that are likely to be weapons for the purpose of the reviewing state's legal review obligation. These are intended to provide additional clarity to members of the relevant areas of government, including the legal reviewers, the capability managers and others responsible for the acquisition or adoption of new weapons. Australia's definition includes:

> It includes weapon systems, munitions, sub-munitions, ammunition, targeting devices, and other damaging or injuring mechanisms.[102]

In contrast to the US and Australia, Boothby adopts a broad approach defining a weapon as 'an object, device, munition, or equipment used to apply an offensive capability'.[103] His definition usefully avoids the requirement to injure personnel or destroy property and may be more relevant to new weapon technologies that may not be purely offensive or intended to cause direct injury or damage. The definition does, however, introduce 'offensive capability' as a criterion, excluding, without explanation, 'defensive capability'. This approach is consistent with that of McClelland, who defines a weapon in similarly broad terms as 'an offensive capability that can be applied to a military object or enemy combatant'.[104]

100 SJ White, 'The Legal Review of Weapons, Means and Methods of Warfare ' (Presentation, September 2020) <https://documents.unoda.org/wp-content/uploads/2020/10/Weapons-reviews-2020-Australia.pdf>.
101 US Army Regulation (n 19).
102 DI OPS 44–1 (n 82).
103 Boothby (n 13) 169.
104 McClelland (n 46) 404.

An even broader definitional approach is proposed by Liivoja, who makes several observations. First, it is unnecessary to expand the definition to include reference to offensive or defensive capability as 'weapons that may be considered defensive in nature, such as anti-aircraft missiles, entail the use of an offensive capability to a defensive end'.[105] This is consistent with the AP 1 definition of an 'attack'.[106] Second, any reference to military objects or enemy combatants is unnecessary, as IHL imposes limitations on the use of weapons. As such, whether a weapon is used in a manner consistent with them does not change the nature of the weapon itself. Finally, he observes that a reference to capability in the definition is unnecessary as capability refers to an ability to do something, whereas a weapon is an instrument or a thing.[107]

Liivoja's approach to the definition of a weapon is attractive in its simplicity; however, as it is a far broader approach than that of many legal review states, it is a minority view. The better approach may be to maintain a broad definitional gate to consider the application of the legal review obligation to new weapons to ensure that their legality is sufficiently considered by states. There are clear humanitarian advantages to adopting a broad definition of a weapon. However, Blake and Imburgia warn that a state may be reluctant to recognise a new technology as a weapon to avoid the conduct of a legal review and questions regarding its use in terms of a 'use of force' for the purpose of art 2(4) of the UN Charter.[108]

It is evident that definitional approaches to the term 'weapon' vary in content and breadth. They are designed with traditional weapons in mind, which cause harm, either offensively or defensively, to enemy combatants or military objectives. They appear to be broadly drafted to enable wide application. This is consistent with the ICRC's recommended broad approach and the object and purpose of art 36 to ensure the legality of weapons prior to their use in armed conflict. State definitions generally include two elements:

a) first, a focus on the intended use or design intent of the object, for use in armed conflict against enemy combatants or military objectives; and
b) second, a non-exhaustive list of what is intended to be included within the state's definition. Some states include the essential components of a weapon, including its ammunition.

---

105 R Liivoja and L Chircop, 'Enhanced Warfighters, Weapons, Means or Methods of Warfare?' (2018) 94 *International Law Studies* 161, 175.

106 AP 1 (n 1) art 49(1) states, '"Attacks" means acts of violence against an adversary, whether in offence or in defence'.

107 Ibid.

108 Imburgia and Blake (n 67) 160.

The definition of a weapon is influenced by the state's definition of 'means of warfare'. Some states regard the terms 'weapon' and 'means of warfare' as synonymous and, therefore, will generally include within their definition of a 'weapon' equipment that makes up a weapon system (e.g., 'sensors'). In contrast, other states may regard equipment such as sensors as a 'means of warfare'.

2.3.1.2 *Means of Warfare*

In contrast to the term 'weapon', 'means of warfare' is less clearly understood. State practice indicates two broad approaches to defining this term. The first approach, adopted by several states, including Australia, the US and the UK, regards the terms 'weapon' and 'means of warfare' as synonymous[109] or interchangeable.[110] This position is consistent with the ICRC's Guide, which regards the terms 'weapons, means and methods of warfare' as designating the 'tools of war and the ways in which they are used'.[111] In contrast, other states have suggested the term 'weapon' is a subset of the more broadly defined term 'means of warfare'.

Several national legal review policies categorise weapons as a specific subcategory of a broader term, 'means of warfare'. For example, according to the UK's Development, Concepts and Doctrine Centre 2016 policy document titled *UK Legal reviews*, the definition of means and methods of warfare is 'weapons in the broader sense of the word but it also includes ways in which weapons are used and warfare is conducted'.[112] The UK policy provides examples of means or methods of warfare such as 'sighting equipment, laser designators, target acquisition equipment, data links and software used for processing target data'.[113] The Australian and US approaches to defining 'means or method of warfare' are similarly broad.

Academics have attempted to provide greater clarity to the phrase 'means of warfare'. McClelland argues that means of warfare include military equipment that, while not a weapon per se, 'nonetheless has impact on the offensive capability of the force to which it belongs'.[114] He goes on to discuss how terms in art 36 can be applied to new technology weapons and cites communications as a

---

109 Hays Parks (n 7) 118.

110 Daoust, Coupland and Ishoey (n 36) 352.

111 ICRC Guide (n 9) 3.

112 UK Ministry of Defence, Development, Concepts and Doctrine Centre, *UK Weapons Reviews* (Web Page, 11 March 2016) <https://www.gov.uk/government/publications/uk-weapon-reviews>.

113 Ibid.

114 McClelland (n 46) 405–6.

good example. While communications systems are not ordinarily regarded as a means of warfare, where 'they have the capacity to collate, analyse, disseminate, store, retrieve and display information produced in preparation for and in the prosecution of military operations', they may fall within a state's understanding of 'means or method of warfare'.[115]

States have adopted numerous approaches to defining the individual words within this art 36's threshold phrase. However, the more integral the intended design of an object to causing injury to persons or damage to objects, the more likely it is to be considered within the art 36 phrase 'weapon, means or method of warfare' and subject to a legal review. This includes components of a weapon system that enable the weapon's normal or expected use. This is consistent with a reasonable interpretation of the object and purpose of art 36 of AP 1, which is to ensure that all weapons, means or methods of warfare' are assessed, prior to their use in armed conflict, as compliance with the reviewing states' legal obligations.

Therefore, there appear to be two approaches to defining 'means of warfare'. The first, narrow approach, used by states, including Australia, the US, Canada and the UK, treats the term as synonymous with the term 'weapon' and, therefore, as an alternate term for a weapon. Thus, the term includes the other components of the weapon system, including munitions. This approach is attractive from a practical perspective as it enables an intuitive approach to be applied to the components of a weapon system. However, it does not provide clear guidance to the legal reviewer about inclusion (or not) of those components of a weapon that, while themselves are not harming implements, nonetheless contribute to the function of a weapon or munition.

The second, broad approach to defining the term 'means of warfare' treats 'weapons' as a subset of 'means of warfare'. This approach seeks a more nuanced approach to the term 'means of warfare' and recognises that while some objects are not themselves harming implements, they may be considered during a legal review on the basis that they are components of a broader weapon system. This approach allows states to consider a broader range of military capabilities in the context of legal reviews. This is particularly the case with cyber weapons, which may not always have a physical or kinetic effect on their target. The interesting question is whether states who adopt this approach would also include an AI system designed to enhance the use of a weapon as part of the weapon system.

115 Ibid.

2.3.1.2.1 Is an AI-Based Command Decision Tool a 'Means of Warfare'?

The use of AI in the military context will not be limited to weapons and includes the command decision tools designed to assist military commanders. Use of AI to inform human decision-making is found in Lockheed Martin's F-35 fighter aircraft, which include helmet-mounted display systems for pilots. The helmets provide pilots with a range of information, including targeting information such as target identity and location and even the recommended weapon system.[116] This system may self-determine which information is most important to the human decision-maker and, in doing so, filter out other available information. The question is whether such a tool is considered to be a 'weapon, means or method of warfare' and therefore subject to an art 36 review.

As noted above, a state can interpret the art 36 phrase 'new weapons, means or method of warfare' to define their understanding of the scope of the legal review obligation. If a command decision tool was designed to enhance commanders' decisions concerning the use of force in armed conflict, a state may determine that this is within their definition of a 'means of warfare' and, therefore, subject to review. Alternatively, if the command decision tool enhanced commanders' decisions unrelated to the use of force or methods of warfare (e.g., concerning the resupply of food and water to troops or maintenance of equipment), it is unlikely to be the subject of a legal review.

An important question for a legal review of such AI systems is the whether the information provided by the AI is sufficient to comply with art 57 of AP 1 which requires those who plan or decide upon an attack to 'do everything feasible to verify' and take 'all feasible precautions'.[117] This may be a difficult question to answer, particularly where the AI system relies on deep neural networks, which restrict a user's ability to understand how the AI arrived at a particular answer or recommendation.

2.3.1.3 *Method of Warfare*

The final element in the phrase 'weapon, means or method of warfare' requiring analysis is 'method of warfare'. While also lacking an international law definition, it is commonly understood to refer to how a weapon or means of warfare is used. The ICRC Guide explains, 'The terms "means and methods of warfare" designate the tools of war and the ways in which they are used'.[118] This

116 R Mola, 'Super Helmet, F-35 Pilots Get X-ray Vision and Other Magic Powers', *Air and Space Magazine* (online, September 2017) <https://www.airspacemag.com/military-aviation/super-helmet-180964342/>.

117 AP 1 (n 1) art 57(2).

118 ICRC Guide (n 9) 3.

interpretation is commonly accepted by states and academics. The 2016 US Law of War Manual states that 'method of warfare has referred to how warfare is conducted, while means of warfare has referred to weapons or devices used to conduct warfare'.[119]

However, if we address the method of warfare independently of a specific means of warfare, it is less clear whether the term 'method of warfare' is intended to be the subject of a legal review. AP 1 regulates specific forms of military tactics, such as blockade and starvation,[120] as 'methods of warfare'. There is no evidence in national legal review doctrine requiring the review of a 'method of warfare' in isolation of a means. This does not mean that a state cannot conduct a review of such methods of warfare. While there is no evidence of support for this position, a state may regard the use of autonomy in armed conflict as a 'method of warfare'. Similarly, offensive cyber operations may be included in a state's definition of 'method of warfare' and be subject to a legal review.

The determination of whether an AWS falls within the threshold phrase 'weapon, means or method of warfare' will focus primarily on the weapon component of the weapon system. An AWS system will generally consist of the weapon, the sensors that provide data to the AI and weapon operator, the mobility platform and the AI system.

2.3.2 Is Autonomy in Weapons a Means or Method of Warfare?

Autonomy in weapons raises the question of whether the use of AI to operate a weapon is a 'method' of warfare. Is it possible to regard autonomy in a weapon system as a 'manner in which is it used' and, therefore, a method of warfare? This question is relevant for a state to determine whether art 36 requires a legal review of AI intended to enhance a weapon system in isolation from an actual weapon.

It is possible that a state may study and develop the application of AI to a range of weapon capabilities well in advance of and separate to the development of an individual weapon system. This study could include research into aspects of autonomy that, while far from fielding in armed conflict, may represent the initial stages of future weapon capability. DSTG's research into 'fusion of machines, computing, sensing and software to create intelligent systems capable of interacting with the complexities of the real world' illustrates

119 US Department of Defense, *Law of War Manual* (Office of General Counsel, June 2015, revised December 2016) ('US Law of War Manual'), paragraph 5.1.1.

120 AP 1 (n 1) art 54(1) states, 'Starvation of civilians as a method of warfare is prohibited'.

this point.[121] Their research considers applications of AI that are removed from specific weapon capabilities but may be considered 'methods of warfare' for the purpose of art 36. Their website describes the research as 'Research consists of developing unique hardware platforms, algorithms for managing autonomous platforms and systems, human/unmanned systems interface, machine learning and intelligent decision-making, scalable and robust distributed networking and collaboration'.[122]

The US Department of Defense Directive on 'Autonomy of Weapons' does not address this issue specifically but applies a broad approach scope to include: '(2) The design, development, acquisition, testing, fielding, and employment of autonomous and semi-autonomous weapon systems, including guided munitions that can independently select and discriminate targets'.[123]

The use of the word 'system' allows the US to consider an AI operating system in isolation from the weapon component of the system that it operates, but this is not a clear intention. Additionally, the US Directive states that it is policy that 'Systems will go through rigorous hardware and software verification and validation (V&V) and realistic system development and operational testing and evaluation (T&E)'.[124]

2.3.3 Methods to Identify Reviewable Components of an AWS System

An AWS may be made up of multiple systems, not all of which require legal analysis during an art 36 legal review. A state may employ a range of methods to identify which components of an AWS are required, either as a matter of law or policy, to be analysed during a legal review. These methods could include:

a. *reviewing only those components that enable the weapon's normal or expected use*. This broad approach may capture those components that enable a weapon to detect, select and engage its target. This may also capture those AI components that indirectly enable the weapon's normal or expected use. For example, an unmanned aerial system that employs an autonomous pilot system, removing the requirement for a remote human pilot, may be the subject of the review. As the aerial delivery of the missile is essential to its normal or expected use, the legal review of the autonomous pilot would be necessary.

---

121 Defence Science and Technology Group, *Autonomous Systems* (Web Page) <https://www.dst.defence.gov.au/research-area/autonomous-systems>.

122 Ibid.

123 US Directive 3000.09 (n 18) 1.

124 Ibid 2.

b. *reviewing only those autonomous components that directly enable weapon functions.* This method would exclude consideration of weapon platforms and other systems that are not involved in target acquisition and engagement. If the weapon included autonomous systems that identified targets for human decision, the accuracy and reliably of the sensors and systems responsible for target identification would form an integral part of the legal review.
c. *reviewing only those autonomous systems that engage the state's IHL or international law obligations.* This would ensure that all components relevant to the art 36 review obligation are considered. This could include components that indirectly or directly enable the identification, selection, planning and decision to launch an attack.
d. *adopting a risk methodology to identify reviewable autonomous components.* This approach is consistent with the regulation of 'safety-critical' software in the aviation, space and automotive industries. Industry standards distinguish different classes of 'safety integrity levels' to 'reflect the degree of severity of possible consequences of failures'.[125] In this way, those autonomous components that can cause significant harm to persons or property would be the subject of the art 36 legal review.

In relation to the last point, in 2016, the UN Institute for Disarmament (UNIDIR) published a report titled *Safety, Unintentional Risk and Accidents in the Weaponization of Increasingly Autonomous Technologies*.[126] The report highlighted the broader range of risks that increasingly autonomous weapons present. The report identifies potential causes of failure in AWS, including human error, human–machine interaction failures, malfunctions, communications degradation and software encoding errors.[127] As weaponry becomes more technically sophisticated, the legal review will increasingly rely on the advice of subject matter experts from a range of fields. It will also require a broader approach to the internal test and evaluation process.

125 M Hagstrom, 'Complex Critical Systems: Can LAWS be Fielded?' in Robin Geiss and Henning Lahman (eds), *Lethal Autonomous Weapon Systems: Technology, Definition, Ethics, Law & Security* (Federal Foreign Office, 2016) 132.

126 United Nations Institute for Disarmament Research, Safety, *Unintentional Risk and Accidents in the Weaponization of Increasingly Autonomous Technologies* (UNIDIR Resources No 5, 2016) <https://www.unidir.org/files/publications/pdfs/safety-unintentional-risk-and-accidents-en-668.pdf>.

127 Ibid 5.

2.3.4 Meaning of 'of Warfare'

The final part of the phrase 'weapons, means or methods of warfare' requiring analysis is the phrase 'of warfare'. The clear intention is to limit the scope of the art 36 legal review to only those weapons intended for use in armed conflict. Moreover, a strict interpretation limits the qualification to only those weapons intended for use in international armed conflict.[128]

This qualification does not, however, create a practical impediment for the legal review of all weapons under art 36. This is because states do not equip their militaries according to the legal categorisation of the armed conflict they are engaged in.[129] The application of the customary international law prohibitions against unnecessary suffering and indiscriminate effects to non-international armed conflict are addressed in the ICRC's 2005 Study of Customary International Humanitarian Law.[130] This conclusion reflects the 1995 decision of the International Criminal Tribunal in Yugoslavia in *Tadic* that:

> elementary considerations of humanity and common sense make it preposterous that [the] use by States of weapons prohibited in armed conflicts between themselves be allowed when States try to put down rebellion by their own nationals on their own territory. What is inhumane, and consequently proscribed, in international wars, cannot but be inhumane and inadmissible in civil strife.[131]

The practical reality is that a state undertaking a legal review would potentially use the weapon in circumstances that do not meet the threshold of armed conflict. History has shown that states often use their militaries for roles outside the context of an armed conflict. A recent example occurred following the August 2021 collapse of the Government of the Islamic Republic of Afghanistan and the Taliban's capture of Kabul. Several states deployed military forces to Kabul

---

128 International armed conflict as defined in art 1(1) of Additional Protocol I and Common art 2 of the Geneva Conventions of 1949.

129 D Turns, 'Weapons in the ICRC Study on Customary International Humanitarian Law' (2006) 11(2) *Journal of Conflict and Security Law* 201, 210.

130 JM Henckaerts and L Doswald-Becks, *Customary International Humanitarian Law* (Cambridge University Press, 2005) ('ICRC CIL Study') rule 70 prohibits the use of means and methods of warfare of a nature to cause superfluous injury or unnecessary suffering. Rule 71 prohibits the use of weapons that by their nature are indiscriminate, are applicable in non-international armed conflict. See also Turns (n 129) 201–37.

131 *Prosecutor v Tadic* (Jurisdiction), 105 LL.R. 419, 504–20 (1995), Appeals Chamber, Decision on the Defence Motion for Interlocutory Appeal on Jurisdiction, 2 October 1995, 105 ILR 419, 128.

to conduct 'non-combatant evacuation operations' to rescue their citizens and nationals from the danger presented by the Taliban.[132] The legal basis for such operations is often argued to be an exercise of self-defence under art 51 of the UN Charter on the basis that self-defence extends to the protection of nationals abroad.[133] Alternatively, a state may obtain the consent of the territorial state to enter its territory to rescue its citizens.

Regardless of the legal basis for the evacuating state to enter the territory, such operations are considered non-warlike and are not regulated by IHL. Military forces undertaking such operations are often issued with rules of engagement restricting the use of lethal force to only circumstances of self-defence. Such operations are generally conducted in circumstances of internal disorder. Therefore, military forces are generally armed for self-protection and the protection of their evacuating citizens. The military is likely to deploy with weapons that enable limited law enforcement tasks such as crowd control. This may include non-lethal weapons such as tear gas or CS gas, commonly used as a riot control agent.

In a domestic setting, a government may call upon its military forces to assist local authorities to respond to tasks ranging from civil emergencies, including bushfires, floods and COVID-19, to civil law enforcement. While such tasks are predominately unarmed, support to police forces may include weapon carriage for self-defence or law enforcement tasks. This is particularly so for specialist military units trained to conduct counter-terrorist operations.

Militaries rarely possess separate weapon arsenals for use in armed conflict and non-armed conflict role. With some notable exceptions,[134] many small arms, such as rifles and pistols, are employed across the spectrum of military operations, including domestic law enforcement/security operations. Consequently, many weapons, means or methods of warfare acquired by the military for use in a broad range of operational circumstances are subject to legal reviews.

---

132 For example, ABC News, *Australian Military Rescue Afghanistan to Proceed when Possible* (16 August 2021) <https://www.abc.net.au/news/2021-08-16/australian-military-rescue-afghanistan-proceed-when-possible/100381278>.

133 R Alcala, 'Afghanistan and Non-combatant Evacuation Operations', *Articles of War Blog* (Blog Post, 5 August 2021) <https://lieber.westpoint.edu/afghanistan-noncombatant-evacuation-operations/>.

134 Hollow-point rounds are often used in domestic counter-terrorist roles to minimise the risk of collateral damage resulting from rounds penetrating their intended targets and harming innocent by-standers or infrastructure. Most states consider hollow-point rounds as being prohibited for use in international armed conflict by *Declaration (IV, 3) Concerning Expanding Bullets*, signed 29 July 1899 (entered into force 4 September 1900).

There are some exceptions to this 'dual-use' rule. For example, specialist munitions such as hollow-point bullets are procured specifically for domestic counter-terrorism roles. Such bullets are designed not to over-penetrate their targets and, therefore, are preferable for operations conducted near civilians and in confined spaces such as aircraft. The need to conduct a legal review of such a munition is an issue of state policy, especially where AWS are designed for a broad spectrum of military operations, including domestic counter-terrorist operations, which are governed by national laws.

2.4 *Meaning of 'in Some or All Circumstances'*

The art 36 phrase 'in some or all circumstances' is important as it determines the breadth of the legal analysis of a legal review. A plain reading of the suggests a broad responsibility on reviewing states to consider 'all circumstances' in which the use of a weapon or munition may be unlawful. It is recognised that any lawful weapon can be used unlawfully.[135] The ICRC Guide relevantly states that the aim of art 36 is to 'prevent the use of weapons that would transgress international law in all circumstances and to impose restrictions on the use of weapons that would transgress international law in some circumstances'.[136]

The Committee Report on the Diplomatic Conference responsible for drafting AP 1 provided some clarity as to the breadth of the phrase, 'in some or all circumstances'. The report stated that 'The determination is to be made on the basis of normal use of the weapon as anticipated at the time of evaluation'.[137]

This is reflected in the ICRC Commentary of AP 1 which clarifies that:

> It should also be noted that the article is intended to require States to analyse whether the employment of a weapon for its *normal or expected use* would be prohibited under some or all circumstances. A State is not required to foresee or analyse all possible misuses of a weapon, for almost any weapon can be misused in ways that would be prohibited [emphasis added].[138]

The phrase 'normal or expected use' is an interpretive mechanism that limits the legal review analysis to only those uses that are intended and anticipated at the time of the review. While a weapon may have numerous roles that fall

135 Hays Parks (n 7) 119.
136 ICRC Guide (n 9) 4.
137 ICRC Commentary (n 16) [1466].
138 Ibid [1469].

within the 'normal or expected use', the list is finite. Some scholars are critical of this approach. For example, Fry suggests that this approach is too limited:

> However, it does indicate that the commentators are far too passive in interpreting Article 36. Indeed, 'in some or all circumstances' suggests that these legal reviews must consider anticipated uses of weapons beyond those that are considered 'normal'. The Rapporteur's comment actually supports this latter interpretation by referring to states' obligations to analyze 'expected use' of a weapon. This is much broader than just normal use that the commentators assert must be reviewed.[139]

Fry's view is supported by Jevglevskaja, who argues that the scope of a legal review should include 'certain non-intended uses where such uses are reasonably expected or foreseeable'.[140] There does not appear to be evidence of state practice to support this position; however, there is merit in the argument. Of course, a state can adopt a broad analysis of a weapon or munition beyond what a manufacturer describes as the weapon use.

Therefore, a legal review will, as a preliminary question, identify the subject weapon's normal or expected use and undertake the analysis of whether a specific or general prohibition or restriction that is binding on the reviewing state applies.[141]

A further consideration is whether the phrase 'normal or expected use' requires analysis of the state's legal obligations in different operational contexts. For example, IHL recognises two forms of armed conflict: international and non-international armed conflict. In addition, militaries may employ weapons in situations other than armed conflict, such as UN-mandated peace operations, domestic security roles (e.g., counter-terrorism) and even humanitarian relief operations. Does the phrase 'in some or all circumstances' require consideration of a new weapon, means or method of warfare in the context of the various international law regimes applicable to different situations? The international laws protecting human rights are particularly relevant to this question. While AP 1 is relevant to international armed conflict, there is no evidence to suggest that the legal analyses are limited to the law regulating international armed conflict. Second, most weapons acquired by militaries are used across the spectrum of military operations. There are notable exceptions.

---

139 J Fry, 'Contextualised Weapons Reviews for Means and Methods of Warfare: Cave Combat and IHL' (2006) 44 *Columbia Journal of Transnational Law* 453, 471.

140 Jevglevskaja (n 3) 147.

141 ICRC Guide (n 9) 8–14.

For example, hollow-point rounds, prohibited in IAC by Hague Convention III, are used in certain domestic counter-terrorism operations where their limited penetration lowers the risk of civilian collateral harm and penetration of aircraft hulls.[142] There is no evidence in state practice of any state undertaking multiple legal reviews for the separate legal regimes applicable to IAC, NIAC and other forms of military operations. There is, however, evidence that IHRL is considered by some states during the conduct of a legal review.[143] The application of IHRL to armed conflict remains the subject of debate.

The question that arises is whether this widely accepted interpretation of this phrase is appropriate for the art 36 legal review of an AWS system. In this regard, there are three issues that the legal review of an AWS raises. First, is it possible to apply ICRC's interpretation to the legal review of an AWS that is capable of machine learning. Given the risks associated with machine decision-making in unstructured environments, does a legal review need to 'foresee or analyse all possible [technical] misuses of a weapon' and any changes made by a machine learning system? Second, is there a need for an ongoing in-service art 36 legal review to address any modification to the weapon or its operating software, such as if an anti-material weapon is later used in an anti-personnel role? Third, if a weapon is enhanced by AI capable of machine learning, how does the legal reviewer identify and define the weapon's normal or expected use? The latter issues are addressed in the context of AWS in Chapter 5.

2.4.1 Does a Legal Review of an AWS Need to 'Foresee or Analyse All Possible [Technical] Misuses of a Weapon'?

As noted above, the ICRC's Commentary on Additional Protocol 1 interprets the nature of the art 36 obligation to determine the legality of a new weapons 'in some or all circumstances' to mean in its 'normal or expected use'.[144] It further argued that, 'a State is not required to foresee or analyse all possible misuses of a weapon, for almost any weapon can be misused in ways that would be prohibited.'[145]

This practical interpretation of the scope of the art 36 legal review obligation avoids the need to analyse the potentially infinite ways that a weapon can be deliberately misused. While neither the ICRC Commentary nor the Rapporteur

142 See NSW Coroner, *Report into the Inquest into the Deaths Arising from the Lindt Café Siege* (24 May 2017) <https://www.lindtinquest.justice.nsw.gov.au/Pages/Findings.aspx>.

143 S Casey-Maslen (ed), *Weapons Under International Human Rights Law* (2014 Cambridge University Press: Cambridge).

144 ICRC Commentary (n 16) [1469].

145 Ibid.

of Committee III explains the rationale behind this statement, the ICRC relied upon the presumption that weapons would be under direct human control and, therefore, the IHL rules would hold individuals accountable for misuses of a weapon that amount to grave breaches of the Geneva Conventions.[146]

The question is whether the ICRC's interpretation of the scope of the art 36 legal review obligation remains valid for the legal review of an AWS? It may be observed that the ICRC's Commentary on AP 1 was written in the context of human-operated and controlled weapons and so took it as fundamental that IHL rules apply to the humans who operate the weapons and not to the weapons themselves.[147] Similarly, individual criminal responsibility requires a human, rather than a machine, to form an intention to commit, or in the case of a military commander, have knowledge of an unlawful act. The ICRC's interpretation is appropriate in the context of the accountability mechanisms for the possible misuse by humans of weapons.

However, the application of this limited interpretation of the phrase 'in some or all circumstances' may need to be reconsidered in light of AWS which present a range of legal risks as a result of using autonomy in a weapon system. These risks include the AI system misinterpreting data, relying on general data that is inappropriate to a specific operating environment, inaccurate or incomplete understanding of IHL rules by those responsible for designing, programming and training, or the programming of bias in AI decisions. Any of these risks, or a combination of them, may risk an AWS operating in violation of IHL. To minimise this risk, a legal review of an AWS may apply a broader interpretation that requires a state to address the potential consequences associated with the risk of AI technical 'misuses' of a weapon. While the AI system will not form an intent in the way a human may do so, it may perform its programmed function in a way that was not contemplated by its programmers or commanders.

146 *Convention (I) for the Amelioration of the Condition of the Wounded and Sick in the Armed Forces in the Field*, 12 August 1949, 75 UNTS 31, art 50; *Convention (II) for the Amelioration of the Condition of the Wounded, Sick, and Shipwrecked Members of Armed Forces at Sea*, 12 August 1949, 75 UNTS 85, art 51; *Convention (III) Relative to the Treatment of Prisoners of War*, 12 August 1949, 75 UNTS 135, art 130; *Convention (IV) Relative to the Protection of Civilian Persons in Time of War*, 12 August 1949, 75 UNTS 287, arts 146, 147 (collectively 'GC grave breaches').

147 ICRC Commentary (n 16) [1469].

2.5 *Meaning of 'Prohibited by This Protocol or by Any Other Rule of International Law'*

The last operative phrase employed by art 36 reinforces the context in which the state is to undertake a legal review. This phrase ensures that the legal reviewer is only concerned with those obligations binding upon the state as a matter of international law or that a state may choose to apply for policy reasons. The ICRC Commentary emphasises this and adds that 'The determination of legality required of States be this article is not intended to create a subjective standard'.[148]

This reinforces that a determination of legality by a state is only relevant to the reviewing state and does not affect the use of the weapon by other states.

The application of AP 1 to a weapon is, in practice, limited to the specific prohibitions or regulations concerning the type, use and nature of the subject weapon. For example, a legal reviewer would consider the prohibition against indiscriminate attacks[149] but not consider whether the human operator of the weapon was able to 'do everything feasible to verify that the objectives to be attacked are neither civilians nor civilian objects' as required by art 57(2)(a)(i) of AP 1. This is logical given that the obligation to take 'precautions in attack' rests upon 'those who plan or decide upon an attack'.[150]

The determination of legality required by art 36 is limited by the phrase 'this Protocol or by other rule of international law applicable to the High Contracting Party'. There are two limbs to this phrase. The first limb refers to 'this Protocol' referring to AP 1. Article 1(3) of AP 1 states that the Protocol applies primarily in situations referred to in art 2 common to the Geneva Conventions, which, in turn, applies in situations of 'declared war or any other armed conflict which may arise between two or more of the High Contracting Parties, even if a state of war is not recognised by one of them'.[151] AP 1 regulates means of methods of warfare in an international armed conflict; however, there is no equivalent rule in AP 2 regulating non-international armed conflict. It follows that the first limb of art 36 requires a determination of legality in the context of the rules of IHL, including customary international law, as they apply to international armed conflict. The second limb, 'any other rule of international law', broadens the scope of the legal review significantly to thus include literally 'any other rule of international law'. It is open to a reviewing state to include those rules

148 Ibid.

149 AP 1 (n 1) art 51(4).

150 Ibid art 57(2)(a).

151 Ibid art 1(3).

of international law concerned with disarmament, arms control, the proliferation of weapons and IHRL that bind the state.

2.5.1 Should a Legal Review Consider IHRL?

As noted above, it is possible that weapons procured for use in armed conflict could also be used by the military for domestic law enforcement purposes. This is particularly true where a state authorises its military to undertake domestic counter-terrorism roles. The Australian *Defence Act 1903* (Cth) provides an example of this. This legislation enables the Australian Government to authorise the ADF to undertake limited domestic military action in response to 'acts of violence' within a state or territory or against 'Commonwealth interests' where the civil authorities are unable to do so.[152] Weapons and munitions employed in armed conflict may also be employed in the domestic counter-terrorism role.

This raises the question of whether the legal review of such weapons should consider a state's international human rights obligations. While states possess different views on the application of IHRL in armed conflict,[153] there is no debate concerning its application to situations of domestic law enforcement. States may decide, as a matter of policy, whether they are to consider IHRL in their legal review of weapons that are likely to be employed by their armed forces in domestic roles such as counterterrorism. This issue is not addressed in the ICRC Guide; however, the UN has encouraged states to consider human rights law in the review of weapons.[154] Moreover, there are several examples of state practice by Sweden, Switzerland and the UK.[155]

---

152 *Defence Act 1903* (Cth). See, e.g., pt IIIAAA, s 51B.

153 See M Sassòli, 'The Role of Human Rights and International Humanitarian Law in New Types of Armed Conflicts' in Orna Ben-Naftali (ed), *International Human Rights and Humanitarian Law* (Oxford University Press, 2011) 34, 34–94; G Corn, 'Mixing Apples and Hand Grenades: The Logical Limit of Applying Human Rights Norms to Armed Conflict' (2010) 1(1) *Journal of International Humanitarian Legal Studies* 52, 52–94.

154 The 1990 United Nations Basic Principles on the Use of Force and Firearms by Law Enforcement Officials encourage states to review less lethal weapons used for law enforcement purposes: 'Government and law enforcement agencies should develop a range of means as broad as possible and equip law enforcement officials with various types of weapons and ammunition that would allow for a differentiated use of force and firearms'.

155 See, eg, the Swedish approach described in *Förordning om folkrättslig granskning av vapenprojekt* [Ordinance on the International Law Review of Arms Projects] SFS 2007:936 (15 November 2007) <https://www.riksdagen.se/sv/dokument-lagar/dokument/svensk-forfattningssamling/forordning-2007936-om-folkrattslig-granskning_sfs-2007-936>. See also Casey-Maslen (n 143).

The application of IHRL is central to the ongoing UN debate concerning the legality of AWS. While the debate is concerned primarily with the use of AWS in armed conflict, there are clearly IHRL dimensions to the ethical concerns raised on the use of AWS to target humans and the need for human control over autonomous weapons. These concerns apply equally to the use of AWS for domestic law enforcement purposes. It is likely that such concerns will need to be, or are already, addressed in national laws and policies and that they will therefore be considered during the conduct of a legal review of an AWS.

3 Conclusions Concerning the Art 36 Operative Terms

After tracing the sources and scope of the legal review obligation, this chapter analysed art 36's operative terms in relation to AWS. It identified that autonomy in weapons challenges many of the existing interpretations of these terms and argues that this may affect how states conduct legal review of AWS. The conclusions that are drawn from this analysis can be summarised as follows:

a) The interpretation of terms the terms 'study and development' may, either as a matter of law or national policy, need to include study and development of AWS by private defence industry, academia and research organisations. This may also include the study and development of AWS for export to other states. A reviewing state may need to consider whether such study and development triggers their art 36 obligation as a matter of law or whether they engage with defence industry, academia and research organisations as a matter of good practice to ensure they are aware of the art 36 obligation and the state's international law obligations.

b) The interpretation of the term 'new' will require further consideration in the context of AWS. For example, the enhancement of existing weapons with AI and the ability of AWS to employ machine learning are examples where an AWS may be considered 'new' for the purpose of art 36.

c) States may require a more nuanced interpretation of the terms 'means or methods of warfare' to determine when the art 36 obligation arises in relation to AWS and its related AI systems. This may assist in determining whether an AI targeting decision tool is a means of warfare or identify what components of an AWS, for example an AWS AI system, require a legal review separately from the weapon system itself.

d) The interpretation of 'in some or all circumstances' limit a legal review to an analysis of a weapon's normal or expected use at the time of the legal review and excludes all possible misuses. This interpretation may not be appropriate for an AWS that is designed to perform autonomous functions that are governed by IHL. This is particularly the case where the AWS is capable of machine learning. This is because it is arguable that a weapon review of an AWS must consider all possible uses and technical misuses to properly identify and analyse legal risks associated with the weapon.

Having outlined the sources of the legal review obligation and analysed the operative terms within the art 36 text in this chapter, the next chapter identifies how states apply their legal review obligation in practice. The following chapter also surveys how those states with national legal review mechanisms determine the legality of weapons and identifies the common steps in the traditional legal review process.

CHAPTER 5

Identifying the Traditional Legal Review Process

Chapter 5 concludes Part 1 of this book by bringing together the analysis from the proceeding chapters into a practical focus to identify the traditional legal review process. This permits a detailed consideration of whether the traditional legal review process is sufficient to determine the legality of AWS.

Having examined how international law regulates a state's possession and use of weapons in Chapter 3 and the sources, scope and interpretation of the operative terms of the art 36 legal review obligation in Chapter 4, this chapter identifies both the content and process of national legal reviews. In doing so, this Chapter identifies gaps in the traditional weapon reviews analysis and provides a basis for the proposed amendments to the legal review process set out in Part 2.

The Chapter commences in section 2 by emphasising the scarce evidence of state weapon review practice. This is consistent with the findings of the Chapter 2 literature review. Section 3 then identifies the two common methods used by states to conduct legal review, namely the committee method and the single reviewer method. These methods differ in process, but both address the same legal issues. The common issues identified in Section 4 flow from the scope of the legal review obligation and are summarised as four steps of a legal review: a preliminary step to consider the requirement and parameters of the legal review, step 1 which analyses the specific weapons law prohibitions and restrictions, step 2 which addresses the general prohibitions and restrictions, and step 3 to consider the application of the Martens clause, national policy and future developments in international law.

The chapter concludes that while the traditional legal review process is suitable for human-controlled weapons – with weapon operators responsible under international law for the lawful use of a weapon – the traditional approach is too narrow for AWS as it does not determine an AWS ability to operate in compliance with targeting law. An expanded legal review process will be necessary where autonomous functions are governed by law, particularly targeting law. This requirement is likely to extend throughout an AWS life cycle.

 | DOI:10.1163/9789004707047_007

1 Limited State Practice

As noted in Chapter 2, there is limited evidence of state legal review practice for conventional weapons and no evidence in relation to AWS. Relative to the total number of states party to AP 1, there is only evidence that a small proportion of states party to AP 1 undertake national legal reviews. In 2006, the ICRC Guide identified only seven states which were known to have established national legal review processes.[1] The ICRC Guide cites Australia,[2] Belgium,[3] the Netherlands,[4] Norway,[5] Sweden,[6] the US[7] and the UK as examples of countries with formal legal review mechanisms. Since 2006, several more states have established formal legal review processes.[8] However, legal reviews are far from universal among states party to AP 1. Of those states that do conduct legal reviews, there is a divergence of practice. It is possible that increased sophistication in weaponry will therefore further impede rather than encourage the conduct of legal reviews. For example, SIPRI identifies the complexity and cost

1 ICRC, *A Guide to the Weapons Review of New Weapons, Means and Methods of Warfare: Measures to Implement Article 36 of Additional Protocol I of 1977* (2006) ('ICRC Guide') 5.

2 Australian Government, ADF, Defence Instruction (DI) Operations 44–1 *Weapons Review of New Weapons* (2 June 2005) ('DI OPS 44–1').

3 Défense, Etat-Major de la Défense, *Ordre Général – J/836* (18 July 2002), establishing *La Commission d'Evaluation Juridique des nouvelles armes, des nouveaux moyens et des nouvelles méthodes de guerre* (Committee for the Weapons Review of New Weapons, New Means and New Methods of Warfare).

4 *Beschikking van de Minister van Defensie* (Directive of the Minister of Defence) nr.458.614/A, 5 May 1978, establishing the *Adviescommissie Internationaal Recht en Conventioneel Wapengebruik* (Committee for International Law and the Use of Conventional Weapons).

5 *Direktiv om folkerettslig vurdering av vapen, krigforingsmetoder og krigforingsvirkemidler* (Directive on the Weapons Review on Weapons, Methods and Means of Warfare), Ministry of Defence, 18 June 2003.

6 *Förordning om folkrättslig granskning av vapenprojekt* [Ordinance on the International Law Review of Arms Projects] SFS 2007:936 (15 November 2007) <https://www.riksdagen.se/sv/dokument-lagar/dokument/svensk-forfattningssamling/forordning-2007936-om-folkrattslig-granskning_sfs-2007-936>.

7 US Department of Defense, Instruction 5500.15 *Review of Legality of Weapons under International Law* (16 October 1974); US Army Regulation 27–53 *Legal Review of Weapons and Weapon Systems* (September 23, 2019); US Department of the Navy, Instruction 5000.2E *Implementation and Operation of the Defense Acquisition System and the Joint Capabilities Integration and Development System* (1 September 2011); Department of the Air Force, Instruction 51–402 *Weapons Reviews of Weapons and Cyber Capabilities* (27 July 2011).

8 For example, Canada, Germany and Denmark. See Asia-Pacific Institute for Law and Security, (2024) Portal on the Legal Review of Weapons (Website) <https://apils.org/>.

of testing and evaluation (T&E) procedures as being a future challenge to the legal review of AWS.[9]

Publicly available evidence of state legal review processes relates predominately to the review of conventional weapons. For example, Australia published its first policy addressing the legal review of new weapons in 2005. The classified document titled Defence Instruction (General) Operations 44–1 *Legal review of New Weapons* was issued under s 9A of the *Defence Act 1903* (Cth), giving its content the legal status of an 'order' for the purpose of the *Defence Force Discipline Act 1982* (Cth). This compels members of the ADF to comply with the instructions within the directive. This instruction was replaced by an interim manual in May 2020.[10] Neither the 2005 nor the 2020 document refer specifically or indirectly to the legal review of AWS.

In contrast, the US Department of Defense published Directive 3000.09 *Autonomy in Weapon Systems*, outlining broad policy guidelines regarding the development and use of autonomous and semi-autonomous weapons.[11] This directive reinforces the need for legal reviews during the development of autonomous weapons and for thorough, realistic T&P processes.[12] However, it does not describe a particular process or method for the legal review. Several states have, however, made public statements concerning the relevance of the legal review to autonomous weapons, but few have committed themselves to written policy.[13]

For reasons of national security, and potentially commercial propriety, a state may be reluctant to publish detailed information regarding the legal review of specific AWS capabilities. States may seek to avoid public knowledge that it is developing and procuring AWS. It is unclear how states will develop their practice of legal review to address autonomy in weapons. This is not to suggest that states are not concerned about doing so. For example, in 2016,

9 V Boulanin and M Verbruggen, *SIPRI Compendium on Article 36 Reviews* (SIPRI, December 2017) 24 <https://www.sipri.org/publications/2017/sipri-background-papers/sipri-compendium-article-36-reviews>.

10 Australian Government, ADF, *Defence Article 36 Review of New Weapons Guide* (May 2020) 4 ('Australian Article 36 Review Guide') (obtained under *Freedom of Information Act* (187/20/21)).

11 US Department of Defense, Directive Number 3000.09 *Autonomy in Weapon Systems* (21 November 2012, updated Jan 25, 2023) enclosure 3 ('US Directive 3000.09') <https://media.defense.gov/2023/Jan/25/2003149928/-1/-1/0/DOD-DIRECTIVE-3000.09-AUTONOMY-IN-WEAPON-SYSTEMS.PDF>.

12 Ibid 2.

13 At the time of writing (March 2024), the only state known to have publicly released a weapons review policy concerning the acquisition and development of autonomous weapons is the US.

the UK sponsored a Second International Weapons Conference to consider the legal review of autonomous weapons, demonstrating a concern for establishing internal legal review practices.[14]

A central issue regarding the adequacy of the traditional legal review for determining the legality of AWS is the traditional reliance on the presumption that the weapon operator (i.e., the human) will use the weapon lawfully. This presumption is appropriate as individual weapon users are subject to regulatory measures intended to ensure compliance with the rules of the Geneva Conventions and their Additional Protocols. These include a regime of grave breaches, imposing a duty upon military commanders to prevent and, where necessary, suppress breaches of the rules by persons under their control,[15] and ensuring that legal advisers are available to military commanders at the appropriate level.[16] However, this presumption may not be appropriate for weapons that are designed to make targeting-related decisions, as the weapon itself is not subject to legal accountability.

Some may argue that a weapon that has not been, or cannot be, legally reviewed is unable to be used in armed conflict without the user state placing itself at significant risk of breaching its international legal obligations. Therefore, the question is whether the traditional review process, including the reliance on the presumption of lawful weapon use, is appropriate for the review of weapons with AI, which may be able to not only make decisions independently of their human operators but also learn how to solve new problems. If not, how can the review process be improved to provide states with sufficient legal analysis to ensure that their development and use of AWS is lawful?

2 Traditional Legal Review Process

As previously identified, international law does not require particular process or standards of review in their domestic application of the legal review obligation.[17] The legal review obligation is one of result, not process. It is fulfilled by a

14 J Farrant and C Ford, 'Autonomous Weapons and Weapons Reviews: The UK Second International Weapons Review Forum' (2017) 93 *International Law Studies* 389 <https://digital-commons.usnwc.edu/cgi/viewcontent.cgi?article=1710&context=ils>.

15 *Protocol Additional to the Geneva Conventions of 12 August 1949, and relating to the Protection of Victims of International Armed Conflicts (Protocol I)*, opened for signature 8 June 1977, 1125 UNTS 3 (entered into force 7 December 1978) art 82 ('AP I').

16 Ibid.

17 W Boothby, *Weapons and the Law of Armed Conflict* (Cambridge University, 2009) 343.

state's determination of whether its weapon capability complies with its international legal obligations. The ICRC's Commentary to AP I recognises that art 36 does not contain procedural guidance but 'implies the obligation to establish internal procedures for the purpose of elucidating the issue of legality'.[18]

A central question is whether the traditional legal review methodology needs to be adapted to accommodate AI or does 'one size fit all'? Hays Parks argues that 'It is not a situation in which "one size fits all", nor one in which one government's legal review programme would be suitable for another government. Establishing and maintaining a legal review programme is more important than the form it takes'.[19]

The traditional legal review methodology, as it is applied to human-operated weapons, focusses the determination of legality per se. Does the autonomous operation of an AWS raise legal risks that are not fully addressed by the traditional legal review process? First, where the AWS performs autonomous functions that are governed by targeting law (e.g., distinguishing between lawful and unlawful targets), it is not possible to rely on a presumption that a human operator will use the weapon lawfully. Second, the weapon's algorithms may be programmed and trained using data that is specific to a particular operating environment and not suitable for other environments. It may require reprogramming, retraining and retesting of its programming to minimise legal risk in new operating environments. Finally, the AWS may be capable of machine learning, which enables it to modify its normal or expected use. Accordingly, the weapon may be able to identify and explain any changes, which then enables a decision regarding the need for further legal review to ensure that any self-learned modifications remain consistent with the state's international law obligations.

In essence, the traditional legal review methodology for human-operated weapons focuses on the 'study, development, acquisition or adoption' that occurs during the capability development stage of a weapon's life cycle. This means, in practice, a legal review is completed prior to its introduction into service and then, excepting material modifications or changes to methods of use, the weapon is not considered again from a legal review perspective.

This approach may be insufficient for AWS, which require broader art 36 input not only during the acquisition process but throughout the AWS life

18 Y Sandoz, C Swinarski and B Zimmerman (eds), *Commentary on the Additional Protocols of 8 June 1977 to the Geneva Conventions of 12 August 1949* (ICRC and Martinus Nijhoff, Geneva, 1987) ('ICRC Commentary') [1470].

19 W Hays Parks, 'Conventional Weapons and Weapons Reviews' (2005) 8 *Yearbook of International Humanitarian Law* 55, 55–142, 107.

cycle. This includes during the initial study, development and training of the underlying AI technology to ensure that it is capable of functioning in a manner consistent with the reviewing state's legal obligations. In addition, during the acquisition and adoption phase, a more rigorous test and verification process is necessary to identify circumstances where the AI performance is affected by factors including programming and data; environment; unforeseen events and adversary actions; and, finally, ongoing oversight during their operational lifecycle.

However, before considering the requirements for an expanded legal review methodology to address the unique challenges presented by AWS, it is important to consider the current approaches to legal review of human-operated weapons to understand why the existing methodology is insufficient to enable the legal review of AWS. This is not an entirely straightforward process.

Despite the importance of the legal review process, there is limited state practice to provide a clear understanding of the methods employed by states to review new weapons.[20]

2.1 *Evidence of State Practice*

It is implicit that a state will need to develop a method for the legal review of its weapons.[21] A survey of state practice suggests that there are three broad legal review methodologies applied: the committee method, the single official method and the hybrid method. The most common method, especially in continental Europe and Scandinavia, is the committee method. This method enables multi-disciplinary experts from relevant fields to consider and determine the legality of a weapon, means or method of warfare collectively. In contrast, a single official method is employed by Australia, the US, the UK, Canada and New Zealand which centres on a single official, often a legal adviser within the state ministry of defence. In contrast to the committee method, the legal advisor is responsible for obtaining multidisciplinary input to inform the legal review that ultimately informs departmental and government decision-making.

The key distinctions between these two methods are the level of decision-making. A committee may enable a senior official, advised by expert members of the committee, to determine the legality of a particular weapon. This

20 ICRC Guide (n 1) 5.

21 The ICRC Commentary states that the art 36 legal review obligation 'implies the obligation to establish internal procedures for the purpose of elucidating the issue of legality', ICRC Commentary (n 18) [1470].

contrasts with the single official method, where a legal review may be done by a less senior official with the ministry of defence. Therefore, the legal review will make recommendations for approval at a higher level.

The third, less common, method of conducting a legal review is a hybrid of the committee and single official methods. It involves a single official undertaking a legal review and presenting a report to the committee for determination.

Before considering the steps that a legal review must take to determine the legality of AWS, it is useful to survey in more detail existing state practices and domestic implementation of legal review obligations.

2.1.1 Committee Method

A common method employed by European nations to implement their legal review obligation is via committee. A legal review committee will often include multi-disciplinary experts to provide military, legal, environmental and health-related input to the review process. A committee may use a voting system or rely upon the committee chair to act as the decision-maker responsible for the procurement of the weapon. Sweden,[22] Norway,[23] Belgium[24] and the Netherlands[25] employ a committee method.[26] A legal review committee may be established either within the ministry of defence or externally. The most mature committee processes are found in Scandinavia, where Sweden and Norway have both developed mature review processes.

A strength of the committee method is in its use of a broad range of expert views to be considered in a collective forum. Inter-disciplinary input is increasingly important to address those issues raised by the development and use of AWS, which are not clearly addressed by international law. A reviewing state may need to determine its own policies to address issues such as meaningful human control, autonomous target selection and restrictions on the type of targets that may be engaged by an AWS.

The committee method is not without its critics. McClelland argues that the benefit of bringing together high-level experts may also be a disadvantage by reducing the flexibility of the process. He suggests that such representation may result in less frequent meetings or delays where additional evidence is

22 *Förordning om folkrättslig granskning av vapenproject* (n 6).

23 *Direktiv om folkerettslig vurdering av vapen, krigforingsmetoder og krigforingsvirkemidler* (n 5).

24 *La Commission d'Evaluation Juridique des nouvelles armes, des nouveaux moyens et des nouvelles méthodes de guerre* (n 3).

25 *Beschikking van de Minister van Defensie* (n 4).

26 ICRC Guide (n 1) 21.

required by the committee.[27] Hays Parks points out a practical limitation of the committee method: that any need for further information or a lack of consensus within the committee may cause delay in the decision-making process and ultimately affect the acquisition of a weapon.[28] It is noted that both critics are practitioners of the single official method of legal review.

It remains to be seen whether the committee method is appropriate for the legal review of AWS. One issue evident from the summary in Table 5.1 is that, of the states that use a committee method for legal reviews, few have publicly identified how they will consider autonomy in weapons.

2.1.2 Single Official Method

The single official approach to the legal review of weapons is employed by Australia, the US, the UK, Canada and New Zealand (see Table 5.2). In each case, a single official from the respective department or ministry of defence undertakes the legal review on behalf of a responsible authority. The legal reviewer is generally a lawyer, either a military legal adviser or civilian public servant, who obtains technical and operational input and advice from experts from within the department.

2.1.3 Hybrid Method

The hybrid method utilises components of both the committee and single official methods. This approach enables a single committee to endorse recommendations made by a draft legal review prepared by a single legal review officer.

A hybrid method may include both a committee and a single official approach depending on the specific weapon types. For example, Australia's 2018 paper 'The Australian Article 36 Review Process', submitted to the UN GGE on LAWS, indicates that 'For sensitive and/or technically complex weapons, the Article 36 Review may be undertaken by a multi-disciplinary board rather than the traditional two-person legal team'.[29]

While methods for conducting legal reviews vary between states, there are common elements. These are likely to flow from sharing of national legal review practices between allies.[30] This may account for the use of the committee method by Scandinavian and western European states and the single

27 J McClelland, 'The Weapons Review of Weapons under Article 36 of Additional Protocol 1' (2003) 850 *International Review of the Red Cross* 397, 403.

28 Hays Parks (n 19) 108.

29 Australian Article 36 Review Guide (n 10).

30 Farrant and Ford (n 14) 392.

TABLE 5.1 Summary of states utilising a legal review committee

State	Source of legal review obligation[a]	Method of review	Content of review	Public access to review via FOI?	Addresses AWS?
Sweden	AP 1 – ratified 31 Aug 79	Committee established by Ordinance – 1976[b]	IHL, IHRL	Yes[c]	No
Norway	AP 1 – signed 14 Dec 81	Committee established by Directive – 1994	IHL	Unknown	No
Belgium	AP 1 – signed 20 May 86	Committee established by General Order – 2002	IHL, IHRL	Unknown	No
Germany	AP 1 – signed 14 Feb 91	Committee established by regulation – 2015	IHL	Unknown	No
Netherlands	AP 1 – signed 26 Jun 87	Committee established in 1978	IHL, IHRL	Unknown	No

a ICRC Database, *Protocol Additional to the Geneva Conventions of 12 August 1949, and relating to th Protection of Victims of International Armed Conflicts (Protocol I)*, (8 June 1977) <https://ihl-datab ses.icrc.org/applic/ihl/ihl.nsf/States.xsp?xp_viewStates=XPages_NORMStatesParties&xp_treaty elected=470>.

b *Förordning om folkra¨ttslig granskning av vapenproject* (n 6).

c I Daoust, R Coupland and R Ishoey, 'New Wars, New Weapons? The Obligation of States to Asse the Legality of Means and Methods of Warfare' (2002) 84 (846) *International Review of the Re Cross* 245, 345–362, 355.

TABLE 5.2 Summary of states utilising single legal reviewers

State	Source of legal review obligation[a]	Method of review	Content of review	Public access to review via FOI?	Addresses AWS?
United Kingdom	AP 1 – ratified 28 Jan 98	Single reviewer established by policy updated in 2016[b]	IHL	Unknown	No
United States	General obligation	Single reviewers established by directives in each military branch[c]	IHL	Yes[d]	Yes[e]
Australia	AP 1 – signed 21 Jun 91	Single reviewers[f] established by policy (manual)[g]	IHL, IHRL	No	No
Canada	AP 1 – signed 20 Nov 90	Single reviewers[h]	IHL	Unknown	No
New Zealand	AP 1 – signed 8 Feb 88	Single reviewers[i]	IHL	Unknown	No

a ICRC, *Customary International Humanitarian Law Database* (Website) <https://ihl-databases.icrc.org/customary-ihl/eng/docs/v1_rule> ('ICRC CIHL Database').

b UK Ministry of Defence, Development, Concepts and Doctrine Centre, *UK Weapons Reviews* (Web Page, 11 March 2016) <https://www.gov.uk/government/publications/uk-weapon-reviews>.

c US, *Interim Guidance-Defence Acquisition* (30 October 2002).

d ICRC Guide (n 20) fn 95.

e US Directive 3000.09 (n 11).

f Australian Government, *The Australian Article 36 Review Process*, UN Doc CCW/GGE.2/2018/WP.6 (30 August 2018) ('Australian Article 36 Review Process').

g Australian Government (n 10).

h US Department of Defence, Joint Doctrine Manual, *Law of Armed Conflict at the Operational and Tactical Levels*, B-GJ-005-104/FP-021 (13 August 2001).

i New Zealand Defence Force, *Manual of Armed Forces Law, Law of Armed Conflict* (DM 69, 2 ed, Vol 4, 8 August 2017).

reviewer methods predominately among the US and its allies. The following sections identify two notable influences in the way states undertake legal reviews.

2.2 ICJ – *Nuclear Weapons Advisory Opinion*

In 1996, at the request of the United Nations General Assembly, the ICJ provided an advisory opinion concerning the question, 'Is the threat or use of nuclear weapons in any circumstances permitted under international law?'[31] While the ICJ's judgement did not specifically consider art 36 of AP 1, it did illustrate an approach to analysing the legality of weapons. In summary, the ICJ applied a two-part approach to the consideration of the legality of nuclear weapons:

a. Is there international law specifically prohibiting the threat or use of a weapon in general or in certain circumstances? and
b. Without a specific prohibition, is there a general prohibition of the threat or use of a weapon in general or in certain circumstances?[32]

The ICJ's approach is reflected in the processes adopted by numerous states.[33] The ICRC Guide does not refer specifically to the ICJ Advisory Opinion but does adopt a similar approach to the review of weapons.

The immediate question is whether the ICJ's approach assists in the determination of the legality of an AWS. Noting the absence of a specific prohibition or regulation of autonomy in weapons, the ICJ Advisory Opinion relevantly affirms the view that 'the illegality of the use of certain weapons as such does not result from the absence of authorization, on the contrary, is formulated in terms of prohibition'.[34] This reinforces the application of general law prohibitions, which are concerned with the effects of all weapons.

It is noteworthy that while the advisory opinion identifies the 'cardinal principles contained in the texts constituting the fabric of humanitarian law' as the principles of distinction and unnecessary suffering,[35] it does not address the application of IHL rules governing methods of warfare beyond an observation that nuclear weapons are unable to be used discriminately.[36]

---

31 *Legality of the Threat or Use of Nuclear Weapons (Advisory Opinion)* [1996] ICJ Rep 226 [260] ('Nuclear Weapons Case') [20].
32 Ibid [49]–[73].
33 For example, Australian Article 36 Review Guide (n 10).
34 Nuclear Weapons Case (n 43) [52].
35 Ibid [78].
36 Ibid [92].

The ICJ's analysis of the legality of nuclear weapons was not intended to address autonomy in weapons. However, it does provide an authoritative approach for determining the legality of weapons. This is reflected in the common legal review approach described later in this chapter.

2.3 *ICRC Guide*

As noted in Chapter 2, in 2006 the ICRC published their Guide to provide practical guidance to states on how to fulfil their legal review obligations. The ICRC Guide is divided into two parts. First, Part 1 addresses the 'material scope of application' of the legal review. This includes considering the types of weapons that are the subject of legal review, what rules must be applied and what data should be considered in undertaking the review. Second, Part 2 of the ICRC Guide considers the practical state review mechanisms, such as under whose authority a legal review is to be conducted, what procedures should be applied, when a review should be completed and how decisions are reached.

Part 1 of the ICRC Guide is the most important part for the purpose of this book, as it addresses the key legal issues to be assessed during a legal review. It is not written to address any one particular means or method of warfare but casts a wide net to include 'weapons of all types – be they anti-personnel or anti-material, "lethal", "non-lethal" or "less lethal" – and weapons systems'.[37] It also includes 'the ways in which these weapons are to be used pursuant to military doctrine, tactics, rules of engagement, operating procedures and countermeasures'.[38] It is possible that an AWS utilises a weapon that has already been the subject of an earlier legal review. In this case, the ICRC Guide includes 'an existing weapon that is modified in a way that alters its function, or a weapon that has already passed a legal review but is subsequently modified'.[39]

While the ICRC Guide was not written for specific weapons, there is little doubt that an AWS would fall within the scope of the legal review obligation. It also raises the interesting question of whether the enhancement of a weapon with AI brings the weapon within the scope of a further review. The enhancement of weapons normally operated by humans is more a modification to the method of use rather than the creation of a new means of warfare. However, this is a theoretical argument, as such a weapon would fall within the scope of a legal review in either case.

Part 1 of the ICRC Guide, in addition to specific and general international law rules, refers to 'Prohibitions or restrictions based on the principles of humanity

37 ICRC Guide (n 1) 9.
38 Ibid.
39 Ibid 10.

and the dictates of public conscience (the Martens clause)'.[40] While there are various views concerning the legal status of the Martens clause, it does provide an opportunity for states to consider broader issues that may be relevant to the legal review of novel technologies. The difficulty in an assessment of a weapon in the context of the Martens clause is identifying an objective standard of the principles of humanity and dictates of public conscience. This practical application of the Martens clause is not addressed by the ICRC Guide.

2.4 *Article 36 Legal Review and the National Defence Acquisition Process*

Chapter 4 identified that many states have developed formal government-led, bureaucratic processes to enable the efficient and cost-effective procurement of military capabilities, including weapons, needed to meet current and anticipated security needs. These processes are generally internal to a state; however, given the increasing complexity and costs of military technology, they are also done on a bilateral and multilateral basis. Examples include the 2010 Defence and Security Treaty between the UK and France,[41] the Nordic Defence Cooperation[42] and Australia's Joint Strike Fighter program.[43]

US Department of Defence Directive 5000.01 *The Defense Acquisition System* states that the objective of the Defence Acquisition System (DAS) is to 'support the National Defence Strategy, through the development of a more lethal force based on US technological innovation and culture of performance that yields a decisive and sustained US military advantage'.[44]

This directive emphasises that the acquisition and procurement of weapons and information systems must be consistent and comply with 'applicable treaties and international agreements, customary international law, and the law of armed conflict'.[45]

40 Ibid 16.

41 *Treaty between the United Kingdom of Great Britain and Northern Ireland and the French Republic for Defence and Security Co-operation* (Treaty Series No 36, 1 July 2011) <https://assets.publishing.service.gov.uk/government/uploads/system/uploads/attachment_data/file/238153/8174.pdf>.

42 Nordic Defence Cooperation (Web Page) <https://www.nordefco.org/the-basics-about-nordefco>.

43 Australian Department of Defence, *Joint Strike Fighter Program* (Web Page) <https://www1.defence.gov.au/about/capability-acquisition-sustainment-group/our-structure/air/jsf>.

44 US Department of Defense, Directive 5000.01 *The Defense Acquisition System* (12 May 2003) ('US Department of Defense Directive 5000.01').

45 Ibid 9.

State acquisition processes are variously referred to as the material acquisition process, the procurement system or the capability development process. In Australia, the process is referred to as the capability acquisition process, and it is represented by the One Defence Capability System (ODCS).[46] The ADF identifies 'fundamental inputs to capability' which combine 'equipment, workforce, organisation, estate, logistics and other systems'.[47]

A key concept of the ODCS is the centralised planned process, which is informed by the Force Design process to 'translate strategic direction into a future force structure' by assessing 'current and planned defence capabilities to identify gaps and opportunities in the development of the future force'.[48] In effect, the process enables 'an expression of the intended set of capabilities that provide the optimised range of options for addressing strategic risks'.[49] Decisions regarding how these gaps are filled and opportunities exploited are made during the ODCS, which consists of four discrete stages linked by decision 'gates'. Importantly, and consistent with the Westminster system of government, these defence procurement decisions are made by the executive government. The more significant procurement decisions are made by the government's National Security Committee of Cabinet, while others are delegated to the minister for defence and the minister for finance.[50]

Decisions made at the decision gates of Australia's ODCS consider a range of issues relating to how an identified capability need can be filled. The consideration of these issues may be informed by the legal and ethical analysis conducted during the legal review.

The Australian ODCS incorporates key milestones or decision points at which the Defence Department makes recommendations to the federal government concerning funding subsequent phases of the acquisition. These decisions may be supported by interim legal reviews to inform government decision-making. The UK applies a similar approach to Australia by conducting interim reviews to inform key decisions during the procurement process.[51]

46 Australian Government, ADF, *Defence Capability Manual*, Version 1.2 (4 April 2022) ('Defence Capability Manual').

47 Ibid 12.

48 Ibid 28.

49 Ibid 29.

50 Ibid 14–15.

51 UK Ministry of Defence, Development, Concepts and Doctrine Centre, UK Weapons Reviews (Web Page, 11 March 2016) <https://www.gov.uk/government/publications/uk-weapon-reviews>.

2.4.1 Legal Review of AWS during the National Defence Acquisition Process

The question that follows is whether this ODCS-centric approach is sufficient to ensure the legality of weapons during their life cycle. It is argued that an AWS requires an expanded art 36 legal review methodology that informs critical study and development of the AI, particularly with respect to the development of algorithms and training of neural networks and the ongoing verification during the weapon's in-service life.

The expanded art 36 legal review, argued for in Part 2, will involve additional inputs to inform the critical stages during the lifecycle of an AWS. This includes:

c) *During the study and development of an AWS.* The development of an AWS' AI system designed to inform human decisions that engage IHL obligations requires the AI engineers and programmers to understand the nature of the relevant state's legal obligations and their application in the context of the weapon's normal or expected use. Moreover, the data used to train an AI neural network should be assessed to ensure that risks associated with programming and data are recognised and mitigated. This will require input from the legal review official to inform this work.

d) *During in-service life.* The in-service life of an AWS may be measured in years or even decades.[52] During this time, hardware and software upgrades will likely be required to address defects or improve effectiveness. Where there is a material modification of an AWS, a state will be required to determine whether the modification affects an earlier legal review determination of legality.

3 Common Steps of the Traditional Legal Review Methodology Applied to AWS

Irrespective of the review methodology adopted by the state, national practice suggests four broad steps are common in determining the legality of weapons. A first preliminary step confirms the applicability of art 36 by assessing whether there is a 'new weapon, means or method of warfare'. This step also identifies the normal or expected use of the weapon anticipated at the time of the review.

---

52 For example, the Phalanx Close-In Weapon System was first introduced into service with the US military in the 1970s and remains in service with over 15 countries: <https://www.raytheonmissilesanddefense.com/what-we-do/naval-warfare/ship-self-defense-weapons/phalanx-close-in-weapon-system>.

The second step determines whether the particular type of weapon is specifically prohibited or restricted by treaty or customary law binding the reviewing state. This focuses on the weapon design and how it causes harm or damage. For example, if the weapon employs an asphyxiating gas to cause injury or death to combatants, it may be prohibited by the 1925 Geneva Gas Protocol, the Chemical Weapons Convention and customary international law.[53]

The third step considers general international law prohibitions applicable to all weapons. This includes whether the normal or expected use causes unnecessary suffering or superfluous injury to enemy combatants,[54] is inherently indiscriminate in that it cannot be directed at a specific military objective[55] or causes widespread, long-term and severe environmental damage.[56]

Finally, for some states, the last step in the legal review process includes consideration of non-binding instruments, or so-called 'soft law', and national policy.[57] Reflecting the Martens clause,[58] this step enables consideration of domestic policy reflecting the 'principles of humanity' and 'the dictates of public conscience'. While not determinative of a weapon's legality, states may make policy decisions on relevant issues, such as a political decision not to use a particular type of weapon (e.g., depleted uranium munitions)[59] or requirements for human control over AWS.[60]

---

53 *Protocol for the Prohibition of the Use in War of Asphyxiating, Poisonous or Other Gases, and of Bacteriological Methods of Warfare*, opened for signature 17 June 1925 (entered into force 8 February 1928) ('1925 Gas Protocol'); *Convention on the Prohibition of the Development, Production, Stockpiling and Use of Chemical Weapons and on their Destruction* (13 January 1993) ('CWC').

54 AP 1 (n 15) art 35(2).

55 Ibid art 51(4)(a).

56 Ibid art 35(3).

57 See Australian Government (n 46); SJ White, 'The Legal Review of Weapons, Means and Methods of Warfare' (Presentation, September 2020) <https://documents.unoda.org/wp-content/uploads/2020/10/Weapons-reviews-2020-Australia.pdf>.

58 The Martens clause first appeared in the preamble to the 1899 *Hague Declaration 2 Concerning Asphyxiating Gases* (29 July 1899) and was subsequently reaffirmed in 1907 *Hague Convention (IV) Respecting the Laws and Customs of War on Land*, opened for signature 18 October 1907 (entered into force 26 January 1910) ('1907 Hague Convention IV') and AP 1 (n 15) art 1(2).

59 For example, the Australian Government decided not to continue to use depleted uranium munitions. See Senator Hill's response to questions in the Commonwealth of Australia, Parliamentary Debates, Senate, 15 October 2003, [16585] <https://www.aph.gov.au/binaries/hansard/senate/dailys/ds151003.pdf>.

60 US Department of Defense (n 11) states, 'Autonomous and semi-autonomous weapon systems shall be designed to allow commanders and operators to exercise appropriate levels of human judgment over the use of force'.

These steps focus on the application of the specific and general international law prohibitions that bind a reviewing state. However, when applied to a generic AWS (e.g., an AWS designed to target and destroy military objectives in armed conflict), there appear to be gaps in the consideration of those AWS functions that are governed by IHL rules concerning the lawful use of a weapon.

3.1 *Preliminary Step – Determine Preliminary Questions*

An important preliminary step in the legal review process is to confirm that the AWS, or a component of an AWS, as a matter of law, is required to be legally reviewed. This also assists the legal review to confirm the scope of the legal review analysis and seek information to enable the conduct of the review. A legal reviewer will generally consider three preliminary questions. First, is the object a new weapon, means or method of warfare? Second, what is/are the weapon, means or method of warfare's normal or expected use or uses? Finally, how does the weapon, means or method of warfare achieve its intended effect(s)?

3.1.1 Is the AWS a New Weapon, Means or Method of Warfare?

Assessing whether a traditional rifle or missile is a weapon is generally regarded as a straightforward process.[61] Nevertheless, the preliminary legal review question is necessary to determine if a subject equipment or item is within the scope of the art 36 review obligation. The assessment is an objective one based on the nature and purpose and is measured against the state internal definition of a new weapon, means or methods of warfare.

In considerating the AWS's nature, a legal reviewer will identifying how it is designed to achieve its intended effect (e.g., injury to persons or damage to objects). The analysis should include identifying the harming mechanism, for example, a munition designed to transfer kinetic or chemical energy to the target. If the object is a cyber capability, this review may focus on the programming design. While almost any object can potentially be used as a weapon, for example a truck can be used to attack persons or objects, the legal review obligation only extends to offensive or defensive capabilities intended to cause harm to combatants or damage to military objectives in armed conflict. Article 36 does not use the 'primary purpose' language found in several of the Protocols of the CCW. The definition of a weapon is often

61 McClelland (n 27) 404.

determined by its primary purpose, i.e. to cause harm. This provides a useful way to identifying an object designed to cause a prohibited effect. If there is doubt as to whether an object is a weapon, means or method of warfare for the purpose of art 36, legal advice should be sought from the reviewing authority.[62]

In some cases, an assessment of whether an object is within a state's definition of a 'new weapon, means or methods of warfare' is formally recorded in a written report. The UK Ministry of Defence's Development Concepts and Doctrine Centre complete a 'non-Review' to create a formal government record of the decision not to review a particular object.[63] This decision is monitored for future changes that may affect this assessment. Similarly, Australia's art 36 legal review process notes that where a capability is assessed not to be a new weapon, means or method of warfare, 'a record will be made in writing that the capability does not require an article 36 Review'.[64]

As noted in Chapter 4, AP 1 does not define the phrase 'new weapon, means or method of warfare' and allows the reviewing state to define the scope of its legal review obligation through internal policy. Accordingly, the assessment of whether an object is a reviewable weapon or method of warfare will be determined by consideration of the reviewing state's definition of a weapon. The answer to this question becomes less straightforward where the subject of review is a complex weapon system with autonomous functionality.

3.1.2 What Is the Weapon's Normal or Expected Use at the Time of Evaluation?

As noted in Chapter 4, a traditional legal review will focus on the weapon's normal or expected use at the time of the assessment. It is necessary to define the normal or expected use in terms of the weapon's 'construction, design, control mechanisms, destructive characteristics, intended circumstances of use and intended military effect'.[65]

A multipurpose weapon may be designed to have several 'normal or expected uses'. For example, an assault rifle may be capable of accurate fire out to 300 metres but also be used at short range. It may also be used in close-quarter combat by attaching a bayonet. It is necessary for the art 36 review to

62 ICRC Guide (n 20) 10.
63 UK Ministry of Defence (n 51).
64 Australian Article 36 Review Guide (n 10).
65 Boothby (n 17) 343.

consider each of these anticipated uses. This is particularly the case with AWS, which will likely comprise complex systems of systems.

3.1.3 What Information Is Required to Conduct a Traditional Review?

A legal reviewer will require a range of technical and performance information to conduct the legal review. This information will inform the determination of legality by enabling legal analysis of the specific and general IHL prohibitions and restrictions that apply.

The information needed to inform the legal review will depend on the legal compliance issue being analysed. For example, to consider whether the weapon is unlawful per se because it is the subject of a specific treaty law or customary international law prohibition, the legal reviewer will seek information relating to the intended use of the weapon and technical details about how the weapon achieves its effect. Accordingly, if the reviewing state is party to the Chemical Weapons Convention, the legal reviewer will consider whether the weapon employs toxic chemicals and their precursors to cause death or other harm through the toxic chemicals.[66] Similarly, to determine whether the weapon is indiscriminate by nature, the legal review will require performance data, including its accuracy, reliability, radius of destruction and intended method of use.

A legal review is likely to require the following information:

a. to identify the normal or expected use of the weapon:
   i. the operational analysis of the capability that the procurement is intended to provide
   ii. the documents that set out the concept of use of the weapon to reveal the circumstances in which it is intended to use the weapon, its utility and general employment information
   iii. the manufacturer's information
   iv. scientific reports that are available on the weapon, its performance, technology or related matters;[67]

b. to determine whether the weapon is specifically prohibited or restricted by an international law treaty or customary law:
   i. full technical description of the weapon or weapon system including its speed, range, shape
   ii. details of its construction materials
   iii. the damage mechanism and how it works

---

66 CWC (n 53).

67 Boothby (n 17) 349–50.

   iv. reliability, accuracy, design effect
   v. deployment method;[68]
c. to determine if the weapon is indiscriminate by nature:
   i. the intended radius of destruction[69]
   ii. the intended or designed circumstances of use and the way in which the weapon will be used;[70]
d. to determine if the weapon causes superfluous injury or unnecessary suffering:
   i. the nature of the wounding mechanism and the sorts of wound expected from the intended use of the weapon;[71]
e. to determine whether the weapon is intended to, or likely to cause, widespread, long-term and severe damage to the natural environment:
   i. obtain appropriate data describing the likely environmental impact of the weapon.

3.2 *Step 1 – Analyse Specific Weapons Law Prohibitions and Restrictions*

The next step in a legal review is to determine whether the use of a new weapon, means or method of warfare is prohibited or restricted by an international treaty binding on the reviewing state or by customary international law. These prohibitions or restrictions arise through express treaty law obligations binding on the reviewing state or customary international humanitarian law.

As noted in Chapter 3, there are no specific prohibitions or restrictions against AWS as a class of weapons. However, all specific prohibitions and restrictions apply to AWS that employ the relevant weapon system. For example, an AWS that employs chemical or biological weapons is prohibited because of how it causes its effect, not because it is autonomous.

Where there are no specific prohibitions or restrictions relevant to an AWS, it is necessary to consider the general prohibitions against certain weapon effects.

3.3 *Step 2 – Apply General Prohibitions*

If the weapon type is not prohibited or restricted by a specific treaty or customary international law, the second step requires consideration of the general prohibitions that apply to all weapons. Is the weapon prohibited by one or

68 Ibid.
69 Ibid.
70 Ibid.
71 Ibid.

more of the following general rules applicable to all weapons, means or methods of warfare?

a. Is the weapon of a nature to cause unnecessary suffering or superfluous injury to combatants?[72]
b. Is the weapon indiscriminate by nature in that it cannot be directed at a specific military objective and, consequently, is of a nature to strike military objectives and civilians or civilian objects without distinction?[73]
c. Does the weapon cause widespread, long-term and severe damage to the natural environment?[74]

3.3.1 Is the Weapon of a Nature to Cause Unnecessary Suffering or Superfluous Injury to Combatants?

As noted in Chapter 3, the prohibition against weapons causing unnecessary suffering or superfluous injury is among the earliest with respect to the legality of weapons per se.[75] It is codified in art 35(2) of AP I and is regarded as reflecting customary international humanitarian law and, therefore, binding on all states.[76] The prohibition protects combatants from 'those means and methods of warfare that unnecessarily aggravate the suffering of combatants, that is, which cause suffering serving no military purpose'.[77] The prohibition against unnecessary suffering or superfluous injury reflects the 'delicate balance' between the fundamental IHL principles of military necessity and humanity.[78]

Despite its importance, determining what constitutes unnecessary suffering or superfluous injury is difficult in practice. A reviewing state should consider 'whether the employment of a weapon for its normal or expected use inevitably would cause injury or suffering manifestly disproportionate to its military effectiveness'.[79]

---

72 AP I (n 15) art 35(1).

73 Ibid art 51(4)(b).

74 Ibid art 35(3).

75 M Schmitt, 'Autonomous Weapon Systems and International Humanitarian Law: A Reply to the Critics' (2013) *Harvard National Security Journal Features* 8.

76 JM Henckaerts and L Doswald-Becks, *Customary International Humanitarian Law* (Cambridge University Press, 2005) ('ICRC CIL Study') rule 70.

77 M Schmitt, 'The Principle of Distinction in 21 Century Warfare' (1999) 2 *Yale Human Rights and Development Law Journal* 144, 147–8.

78 M Schmitt, 'Military Necessity and Humanity in International Humanitarian Law' (n 176) 810.

79 W Hays Parks, 'Means and Methods of Warfare, Symposium in Honour of Edward R Cummings' (2006) 38 *George Washington International Law Review* 511.

Accordingly, there are two important questions for the legal reviewer to consider in determining whether a new weapon, means or method of warfare causes superfluous injury or unnecessary suffering:

a. Does the weapon or munition effects, weighted in light of a comparable, lawful weapon or munition in use on the modern battlefield, cause more injury or suffering?
b. Will the employment of the weapon in its normal or expected use inevitably cause injury or suffering manifestly disproportionate to its military effectiveness?

In practical terms, AWS are likely to utilise weapons and munitions that are already within state arsenals. On this basis, they are unlikely to be of a nature of cause superfluous injury or unnecessary suffering. If, however, the AWS employ a new weapon or munition, the legal review will need to consider the two questions described above.

3.3.2 Is the Weapon by Nature Indiscriminate?

IHL prohibits methods or means of combat that cannot be directed at a specific military objective or where the effects cannot be limited as required by IHL.[80] The assessment of indiscriminate effects will consider a range of factors, including 'the accuracy and reliability of the targeting mechanism, the area covered by the weapon, whether the weapon's effects are capable of being limited to the target or being controlled in time and space'.[81] The accuracy and reliability of the weapon are important but must also be considered in the context of the normal or expected use of the weapon. For example, a weapon that is not capable of precision may be employed lawfully in areas where there are only combatants and no civilians or civilian objects. Such weapons are subject to restrictions on their use rather than prohibition.

As noted in Chapter 3, there are two aspects to this prohibition against indiscriminate weapons. The first relates to the weapon design and prohibits weapons that are, by nature indiscriminate. This is a potential risk for AWS which are unable to accurately detect or classify persons and objects in their operating environments. Equally, an AWS that is unable to sense their environment or adapting to changing circumstances may be assessed as indiscriminate by nature.

The second aspect relates to the indiscriminate *use* of a weapon. It is unlawful to conduct an indiscriminate attack by not aiming at a specific military

80 AP I (n 15) arts 51(4)(b)–(c).
81 ICRC Guide (n 1) 18.

objective. This aspect of the prohibition against indiscriminate attacks is not considered by a traditional legal review as it is an application of targeting rules. The dichotomy between weapons law and targeting law in the legal review analysis is discussed later in this chapter.

3.3.3 Will the Weapon Cause Long-Term, Widespread and Severe Damage to the Natural Environment?

International law regulates weapons and the environment in several ways. First, it prohibits excessive damage to the natural environment by prohibited methods or means of warfare, which are intended, or may be expected, to cause widespread, long-term and severe damage. Article 35(3) of the AP 1 states, 'It is prohibited to employ methods or means of warfare which are intended, or may be expected, to cause widespread, long-term and severe damage to the natural environment'.[82]

While the art 35(3) prohibition is concerned specifically with protecting the environment, the prohibition in art 55(1) is directed, in part, towards the harm to the 'health or survival' of the civilian population that may result from significant environmental harm.[83] Article 55(2) prohibits attacks against the natural environment by way of reprisals. The text suggests that the prohibition is directed towards attacks targeting the environment specifically rather than incidental damage resulting from attacks against military objectives in reprisal.

The long-term nature of the damage referred to in arts 35(3) and 55(1) are measured in decades and, therefore, would not include environmental damage caused by conventional warfare, such as from the explosive effects of artillery barrages.[84] Accordingly, prohibition does not apply to short-term, limited environmental damage, such as the use of explosive munitions to prevent enemy access to certain terrain, so-called 'terrain denial' missions.[85]

The risk that an AWS will cause widespread, long-term and severe damage to the natural environment is likely to be low. This is again because the AWS are likely to employ weapons and munitions that are already within the state's arsenal and which are already determined to not cause harm to the natural environment.

---

82 AP 1 (n 15) art 35(3).

83 Boothby (n 17) 95.

84 ICRC Commentary (n 18) [1454].

85 M Montazzoli, 'Terrain Denial Fires on the Modern Battlefield', *Articles of War Blog* (Blog Post, 25 August 2021) <https://lieber.westpoint.edu/terrain-denial-fires-modern-battlefield/>.

3.4 *Step 3 – Other Considerations, Including National Policy*

International law does not regulate all issues concerned with the use of weapons in armed conflict. A state may consider and apply other, non-legal, considerations in the conduct of a legal review, including national policy.[86] Indeed, national policy plays a central role, with many state legal review practices established by policy directives.[87]

As noted earlier, the Martens clause recognises that, in cases not covered by international law rules, civilians and combatants remain under the protection of customary international law, the 'principles of humanity' and 'dictates of public conscience'. A state's interpretation of relevant principles and dictates may be informed by its national AI governance frameworks, ethical AI frameworks and soft law. While views on the legal status of the Martens clause vary,[88] it is argued that the Martens clause provides a theoretical mechanism enabling a state's interpretation of its customary legal obligations to consider national policies and soft law during the conduct of a legal review.

For example, the issue of human control over means and methods of warfare is not covered by international law. During a legal review of an AWS, a state will have regard to national policy of the requirement for, and nature, of human control over AWS. In the case of a US legal review, the weapon reviewer would consider the contents of the US Department of Defence Directive 3000.09, which requires 'Autonomous and semi-autonomous weapon systems shall be designed to allow commanders and operators to exercise appropriate levels of human judgment over the use of force'.[89]

4 Outcomes of the Traditional Legal Review Process

The product of a traditional legal review is generally a report making a determination of the legality of a weapon and recommending whether the relevant

86 Boulanin and Verbruggen (n 9) 9.

87 See, eg, Australian Article 36 Review Guide (n 10).

88 See, eg, C Greenwood, 'The Law of Weaponry at the Start of the New Millennium' in Michael N Schmitt and Leslie C Green (eds), *The Law of Armed Conflict: Into the New Millennium* (U.S. Naval War College, 1999) 206; PA Robblee, 'The Legitimacy of Modern Conventional Weaponry' (1976) 71 *Military Law Review* 95, 125; International Human Rights Clinic and Human Rights Watch, *Losing Humanity: The Case Against Killer Robots* (IHRC and HRW, 2012), 4 ('Losing Humanity'). <https://www.hrw.org/report/2012/11/19/losing-humanity/case-against-killer-robots>.

89 US Directive 3000.09 (n 11) 2.

state should proceed with its development or acquisition.[90] A report will generally reach one of three conclusions regarding the use of the weapon in armed conflict:

a) the normal or expected use(s) is/are lawful
b) the use of the weapon is generally lawful, but particular methods or circumstances may render certain uses unlawful
c) all uses of the weapon are unlawful.[91]

In reaching these conclusions, the report will provide recommendations and guidance to the reviewing state about what limitations or controls should be put in place once the weapon system is introduced into service to ensure its lawful use.[92]

4.1 *Use of the Weapon in Its Normal or Expected Use Is Lawful*

A legal review will determine the legality of a weapon within the context of its normal or expected use. A traditional legal review focuses on the legality of weapons per se; therefore, its determination is likely to be binary in nature. For example, the review of a high-velocity bullet designed to target enemy combatants is prohibited for use because it is of a nature to cause superfluous injury or unnecessary suffering in contravention of art 35(2) of Additional Protocol I. In contrast, the legal review may determine the anti-materiel use of the same bullet is lawful as the issue of unnecessary suffering is not relevant.[93]

4.2 *The Use of the Weapon Is Lawful, but Limitations Are Required on Its Method of Use*

A traditional legal review may recommend that restrictions be placed on the use of a weapon. Such restrictions often ensure the discriminate use of a weapon in a particular circumstance. There are broadly two ways in which a weapon may be indiscriminate. The first relates to the weapon's design: the weapon is unable to be aimed or directed at a specific military objective as required by art

90 ICRC Guide (n 20) [2.4.2].

91 L Sanders and D Copeland, 'Developing an Approach to the Legal Review of Autonomous Weapon Systems', *ILA Reporter*, (27 November 2020) <https://ilareporter.org.au/2020/11/developing-an-approach-to-the-legal-review-of-autonomous-weapon-systems-lauren-sanders-and-damian-copeland/>.

92 D Copeland, R Liivoja and L Sanders, 'The Utility of Weapons Reviews in Addressing Concerns Raised by Autonomous Weapon Systems' (2022) *Journal of Conflict and Security Law*) 300.

93 Ibid.

51(4)(a) of AP 1. The second reason relates to the weapon use: while being technically capable of being directed at a specific military objective, the weapon is used in an indiscriminate way. In such a case, the weapon could be assessed as lawful following a legal review because it is the user of the weapon rather than the weapon itself that must adjust to ensure legal compliance during use. That is, the weapon is capable of being used discriminately, but the weapon user must use it against a lawful target. In this case, limits on the use review determine how the weapon can be used lawfully.[94]

In the case of an AWS that is incapable of being aimed at a specific military objective, for example because is it unable to distinguish between certain military objectives and civilian objects, a legal review may recommend that the weapon not be used to target military objectives located within the civilian population or close to civilian objects unless the military advantage outweighs the risk of collateral damage.

Due to the presumption of lawful use, the traditional legal review will not consider the risks relating to the discriminate use of a weapon. This is gap in traditional process with regard to AWS that are designed to perform targeting functions without direct human control. This gap is basis for an additional legal review step in Part 2.

4.3 *The Weapon Is Unlawful in All Circumstances*

Finally, the determination of a traditional legal review may be that the use of the weapon is unlawful in all circumstances, effectively resulting in the state being unable to utilise the weapon without incurring international responsibility for any wrongful damage resulting from its use in armed conflict. Such a determination may flow from a specific prohibition that prevents a state from possessing the specific weapon technology (e.g., the Chemical Weapons Convention).

Where such a legal review determination is made, significant design and development adjustments may need to be made to enable the system to achieve an alternative, legally compliant outcome (being 1 or 2 above). In the case of a conventional weapon system, this may be possible where componentry that results in non-compliance is identified. For example, an accurate sensor designed to enable the distinction between lawful and unlawful targets may replace an original, inaccurate one.[95]

---

94 Ibid 301.

95 Ibid.

4.4 *Legal Review Outcomes Applied to AWS*

The outcome of the legal review of an AWS may not fit neatly within one of the three options mentioned above. For example, a legal review may advise that the weapon component of the AWS is lawful per se but recommend restricting certain autonomous functionality that may be, or risks being, unlawful. Alternatively, a legal review may recommend that the use of an AWS would be lawful but that, as a matter of national policy, its use should be under direct real-time human control. For example, a review may identify that an AWS can lawfully be used to target combatants, but national policy precludes AWS from being employed against humans without direct human control. Alternatively, because of the inherent complexity of certain operations, state policy may require AWS to be used to target military objectives only, not lawful human targets. Therefore, a legal review report may recommend the AWS is not employed in armed conflict characterised as asymmetric (e.g., in a NIAC) where people (e.g., members of an organised armed group or civilians taking a direct part in hostilities) may be targeted.[96]

If the AWS AI system is capable of machine learning, the legal review may recommend that the AWS actions and operating environments be restricted to those assessed as lawful. In doing so, it may prevent the AI system from implementing new actions until they are assessed as lawful either by the weapon operator, a legal adviser deployed under art 82 of AP 1 or further legal review.

5 Traditional Legal Review Dichotomy between Weapons Law and Targeting Law

As noted earlier, the focus of the traditional legal review analysis is the determination of lawfulness per se of weapons (weapons law) rather than the analysis of the lawful use of weapons in armed conflict in any specific circumstances (targeting law). The recommendations of a legal review inform government decision-makers responsible for weapon procurement and are based on the specific and general international law prohibitions described above. Once procured, the focus turns to the lawful use of the procured weapons in armed conflict. There is a shift in responsibility from government decision-makers to military commanders and individual weapon operators. The latter are advised by military legal advisers deployed in compliance with art 82 of AP 1.[97]

96 Ibid 302.

97 AP 1 (n 15) art 82: 'The High Contracting Parties at all times, and the Parties to the conflict in time of armed conflict, shall ensure that legal advisers are available, when

A practical consequence of this dichotomy is that targeting rules are not analysed in detail during a traditional art 36 legal review. While appropriate for conventional weapons, this approach limits the complete assessment of the legality of an AWS designed to perform targeting functions.

It will be important for an AWS legal review to consider those targeting rules relevant to the autonomous functionality. IHL targeting rules are found predominately in Parts III (Methods and Means of Warfare, Combatant and Prisoner of War Status) and IV (Civilian Population) of AP I. They are premised on the basic rule that 'In any armed conflict, the right of Parties to the conflict to choose methods or means of warfare is not unlimited'.[98] The lawfulness of the use of a weapon on any particular occasion is a matter of targeting law applied by the individual operating the weapon, those who plan or decide upon an attack and potentially a legal adviser deployed to the conflict to advise the military commander.[99]

Haines argues that the legality of a weapon is assessed on two levels.[100] First, the question of whether a weapon is unlawful per se is answered by reference to the specific and general weapons law prohibitions discussed in Chapter 3. Such rules are 'instrument focused' as they are concerned with the physical design and intended effects of the weapon.[101] Second, Haines reinforces that a weapon's use in armed conflict is regulated by IHL rules on the conduct of hostilities. While the previous analysis is concerned with the nature of a weapon, the latter is focused on the IHL rules found in pts III (Methods and Means of Warfare, Combatant and Prisoner of War Status) and IV (Civilian Population) of AP I. These parts include rules relevant to the conduct of an attack in armed conflict and are generally referred to as 'targeting rules'. Targeting rules are not traditionally considered to be part of weapons law as they do not determine the legality of weapons per se and are concerned with the legality of their use.[102]

---

necessary, to advise military commanders at the appropriate level on the application of the Conventions and this Protocol and on the appropriate instruction to be given to the armed forces on this subject'.

98 Ibid art 35(2).

99 M Schmitt and J Thurnher (2013) '"Out of the Loop": Autonomous Weapon Systems and the Law of Armed Conflict' (2013) 4(2) *Harvard National Security Journal* 231, 273–4.

100 S Haines, 'The Developing Law of Weapons: Humanity, Distinction, and Precautions in Attack' in Andrew Clapham and Paola Gaeta (eds), *The Oxford Handbook of International Law in Armed Conflict* (Oxford University Press, 2018) 4.

101 A Tattersall and D Copeland, 'Reviewing Autonomous Cyber Capabilities' in R Liivoja and A Väljataga (eds), *Autonomous Cyber Capabilities Under International Law* (NATO CCDOE Publications, 2021) 227.

102 Boothby (n 17) 44; T Vestner and A Rossi, 'Legal Reviews of War Algorithms' 97 *International Law Studies* 509 (2021), 529–534.

5.1 *Applying Targeting Law in the Legal Review of an AWS*

A traditional legal review of a conventional, human-controlled, weapon will determine whether the weapon is (a) lawful per se and (b) capable of lawful use. In doing so, it does not have to determine whether the weapon is able to be used in compliance with targeting law in specific circumstances. The traditional legal review will identify any intended or obvious uses that would not be lawful, particularly in the context of the basic rule of distinction in art 48 of AP 1. In this way, the traditional legal review process relies on the individual weapon operator. This book argues that it will be necessary for the legal review of an AWS to consider the application of IHL rules regulating methods of warfare, including the rules of distinction, proportionality and precautions in attack.

5.1.1 Distinction

An AWS designed to identify a person or object to attack must be capable of doing so in compliance with the IHL rule of distinction, which is recognised by the ICJ as a 'cardinal principle contained in the texts constituting the fabric of humanitarian law'.[103] The principle is recognised as a norm of customary international law[104] and underpins the fundamental aim of IHL to protect the victims of armed conflict by distinguishing at all times between civilians and combatants and between civilian objects and military objectives. Article 48 of AP 1 codifies the principle of distinction as a 'basic rule' in the following terms:

> In order to ensure respect for and protection of the civilian population and civilian objects, the Parties to the conflict shall at all times distinguish between the civilian population and combatants and between civilian objects and military objectives and accordingly shall direct their operations only against military objectives.[105]

An AWS designed to search for, identify and recommend targets to a human weapon operator or commander will need to do so applying art 48 of AP 1 and other targeting related rules. The ability to accurately distinguish between persons and objects will be influenced by a range of technical and environmental

---

103 Nuclear Weapons Case (n 43) [78].

104 ICRC, *Customary International Humanitarian Law Database* (Website) <https://ihl-databases.icrc.org/customary-ihl/eng/docs/v1_rule> ('ICRC CIHL Database') rule 1: 'The Parties to the conflict must at all times distinguish between civilians and combatants. Attacks may only be directed against combatants. Attacks must not be directed against civilians'.

105 AP 1 (n 15) art 47(1).

factors, which will need to be considered in the art 36 legal review. In some cases, an AI neural network visual classifier will be able to accurately distinguish certain objects based on distinct physical characteristics or electronic signatures. An AI system may be programmed to classify objects with certain physical or technical indicia as a military objective and, in certain environments, be able to achieve a high probability of accuracy. However, classifying persons as either civilians or combatants may be more difficult for an AI neural network. This is because it will require identification of IHL status not only based on physical characteristics but, in some cases, by their actions. Moreover, the IHL-protected status may change based on a person's actions. For example, an otherwise protected civilian may be lawfully attacked while taking a direct part in hostilities,[106] or an enemy combatant may become protected by clearly expressing an intention to surrender.[107]

Most relevantly to targeting law, art 51(4)(a) of AP 1 prohibits an indiscriminate attack (i.e., the indiscriminate use of a discriminate weapon) that is, where the weapon is not directed at a specific military objective.

This is informed by art 52(2) of AP 1, which strictly limits attacks to 'objects' determined to be 'military objectives', having satisfied a two-part test:

a. by their nature, location, purpose or use makes an effective contribution to military action; and
b. whose total or partial destruction, capture or neutralisation, in the circumstances ruling at the time, offers a definite military advantage.

A military objective can be any object that satisfies this test. Such a subjective determination may be beyond the technical ability of an AWS, but states may pre-program AWS to classify certain objects as military objectives.

The rule of distinction is given practical effect by arts 51(2) and 52(1) of AP 1, which prohibit attacks on the civilian population, individual civilians or civilian objects, respectively. These targeting rules are often confused with the general prohibitions in arts 51(4)(b) and (c) of AP 1. The former prohibits per se weapons that are incapable of being aimed at a specific target, while the latter prohibits per se weapons capable of being aimed at a target but causing uncontrollable effects. The use of some chemical weapons is an example.

A traditional art 36 legal review of a weapon will focus on the rules contained in art 51(4)(b) and (c) as they are relevant to the legality per se of the weapon or munition. These contrast with art 51(4)(a), which regulates the use

106 Ibid art 51(3).
107 Ibid art 40(2)(b).

of a weapon and is, therefore, a targeting rule that will not be considered by the legal review as IHL holds commanders and those who plan or decide upon an attack accountable for failing to direct an attack at a specific military objective.

5.1.2 Military Necessity

The preamble to the 1868 St. Petersburg Declaration[108] provides an early expression of the military necessity principle:

> That the only legitimate object which States should endeavour to accomplish during war is to weaken the military forces of the enemy.[109]

The principle was later captured in the Hague Regulations of 1899 and 1907, stating that it is prohibited to:

> destroy or seize the enemy's property, unless such destruction or seizure be imperatively demanded by the necessities of war.[110]

In 1948, military necessity was authoritatively defined by the American Military Tribunal held in Nuremberg following the Second World War. The *Hostage Case* judgement defined military necessity as a principle that:

> permits a belligerent, subject to the laws of war, to apply any amount and kind of force to compel the complete submission of the enemy with the least expenditure of time, life and money.[111]

Military necessity is the essential counterbalance to humanitarian considerations and is reflected in many IHL rules including the prohibition against superfluous injury or unnecessary suffering, originating in the St. Petersburg preamble.[112]

---

108 *Declaration Renouncing the Use, in Time of War, of Explosive Projectiles under 400 Grammes Weight*, opened for signature 29 November 1868 (entered into force 11 December 1868) ('St. Petersburg Declaration').

109 Ibid.

110 1907 *Hague Convention (IV) Respecting the Laws and Customs of War on Land*, opened for signature 18 October 1907 (entered into force 26 January 1910) art 23(g) ('1907 Hague Convention IV').

111 *USA v List et al*, US Military Tribunal, Nuremberg (1948) 11 *Nuremberg Military Tribunal* 1230, 1253 ('Hostage Case').

112 St. Petersburg Declaration (n 120): 'That this object [weaken the military forces of the enemy by disabling the greatest possible number of men] would be exceeded by the

The development and lawful use of autonomy in armed conflict is subject to but not prohibited by the principle of military necessity. Indeed, the AWS capabilities may, in some circumstances where decision speed and accuracy are critical, result in less harm and destruction.

5.1.3 Proportionality

The proportionality rule is linked to the principle of distinction and prohibits launching an attack that may be expected to cause incidental harm to civilians or civilian objects that would be excessive in relation to the concrete and direct military advantage anticipated. The rule is articulated in arts 51(5)(b) and 57(2)(a)(iii) of AP 1. The former is expressed as an example of an indiscriminate attack, and the latter in the context of taking precautions in attack.

Article 57(2)(a)(iii) states:

> (iii) [those who plan or decide upon an attack shall:] refrain from deciding to launch any attack which may be expected to cause incidental loss of civilian life, injury to civilians, damage to civilian objects, or a combination thereof, which would be excessive in relation to the concrete and direct military advantage anticipated.[113]

This rule is often misunderstood as it requires the comparison of unlike values, namely collateral damage to civilians and civilian objects with an anticipated military advantage. The proportionality rules are difficult to apply both in theory and practice.[114] This assessment is subjective, and it is only when the collateral damage that is expected to result is 'excessive' in relation to the military advantage that an attack is prohibited by IHL. The term 'excessive' is not defined by IHL, but its common understanding is 'more than is necessary'. Applied to an attack during an armed conflict, killing and injuring dozens of civilian casualties in an attack may be considered 'more than necessary' to destroy an enemy tank. A common misunderstanding is that this analysis is mathematical in nature. For example, 20 civilian deaths are excessive in relation to two military deaths. This is not the correct analysis, as the value of an anticipated military advantage is a context-specific concept.[115] Accordingly, 20 civilian casualties may be assessed by a military commander as proportionate to the military advantage anticipated by the death of a senior military commander or the destruction of a significant military capability. Schmitt

employment of arms which uselessly aggravate the sufferings of disabled men or render their death inevitable'.

113 AP 1 (n 15) art 57(2)(a)(iii).

114 Schmitt and Thurnher (n 111) 253.

115 Ibid 256.

emphasises that the standard is 'excessive', a comparative concept, not 'extensive', an absolute term.[116]

To aid attack planning, several militaries use computer programs for collateral damage modelling and simulation. For example, the US Collateral Damage Methodology supports conventional weapon targeting by 'providing commanders with an understanding of weapon effects, incidental consequences and mitigation techniques, enabling more balanced, comprehensive judgments.[117] The methodology relies on empirical data, probability and complex weaponeering models to analyse individual attacks and provide commanders with a collateral damage estimate (CDE). The use of AI to inform commanders' decisions is a likely progression of existing CDE modelling tools and may be available via networking or incorporated into individual weapon systems. For example, an AI visual classifier may notify a weapon operator of a collateral damage risk within the weapon effect radius of a particular target. Where such a capability is incorporated into a weapon system, a reviewing state may assess it as a means of warfare and, therefore, subject to the art 36 legal review obligation.

5.1.4 Precautions in Attack

Parties to a conflict are required to take all feasible precautions to protect the civilian population, civilians and civilian objects from the effects of attacks.[118] It operationalises the rules of distinction and proportionality and is found in art 57 of AP 1. Those who plan or decide upon an attack are required by art 57(2)(a) to:

> (i) do everything feasible to verify that the objectives to be attacked are neither civilians nor civilian objects and are not subject to special protection but are military objectives within the meaning of paragraph 2 of Article 52 and that is it not prohibited by the provisions of this Protocol to attack them;
> (ii) take all feasible precautions in the choice of means and methods of attack with a view to avoiding, and in any event minimizing, incidental loss of civilian life, injury to civilians and damage to civilian objects;

---

116 M Schmitt, 'Military Necessity and Humanity in International Humanitarian Law: Preserving the Delicate Balance' (2010) 50(4) *Virginia Journal of International Law* 795, 803–804.

117 US Chairman of the Joint Chiefs of Staff, Instruction CJCSI 3160.01D *No-Strike and the Collateral Damage Estimation Methodology* (13 February 2009) D-2.

118 ICRC CIHL Database (n 104) rule 15.

(iii) refrain from deciding to launch any attack which may be expected to cause incidental loss of civilian life, injury to civilians, damage to civilian objects, or a combination thereof, which would be excessive in relation to the concrete and direct military advantage anticipated.[119]

Taking precautions in attack is an ongoing obligation that exists throughout the conduct of an attack. This is clear from art 57(2)(b) of AP 1, which requires those who plan or decide upon an attack to 'cancel or suspend an attack where it becomes apparent that the target is not a military objective, is subject to special protection or that the attack may cause excessive collateral damage'.[120]

The obligation to take constant care to spare the civilian population is reinforced by the requirements to give effective advanced warning of attacks that may affect the civilian population and to choose possible targets that may be expected to cause the least danger to civilians. This obligation is, however, a qualified one. Article 57(2)(c) of AP 1 states:

> effective advance warning shall be given of attacks which may affect the civilian population, *unless circumstances do not permit*.[121]

An attacking force may refrain from giving an advance warning were doing so would compromise the element of surprise and so surrender any advantage that may result. Alternatively, an advance warning may increase the risk to own troops by alerting an enemy of a pending attack. The use of AWS to conduct an attack may, however, reduce this risk and enable effective advance warning in circumstances that were not possible using human attackers.

The ADF has incorporated these obligations into its targeting procedure, referred to as the 'IHL 6-Step Targeting Process'.[122] This process is designed to inform target planning and decisions at the operational level. The first four steps support the planning of an attack, and the final two steps address the conduct of the attack. The IHL 6-Step Targeting Process consists of:

1. Locate and observe the potential target and its surrounding area.
2. Assess whether the target is a valid military objective and that it is otherwise unprotected from attack by IHL.

---

119 AP 1 (n 15) art 57(2)(a).
120 Ibid art 57(2)(b).
121 Ibid art 57(2)(c) [emphasis added].
122 I Henderson, *The Contemporary Law of Targeting* (Martinus Nijhoff Publishers, 2009) 237.

3. Take all feasible precautions to minimise collateral damage.
4. Assess whether any expected collateral damage is proportional (i.e., not excessive) to the anticipated military advantage to be gained from the attack.
5. Take such care as is appropriate in the tactical situation to release or fire the weapon to achieve the best possible chance of hitting the selected aim point.
6. Cancel or suspend the attack should it become apparent that any one of the assessments made under steps 2 or 4 is no longer valid.[123]

It is foreseeable that an AI system will be capable of aiding those who plan or decide upon an attack to make decisions concerning several of these steps. For example, a command decision tool based on a neural network classifier is designed to make recommendations for Steps 1 to 3. In each case, the human commander or weapon system operator is ultimately responsible for the decision. However, the immediate question is whether relying on such a recommendation amounts to 'doing everything feasible' as required by the precautions rule.

6 Conclusions

Despite the low number of states with national legal review processes, it is possible to discern a number of common legal questions that form the basis of the traditional legal review analysis. The legal review obligation is recognised as one of substance rather than form, the former being far more important than the latter.[124] The common legal questions are: (a) is the weapon prohibited or restricted by an international law binding the reviewing state? (b) is the weapon of a nature of cause superfluous injury or unnecessary suffering; and (c) is the weapon indiscriminate by nature? These questions, whether undertaken by a committee or a single official, are sufficient to enable a state to make a determination of the legality of the weapon per se. This legal review analysis is commonly conducted in four steps which generally inform decision makers at the key weapon acquisition decision points.

The traditional weapon review process does not analyse the legality of a weapon's use in specific circumstances. It does not need to. A legal reviewer

123 Ibid.

124 Hays Parks (n 19) 107.

reviewing a conventional weapon can rely on a presumption that the human weapon operator, who is legally responsible for his or her actions in armed conflict, will use a lawful weapon lawfully in future armed conflict. This reflects the dichotomy between the two bodies of international law that regulate weapons: weapons law, which is applied during a legal review; and targeting law, which is applied during an armed conflict. The traditional legal review process was developed to determine the legality of human operated weapons, not AWS. The fundamental difference is there is a risk that an AWS, designed to perform targeting functions that are governed by targeting law, will perform the function in a way that was either unexpected, or unlawful or both.

The traditional legal review process is not sufficient to determine the legality of AWS. A legal review process is incomplete if it does not determine the ability of an AWS to perform its targeting functions lawfully. This is the basis for arguing in Part 2 of this book for an expanded approach to the legal review of AWS.

PART 2

How Can a State Determine the Legality of an AWS?

Introduction to Part 2

> The established principles and rules of humanitarian law applicable in armed conflict apply to all forms of warfare and to all kinds of weapons, those of the past, those of the present and those of the future.[1]

∴

Part 1 of this book questions whether the traditional approach to legal reviews is sufficient to determine the legality of AWS. In doing so, it analyses the sources and scope of the international legal review obligation and describes how international weapons law regulates a state's possession and use of weapons, including AWS. It then identifies how states give practical effect to their international law obligation by conducting legal reviews. Part 1 identifies what is referred to as the traditional legal review methodology and the common steps evidenced from state practice. It argues that that the traditional legal review process reflects the dichotomy between weapons law and targeting law by focusing on the legality of the weapon per se and not extending to the contextual application of targeting law. While this is appropriate for conventional weapons under direct human control, Part 1 concludes that this approach is insufficient to determine the legality of AWS that use programming or AI to perform tasks that are governed by targeting law.

The need to reconceptualise the approach to the legal review of AWS is not new. In November 2017, the Swiss Delegation to the CCW[2] GGE on LAWS emphasised:

> We see a number of challenges related to [AWS] distinct from traditional legal reviews. ... Beyond the purely technical challenge of assessing IHL compliance of an [AWS], there is also a conceptual challenge related to the fact that an autonomous system will assume an increasing number of

1 *Legality of the Threat or Use of Nuclear Weapons (Advisory Opinion)* [1996] ICJ Rep 226, [86] ('Nuclear Weapons Case').

2 *Convention on Prohibitions or Restrictions on the Use of Certain Conventional Weapons Which May be Deemed to be Excessively Injurious or to Have Indiscriminate Effects* (10 October 1980) and Amendment to Article 1 (21 December 2001) 1342 UNTS 137 ('*CCW*').

 | DOI:10.1163/9789004707047_008

> determinations in the targeting cycle which traditionally are being taken care of by a human operator ... New evaluation and testing procedures may need to be conceptualized and developed to meet this particular challenge.[3]

Part 2 of this book focuses upon the interpretive and methodological challenges that are likely to arise in the legal review of AWS and proposes a modified legal review process. The modified approach builds upon the traditional legal review process and is intended to enable a reviewing state to determine whether some or all of the AWS' normal or expected uses can be employed in armed conflict, or limited situations within armed conflict, or whether aspects of the weapon's capabilities require modification to ensure the weapon's lawful operation. Moreover, the proposed legal review approach will assist in the identification of gaps in the AWS' ability to perform functions in compliance with the reviewing state's international law obligations.

3 Working Paper submitted by Switzerland, *A 'Compliance-based' Approach to Autonomous Weapon Systems*, UN Doc CCW/GGE.1/2017/WP.9 (10 November 2017) 4–5 <https://docs-library.unoda.org/Convention_on_Certain_Conventional_Weapons_-_Group_of_Governmental_Experts_(2017)/2017_GGEonLAWS_WP9_Switzerland.pdf>.

CHAPTER 6

Interpretive and Methodological Questions in the Legal Review of AWS

To provide a basis for arguing for modifications to the traditional legal review process, this chapter will address the unique interpretive and methodological questions that arise in the legal review of an AWS. These questions arise because an AWS is designed to perform functions that are governed by IHL rules without direct human input. A legal review must determine the ability of the AWS to operate in compliance with the reviewing state's international law obligations. Assuming the absence of a new international treaty regulating autonomy in weapons, states must interpret and apply their existing international law obligations to novel AWS capabilities. In the conduct of a legal review of AWS, this must include not only an assessment of whether an AWS is lawful per se but also require an ongoing determination of whether it is capable of lawful use in compliance with the IHL rules regulating methods of warfare, including targeting law. The requirement to analyse the AWS functions that engage IHL targeting rules arise because legal responsibility and accountability for harm resulting from the AWS use resides in the state and its agents (military commanders and weapon operators)[1] and not in the AWS itself.[2] The analysis of whether the AWS is capable of lawful use requires the interpretation of existing legal norms and this presents interpretive challenges the traditional legal review methodology.

These interpretive challenges give rise to questions of how a state will, in practice, conduct a legal review of an AWS. The methodological considerations reinforce the importance of national policy to address the unique AWS legal review requirements that are in addition to the traditional legal review. This includes the application of national policy on AI ethics and governance.

1 International Law Commission, 'Draft Articles on State Responsibility' in *Report of the International Law Commission on the Work of its 52nd Session*, UN Doc A/55/10 (2000) art 4.

2 *Guiding Principles affirmed by the Group of Governmental Experts on Emerging Technologies in the Area of Lethal Autonomous Weapons System*, Annex III to the Final Report of the Meeting of the High Contracting Parties to the Convention on Prohibitions or Restrictions on the Use of Certain Conventional Weapons Which May be Deemed to be Excessively Injurious or to Have Indiscriminate Effects, UN Doc CCW/MSP/2019/9 (13 December 2019) ('UN GGE Guiding Principles').

 | DOI:10.1163/9789004707047_009

The need for an expanded legal review process in the development and use of AWS is also considered, including where important research and development occurs by private companies or research agencies prior to an AWS entry into a state capability acquisition process.

Building on the analysis of the art 36 operative terms in Chapter 4, Section 1 challenges some additional interpretations of the art 36 obligation in relation to an AWS. This includes whether a legal reviewer can rely on the traditional legal review presumption that weapon will be used lawfully in armed conflict. This is followed by considering whether a legal review must ensure that, for each autonomous function performed by an AWS, there are clear lines of human accountability. Finally, the section raises the difficult question of what legal standards are to be applied in determining the legality of AWS.

Section 2 then identifies the methodological questions that may arise in a legal review of an AWS. This includes whether the complex nature of AWS requires the legal review process to extend to before and after the 'study, development, acquisition or adoption' of an AWS. Noting that much of the technology employed by an AWS is developed by defence industry, the section considers the benefit of the legal review process including an informative stage to ensure the state's legal review requirements and standards are understood by those defence industry developing AWS technology. The need to maintain a legal review oversight or governance of an AWS after it has been acquired and during its in-service use is considered.

The chapter makes five concluding observations. Firstly, the tradition legal review presumption that a human weapon operator will use the weapon lawfully is not possible where AI or programming performs certain task governed by IHL targeting rules. Secondly, the need to maintain clear lines of human responsibility requires consideration during the legal review to the use of AWS resulting in gaps in legal responsibility. Thirdly, the legal review must determine the appropriate legal standards. These standards may be based on human standards but also be influenced by a range of policy, technical, operational and environmental issues. Fourthly, to address risks associated with the development and use of AWS, national legal review process may expand beyond the traditional legal review steps to include analysis prior to and after the 'study, development, acquisition or adoption' of an AWS. Finally, the potential for AWS with machine learning raises the need for an ongoing, in-service legal review process to address self-identified changes in an AWS' method of use.

These interpretive and methodological questions provide the basis for the conclusion that states seeking to develop or acquire AWS may need to review their national legal review processes and consider the requirement to expand beyond the traditional legal review steps identified in Chapter 5. This includes the need for AWS specific national legal review policy that addresses autonomy in weapons. This chapter sets the foundations for chapter 7 that argues the need for an additional legal review step, and chapter 8 which argues for an expanded legal review process across the entire AWS lifecycle.

1 Article 36's Interpretive Questions Arising from Autonomy in Weapons

The traditional approach to legal reviews is informed by several interpretations of art 36 that apply to convention, human operated, weapons. This section considers whether the interpretations analysed in Chapter 5, applied during a traditional legal review, remain suitable for the legal review of an AWS or whether autonomous functions in weapons requires them to be reconsidered. It argues that AWS-specific interpretations may be necessary to address the questions of state and individual responsibility in the use of AWS.

1.1 *Can the Legal Reviewer Presume an AWS Will Be Used Lawfully?*

An important question to consider is whether a legal reviewer may, in determining the legality of an AWS, presume that the weapon operator will operate the AWS lawfully. During the traditional legal review of a conventional weapon, it is generally presumed that a human weapon operator will operate the weapon in compliance with the state's IHL and international law obligations.[3] This book argues that, while appropriate for a human-operated weapon, this presumption of lawful use is not appropriate to the legal review of an AWS for those aspects of the weapon's functionality that are enabled by AI.

The review of AWS will require a determination of whether the autonomous functionality can operate in compliance with the review state's IHL obligations. This will require an expansion of the legal review process. This underscores the central hypothesis of this book, that the traditional legal review process is not sufficient to address the legal issues raised by autonomy in weapons.

The question of how IHL applies to the use of AWS is the subject of ongoing international debate and remains unresolved. The ICRC has identified state, military commanders, manufacturers and programmers as potentially accountable for unlawful actions under numerous distinct legal regimes including: state

3 L Sanders and D Copeland, 'Developing an Approach to the Legal Review of Autonomous Weapon Systems', *International Law Association Reporter* (27 November 2020) <https://ilareporter.org.au/2020/11/developing-an-approach-to-the-legal-review-of-autonomous-weapon-systems-lauren-sanders-and-damian-copeland/>.

responsibility for violations of IHL; international criminal law; manufacturers and product liability; and corporate criminal liability.[4] Noting concern for a potential 'accountability gap', in the author's view, it is more likely that direct criminal responsibility for IHL breaches attributed to the use of an AWS will lie with the individual military operator, the military commander ordering its use and the state who fielded the weapon in armed conflict. The manufacturer of the weapon may be found responsible under domestic product liability laws for latent defects in the weapon that were undiscovered during its development or acquisition.[5] This book will proceed on the basis that the state and its agents will remain legally responsible for IHL breaches involving the use of AWS in the same way that they are responsible for breaches involving the use of other weapons.

The potential for AWS to make decisions after they have been deployed by a human operator requires serious consideration by the responsible state. Where the weapon makes decisions that engage the state's IHL obligations, hereafter referred to as 'IHL functions', the state's legal review process will need to consider these in relation to the level of human input to the task. This should occur during the weapon's development and procurement, which will, in turn, be informed by the state legal review process and testing. This need to test an AWS' ability to perform IHL functions in realistic operational scenarios is likely to present significant technical challenges for a developing state. It underscores the importance of testing and verification of the weapon's ability to perform its IHL functions in a lawful way.

A state will not generally be able to rely on a presumption of lawful use for AWS functions that are governed by IHL. However, the nature of an AWS' operation may permit the presumption of lawful use to be applied to some aspects of the weapon's operation (e.g., those functions directed or overseen by humans). It will be necessary to review the normal and expected use of the weapon to identify which of the state's international law obligations are engaged by it. Having identified those tasks that have IHL or other international law obligations, it is possible to broadly divide the tasks into three categories:

1. those undertaken by humans;
2. those where the AWS makes the decisions with human input or oversight; or

4 ICRC, *Report on the ICRC Expert Meeting on Autonomous Weapon Systems: Technical, Military, Legal and Humanitarian Aspects*, 26–28 March 2014, Geneva (9 May 2014), 2 <https://www.icrc.org/en/document/report-icrc-meeting-autonomous-weapon-systems-26-28-march-2014>.

5 T McFarland and T McCormack, 'Mind the Gap: Can Developers of Autonomous Weapon Systems be Liable for War Crimes?' 90 *International Law Studies* 361 (2014) 361, 385.

3. those where the AWS makes decisions independently of direct human input.

It may be necessary, depending on the complexity of the human command and control of the weapon, for additional IHL task categories to be identified to allow the legal review to analyse them appropriately. However, assuming that there are three broad categories of IHL tasks that may be completed by an AWS, it is possible that a reviewing state will apply the presumption of lawful use to the first of the three categories and subject the tasks that fall within the second and third categories of tasks to greater legal review analysis to determine whether it is able to perform the task lawfully.

1.2 *Does the Legal Review of an AWS Need to Identify Lines of Human Responsibility?*

As noted in Chapter 4, a traditional legal review does not consider or analyse if there are possible gaps in human responsibility in the use of a weapon during armed conflict. This reflects the fact that IHL and international law contain rules designed to hold states and their agents accountable for violations. While IHL does not specifically prohibit or restrict AWS, the prospect that machines will partially or fully replace human decision makers in the application of lethal force raises important questions of legal responsibility and accountability. Does the use of autonomy break the chain of legal accountability between the state, designers/developers of AWS, weapon operators and military commander? As AWS are machines without legal personality there may be an increasing need for states to consider the issue of legal responsibility in the course of a legal review. This is consistent with the UN GGE on LAWS' 2018 Guiding Principles which affirm,

> (d) Accountability for developing, deploying and using any emerging weapons system in the framework of the CCW must be ensured in accordance with the applicable international law, including through the operation of such systems within a responsible chain of human command and control.[6]

The terms responsibility, liability and accountability are often used synonymously. For example, art 91 of AP 1 holds a party to the conflict responsible for 'all acts committed by persons forming part of its armed forces'. The state is therefore both responsible for the conduct of the members of its armed forces

6 UN GGE Guiding Principles (n 2).

and liable for paying compensation to the victims of IHL violations. A state in turn may hold individual members of its armed forces responsible for their conduct through domestic law such as military disciplinary law or criminal law offences. The following paragraphs use the term responsibility collectively except where a specific reference to accountability or liability is necessary.

Identifying legal responsibility for the use of force in armed conflict is not a new problem. In recent decades, the issue of 'who owns the bomb' has arisen regularly in coalition operations where multiple levels of command and multiple states participate in decision making relevant to an attack.[7] However, AWS raise additional considerations and risks. Among these are the concern to avoid ambiguity or gaps in legal responsibility that may arise where AWS perform targeting functions autonomously.

A threshold question is whether international law permits states or individuals to delegate legal responsibility for actions or decisions concerning the use of force in armed conflict to machines. States party to the CCW, participating in the GGE on LAWS, answered this question definitively in the 2018 Guiding Principle (c) which states,

> [h]uman responsibility for decisions on the use of weapon systems must be retained since accountability cannot be transferred to machines.[8]

This is consistent with how international law has sought to regulate remote weapons since the early 20th century. For example, the Hague Convention VIII relative to the Laying of Automatic Contact Mines prohibited the use of unanchored automatic mines that did not neutralise within an hour of loss of control.[9]

The following paragraphs survey the international law mechanisms designed to promote the rule of law by holding states and individuals responsible for the use of force in armed conflict and reflects how they may be considered during a legal review.

It was observed by the trial judges at the International Military Tribunal, conducted in Nuremberg, Germany at the conclusion of WW2, that 'crimes

---

7 P Cronan et al, 'Operations Bastille and Falconer: Legal Support to Commanders' (2011) 184 *Australian Defence Force Journal* 33, 33–9.

8 UN GGE Guiding Principles (n 2).

9 *Hague Convention (VIII) Relative to the Laying of Automatic Submarine Contact Mines*, opened for signature 18 October 1907, 205 CTS 331 (entered into force 26 January 1910) art 1(1).

against international law are committed by men, not abstract entities'.[10] Individual responsibility under international and national criminal law system for the use of AWS in armed conflict will be examined first.

IHL holds states responsible for the actions of their agents.[11] The IHL rule requiring precautions in attack, for example, states that 'those who plan or decide upon an attack' should do 'everything feasible' to distinguish between lawful and unlawful targets and 'take all feasible precautions' to avoid collateral damage. What is 'reasonable' and 'feasible' is contextually dependent. A question for those who plan or decide upon an attack is whether reliance on an AWS action is reasonable in the circumstances. For example, is it reasonable to rely on an AWS' ability to distinguish between civilians and combatants? This question requires commanders and weapon operators to have clear knowledge of both the AWS capabilities and its limitations.

The IHL standards of reasonable and feasible are relevant to an individual's criminal responsibility. A fundamental purpose of international criminal law is to hold individuals who commit grave breaches of IHL to account. This raises challenges in the context of AWS. How can an individual be held criminally responsible for the artificial decisions undertaken by an AWS under the person's control? In the case of *Galić*, the International Criminal Tribunal for the Former Yugoslavia applied a 'reasonable military commander' standard to determine whether an attack was unlawfully disproportionate.[12] The tribunal observed that clothing, activity, age, and gender were relevant to determine civilian status, as were movement, shape, colour and speed in identifying a civilian object.[13]

If an AWS was designed to recognise such indicia and determine the civilian status of persons and objects, the state might determine that an AWS performing a distinction role must achieve an equal or higher standard than reasonable belief required by a human. Ascribing a higher standard to machines may

---

10 Philippe Kirsch, 'Applying the Principles of Nuremberg to the ICC' (Keynote Address at the Conference 'Judgement at Nuremberg' held on the 60th Anniversary of the Nuremberg Judgment, Washington University, 30 September 2006) 3.

11 *Protocol Additional to the Geneva Conventions of 12 August 1949, and relating to the Protection of Victims of International Armed Conflicts (Protocol I)*, opened for signature 8 June 1977, 1125 UNTS 3 (entered into force 7 December 1978) ('*AP I*') art 91 states, 'A Party to the conflict which violates the provisions of the Conventions or of this Protocol shall, if the case demands, be liable to pay compensation. It shall be responsible for all acts committed by persons forming part of its armed forces.'

12 *Prosecutor v Galić* (*Judgement and Opinion*) (International Criminal Tribunal for the Former Yugoslavia, Trial Chamber I, Case No IT-98-29-T, 5 December 2003), [51].

13 Ibid [50].

be fraught however. What is considered 'reasonable' in the context of autonomous decision-making systems requires the fielding state to carefully consider differing conditions applicable in every potential use and make legal and policy decisions accordingly.

A requirement for meaningful human control over the critical functions of the AWS is often argued as a requirement for its lawful deployment in armed conflict.[14] There is international consensus on the requirement for human control; however, whether this is a legal requirement[15] or an ethical or moral obligation has not been settled.[16] If an AWS is under human control and is conducting tasks directed by a human operator, the chain of human accountability and responsibility remains unbroken, regardless of which IHL obligations have been delegated to the machine. A state must also consider the standard and nature of human control and when human intervention is necessary for the control of the autonomous functionality to be considered 'meaningful'.

A person may be held criminally liable under IHL or Rome Statute offences incorporated into domestic law. The latter may apply where the elements of an offence applying the mental standard of 'intent or knowledge' exist.[17] Accordingly, if a military commander deployed an AWS designed to recognise the *Galić* indicia described above, knowing that it is incapable of doing so in the environment in which it was deployed, and if that deployment resulted in the killing of civilians, such action may meet the mental element of intent or knowledge to be criminally responsible under art 8(2)(a)(i) of the Rome Statute for the war crime of wilful killing.[18]

Further obscuring the principle of legal responsibility is the distributive nature of autonomous systems themselves. This means that different people are potentially legally responsible during different phases of the AWS' development and use ranging from algorithm design, programming, testing,

14 See Article 36, *Meaningful Human Control and AWS* (April 2016) <https://article36.org/wp-content/uploads/2016/04/MHC-AI-and-AWS-FINAL.pdf>.

15 For example, N Goussac, 'Safety Net or Tangled Web: Weapons Reviews of AI in Weapons and War-Fighting', *International Committee of the Red Cross Humanitarian Law & Policy Blog* (Blog Post, 18 April 2019) <https://blogs.icrc.org/law-and-policy/2019/04/18/safety-net-tangled-web-legal-reviews-ai-weapons-war-fighting>.

16 E Jensen, 'The (Erroneous) Requirement for Human Judgment (and Error) in the Law of Armed Conflict' (2020) 96 *International Law Studies* 26, 28–31.

17 *Rome Statute of the International Criminal Court*, opened for signature 17 July 1988, 2187 UNTS 90 (entered into force 1 July 2002) art 30 ('Rome Statute').

18 Ibid art 8(2)(a)(i). For an Australian perspective, see B. Oswald and R. McLaughlin, 'Wilful Killing During Armed Conflict: Is There a Defence of Proportionality in Australia?' (2007) *University of Melbourne Legal Studies Research Paper No. 267*, Vol. 18, No. 1, 1–41.

training and deploying the AWS and potentially for authorising specific actions conducted by it. A computer programmer may be unaware of all the circumstances in which an AWS will be employed. The attribution for mistake, negligence, malfeasance, or failure to meet IHL standards may occur cumulatively and will be difficult to trace. How to establish standards for responsibility held by a person in a broad system of controls[19] that disperses responsibility across several actors will prove a challenge for states.

Finally, domestic liability under national consumer laws may hold an AWS designer or developer accountable for technical or manufacturing errors made prior to its acquisition by a state.[20] AWS are complex systems and there may be several manufacturers who produce individual components that collectively form a system that enables the autonomous operation of a weapon. The most relevant components are those enabling a weapon's operation, particularly the software, sensors and communications. However, criminal responsibility for specific actions in armed conflict may be difficult to attribute to a manufacturer once a state completes its legal review and accepts an AWS into service on the basis that the state has certified the system for use through its introduction into service processes. Notwithstanding, domestic product liability and contract laws may provide a state with legal recourse for defective manufacture or programming. For example, a manufacturer may be contractually liable to compensate the state for damage caused to persons or objects during the normal use of the system. This may include unintended harm caused in the context of an armed conflict.

Having identified the international and domestic law mechanisms for state and individual responsibility, unlike a traditional legal review, it may be necessary for the legal review of an AWS to consider how these mechanisms apply to the use of the weapon to ensure that humans remain legally responsible.

1.2.1 Identifying Lines of Human Accountability for AWS Use

To avoid the risk of accountability gaps in use of AWS there must be clear lines of human accountability in all circumstances of use. It may be argued that there are two aspects to this. The first relates to AWS design in that it should enable existing international law mechanisms for legal responsibility to be maintained. That is, human responsibility should be a design feature. It follows

19 See, e.g., United Nations Office for Disarmament Affairs, 'Convention on Certain Conventional Weapons (CCW). Legal Autonomous Weapons Systems. National Commentary – Australia' (20 August 2020) <https://documents.unoda.org/wp-content/uploads/2020/08/20200820-Australia.pdf>.

20 McFarland and McCormack (n 5).

that a legal review of an AWS will include identifying how the lines of human accountability can be maintained during the weapon's normal or expected use. This will involve an analysis of the IHL rules governing the weapon functions and identifying how IHL and international law can hold humans at various levels accountable for violations of the laws of armed conflict, either as state leaders,[21] military commanders[22] or individual combatants.

The second aspect relates to the lawful use of the weapon and is concerned with ensuring that any AWS misuse is able to be identified. The need to identify potential gaps in human responsibility links with the need for the legal review of an AWS to go beyond the traditional legal review process by seeking to foresee all possible technical misuses. The legal review analysis may reflect the Geneva Conventions' regime of 'grave breaches'[23] requiring states to criminalise, investigate and prosecute alleged breaches.[24] This state obligation is supplemented by art 85 of AP 1, which emphasises this requirement to repress breaches and expands upon the acts within the 'grave breaches' regime. However, the risk of 'a fatal gap between the undertakings entered into by parties to the conflict and the conduct of individuals is [to be] avoided'.[25] AP 1 goes further by holding individual commanders responsible for their subordinates' conduct in armed conflict. This notion of command responsibility is central to the definition and status of armed forces, combatants and the corresponding right to participate in armed conflict.[26] The obligation to enforce IHL rules is reflected in art 43(1) of AP 1:

> The armed forces of a Party to a conflict consist of all organised armed forces, groups and units which are under a command responsible to that

21 See Rome Statute (n 17) arts 7 and 8 *bis* prohibit crimes against humanity and the crime of aggression.

22 AP 1 (n 11) arts 86, 87.

23 *Convention (I) for the Amelioration of the Condition of the Wounded and Sick in the Armed Forces in the Field*, 12 August 1949, 75 UNTS 31, art 50; *Convention (II) for the Amelioration of the Condition of the Wounded, Sick, and Shipwrecked Members of Armed Forces at Sea*, 12 August 1949, 75 UNTS 85, art 51; *Convention (III) Relative to the Treatment of Prisoners of War*, 12 August 1949, 75 UNTS 135, art 130; *Convention (IV) Relative to the Protection of Civilian Persons in Time of War*, 12 August 1949, 75 UNTS 287, arts 146, 147 (collectively 'GC grave breaches').

24 For example, *Geneva Conventions Act 1957* (Cth) and div 268 of the *Criminal Code Act 1995* (Cth).

25 Y Sandoz, C Swinarski and B Zimmerman (eds), *Commentary on the Additional Protocols of 8 June 1977 to the Geneva Conventions of 12 August 1949* (ICRC and Martinus Nijhoff, Geneva, 1987) [3550] ('ICRC Commentary').

26 AP 1 (n 11) art 82.

> party for the conduct of its subordinates, even if that Party is represented by a government or an authority not recognised by an adverse Party. Such armed forces shall be subject to an internal disciplinary system which, *inter alia, shall enforce compliance with the rules of international law applicable in armed conflict* [emphasis added].[27]

Articles 86 and 87 of AP 1 impose positive duties upon commanders and hold them responsible for failing to act to prevent their subordinates violating IHL. This responsibility includes the requirement to investigate and punish perpetrators with penal or disciplinary measures.[28]

The Geneva Conventions' grave breaches are largely expressed as war crimes in arts 8 and 28 of the Rome Statute.[29] The ICRC regards these rules as customary international law.[30]AP 1 seeks to further strengthen these accountability measures by ensuring that legal advisors are available to advise military commanders. Article 82 of AP 1 requires states to ensure:

> legal advisors are available, when necessary, to advise military commanders at the appropriate level on the application of the Conventions and this Protocol and on the appropriate instruction to be given to the armed forces on this subject.[31]

As discussed in Chapter 5, the legal review may make recommendations for the lawful use of a weapon. This may include recommending modifications of an AWS' normal or expected use to mitigate risks of accountability gaps. For example, recommending that AWS certain uses are directly controlled by humans to ensure an unambiguous line of accountability.

---

27 Ibid art 43(1).

28 Ibid art 86(2): 'The fact that a breach of the Conventions or of this Protocol was committed by a subordinate does not absolve his superiors from penal or disciplinary responsibility, as the case may be, if they know, or had information which should have enabled them to conclude in the circumstances at the time, that he was committing or was going to commit such a breach and if they did not take all feasible measures within their power to prevent or repress the breach'.

29 Rome Statute (n 17) arts 8 and 28.

30 JM Henckaerts and L Doswald-Becks, *Customary International Humanitarian Law* (Cambridge University Press, 2005) ('ICRC CIL Study') rule 156.

31 AP 1 (n 11) art 82.

1.3 *What Standards of IHL Compliance Are Required to Pass a Legal Review?*

In determining the legality of an AWS, a reviewing state may consider the need for an objective measure, or measures, to determine whether an AWS can perform its normal or expected use in compliance with the reviewing state's IHL and international law obligations. Identifying the appropriate standard of legal compliance is a sensitive issue that reviewing states are unlikely to disclose publicly (e.g., for security reasons).[32] Despite this, some states have called for 'an elaboration of international agreed norms and standards'.[33] Allied states may agree to confidentially exchange national legal review practice and standards, particularly where there is an opportunity to share AWS technology. This may include the recently announced Australia, UK and US (AUKUS) trilateral security partnership enabling enhanced cooperation with Australia's closest allies on critical technologies, including AI.[34]

Legal compliance standards for specific autonomous functions are likely to be expressed as a range or 'statistical confidence bounds' rather than a binary concept.[35] This range may differ depending on:

a. *the legal risks associated with the AWS' normal or expected use.* This includes risks of violations of IHL rules and physical risks to both weapon operators, friendly forces and protected persons; and
b. *potential target types (persons and objects).* The use of AWS to target humans is controversial.[36] While is it not expressly prohibited by IHL a reviewing state may determine, as a matter of national policy, apply a higher standard of legal compliance for human targets as compared to materiel targets.

---

32 V Boulanin and M Verbruggen, 'Article 36: Dealing with the Challenges Posed by Emerging Technologies' (December 2017), *Stockholm International Peace and Research Institute,* 25 ('SIPRI 2017 Report').

33 *Report of the 2018 Session of the Group of Governmental Experts on Emerging Technologies in the Area of Lethal Autonomous Weapons Systems,* UN Doc CCW/GGE.1/2018/3 (23 October 2018) 20 <https://undocs.org/en/CCW/GGE.1/2018/3>.

34 Australian Government, *Australia Pursue Nuclear Powered Submarines Through New Trilateral Enhanced Security* (Web Page, 16 September 2021) <https://www.foreignminister.gov.au/minister/marise-payne/media-release/australia-pursue-nuclear-powered-submarines-through-new-trilateral-enhanced-security-partnership>.

35 A Backstrom and I Henderson, 'New Capabilities in Warfare: An Overview of Contemporary Technological Developments and the Associated Legal and Engineering Issues in Article 36 Weapons Reviews' (2012) 94 (886) *International Review of the Red Cross* 483, 508.

36 International Human Rights Clinic and Human Rights Watch, *Losing Humanity: The Case Against Killer Robots* (IHRC and HRW, 2012), 4 ('Losing Humanity').

c. *the expected operating environment.* There are risks arising from environmental factors, particularly where the environment effects the AWS ability to perform its intended tasks. A higher standard may be required for an AWS operating in a cluttered, urban environment as compared to an uncluttered maritime environment where electronic technologies already outperform human abilities.[37]

d. *the operational circumstances of use* including operational circumstances such as electronic interference or interoperability with other military systems may raise risks that need to be mitigated.

e. *degree of human control.* A reviewing state may create national policy requiring certain degrees of human control over AWS functions. Where there is less direct human control over specific autonomous functions, the state may require a higher standard of legal compliance.

The internal nature of legal reviews raises the concern of a divergence of state interpretation and application of legal norms to AWS. In a submission to the GGE, Austria argued that states applying different legal standards to legal reviews would lead to inconsistency in results and, ultimately, uncertainty.[38] This risk was identified during the Diplomatic Conference responsible for drafting the 1977 Additional Protocols, which agreed that a determination of legality by a state is not intended to create a new subjective standard.[39] The risk of inconsistent legal review determinations is balanced against the reality that few states, for reasons of national security, publicise the results of their legal reviews.

The legal standards applied during a legal review may vary for different AWS functions. As the legal review must consider each IHL rule or principle that governs the AWS functions in the context of its normal or expected use, a test and evaluation process must be designed to provide the legal reviewer with independent information. The immediate question is, what legal standard should be applied to the test results?

In determining legal standards, some scholars argue that a reference point for determining the minimum standard of legality for AWS decision-making should be that of humans. Sassòli observes:

---

37 Kraska, J and Pedrozo, R. A., *Disruptive Technology and the Law of Naval Warfare* (2022) Oxford University Press, 109.

38 Austria, *Statement to the UN CCW Group of Governmental Experts re Guiding Principles* (1 September 2020) <https://documents.unoda.org/wp-content/uploads/2020/09/20200901-Austria.pdf>.

39 ICRC Commentary (n 25) [1469].

> [t]here is widespread agreement that the ability to use autonomous weapons in compliance with IHL should not be evaluated against a hypothetical ideal, but instead the comparison should be to human beings.[40]

This 'human standard' may, however, be difficult to identify with certainty. Human decision-making involves complex, qualitative assessments.[41] To identify such a standard, states would need empirical data on human performance standards for each IHL rule relevant to the AWS in comparable operational circumstances as those envisioned for the AWS. If empirical data were ascertainable, for example from combat video taken from recent conflicts, this would need to be represented in a form capable of programming, such as statistical probability.[42] However, there is no evidence that a study of such data has occurred or whether states have created national standards for compliance with individual IHL rules. This information is extremely sensitive and unlikely to be publicly disclosed by states.

It is likely that the human standard for compliance with IHL rules will not be perfection. States recognise the decisions made in armed conflict may be made with incomplete or inaccurate information.[43] IHL holds humans to a standard of reasonableness.[44] In the case of *Galić*, the International Criminal Tribunal for the Former Yugoslavia required a 'reasonable belief' to determine whether a person or object is a lawful target.[45] The reviewing state may require, from an ethical perspective and as a matter of policy, an AWS to perform its functions to a higher standard than reasonable belief, although what is considered 'reasonable' in the context of autonomous decision-making systems also requires careful national policy and legal consideration by the reviewing state.

Ultimately, a reviewing state may consider these interpretive questions in assessing their national approach to legal reviews of AWS. The questions arise

40 M Sassòli, 'Autonomous Weapons and International Humanitarian Law: Advantages, Open Technical Questions and Legal Issues to be Clarified' (2014) 91 *International Law Studies* 308, 319.

41 Tetyana Kruppy, 'Of Souls, Spirits and Ghosts: Transporting the Application of the Rules of Targeting to Lethal Autonomous Robots' (2015) 16 *Melbourne Journal of International Law* 1, 33.

42 Backstrom and Henderson (n 35) 495.

43 *Australian Declarations Made upon Ratification of Protocol Additional to the Geneva Conventions of 12 August 1949, and relating to the Protection of Victims of International Armed Conflicts (Protocol I), 1642 UNTS 473* (21 June 1991) 47.

44 M Schmitt and J Thurnher (2013) '"Out of the Loop": Autonomous Weapon Systems and the Law of Armed Conflict' (2013) 4(2) *Harvard National Security Journal* 231, 257.

45 *Galić* (n 12) [51].

because of the unique characteristics of AWS and how they relate to the application of IHL norms. They require states to assess IHL rules governing state and individual responsibility require consideration during the conduct of legal reviews. As a traditional legal review does not take into account the relationship between states and individual responsibilities in the use of weapons the question is whether this is required for AWS.

2 Methodological Questions

Having considered the interpretive questions it is useful to also consider whether AWS raise methodological questions in the conduct of the legal review of AWS. The methodological challenges may require states to consider whether their domestic legal review processes and policies allow a determination of legality of an AWS to be made.

As AWS are likely to be complex systems of systems, the question is whether art 36 requires all components to be the subject of a legal review and, if not, how a state may identify what components require a determination of legality to be made. Before suggesting some conclusions, the following sections will consider the need for engagement with civilian industry during a legal review process as well as the whether there is a need for ongoing legal review during an AWS' in-service life.

2.1 *Should a Legal Review of AWS Occur before and after the 'Study, Development, Acquisition or Adoption'?*

As identified in Chapter 5, the traditional approach to legal reviews reflects the express art 36 requirement to determine the legality of weapons during its 'study, development, acquisition or adoption'. However, the increased complexity of the technology that enables autonomy in weapons may require a broader consideration beyond its study, development, acquisition or adoption. For example, where an AWS is capable of machine learning and is theoretically able to self-modify its 'normal or expected' use, a reviewing state may seek to ensure such changes are not only visible to weapon operators and commanders but are able to be the subject of further legal review before such changes are acted upon in armed conflict.

Traditionally, a reviewing state will undertake a legal review in the final stages of a weapon's acquisition process to satisfy their art 36 obligation. This approach is appropriate for most traditional weapons that are determined to be lawful per se as they meet the criteria described in Chapter 5. However, as noted in the preceding section, the risk associated with the lawful use of the weapon is transferred to military commanders and weapon operators, who are subject to international law accountability mechanisms, to ensure the weapon is used in compliance with IHL.

This book argues that this approach is too narrow for AWS which will require ongoing legal review throughout their life cycle. To ensure that AWS operate in compliance with a state's legal obligations the legal review should be an integral part of the AWS design and procurement process, both informing the AWS development and assessing its legality during use. This may require participation in state-sponsored research and development, for example, through organisations such as the US DARPA or Australia's TASDCRC.

Accordingly, a legal review of an AWS is unlikely to be a singular determinative process and will require a broader, iterative, multidisciplinary and ongoing approach. This may extend beyond the 'study, development, acquisition or adoption' and continue throughout the AWS' in-service life. This may be necessary to enable an assessment of an AWS' ability to operate in environments that differ from those considered in an earlier legal review and where advances in technology change an AWS' operation.

In addition to the weapon reviews during the acquisition of an AWS, a state should consider the need for ongoing 'in-service' legal reviews. Where there are small operational changes, these may be assessed by a legal adviser deployed in compliance with art 82 of AP 1. This 'field review' would reference and build upon the legal review conducted pre-introduction into service. More significant changes (e.g., the introduction of machine learning or improvements in the AI's contextual reasoning capability) may require legal review analysis at the national or strategic level.

The need for an expanded approach to the legal review of an AWS is argued in chapter 8 which proposes three broad weapon review phases during an AWS lifecycle.

2.2 *Should States Inform Industry of Their Legal Review Requirements?*

While states are the primary users of military weapons, the technology enabling AWS is increasingly developed by defence industry and research organisations outside state military establishments.[46] AI is being applied to fields ranging from autonomous vehicles, gaming and virtual assistants.[47] This demonstrates

46 H Nasu, 'Artificial Intelligence and the Obligation to Respect and to Ensure Respect for International Humanitarian Law' in Eve Massingham and Annabel McConnachie (eds), *Ensuring Respect for International Humanitarian Law* (Routledge Press, 2020) 4.

47 G Moy et al, *Technical Report: Recent Advances in Artificial Intelligence and their Impact on Defence* (Defence Science and Technology Group, May 2020) 1 ('DSTG Report').

the challenges stemming from the dual-use nature of many AI applications. A range of AI technologies developed for civilian purposes may be capable of military application; however, there is often a disconnect between the military and civilian technology sector.[48] For example, an AI system designed to identify cancerous cells in medical imagery may be adapted to identify enemy personnel or objects on the battlefield.

Those responsible for developing, programming and training the AI that enables AWS functionality must understand the legal risks and consequences of their work. This is especially true for those functions that are regulated by IHL. Translating legal rules and principles cannot be left to the acquisition or legal review process. The legal requirements must be 'built in from the beginning'.[49]

A question that has received little academic attention is whether art 36 requires a state to conduct a legal review of AI technology that is studied and developed by defence industry but not ultimately acquired or adopted by the reviewing state. The study and development may be for commercial sale and exported to a foreign state. There appear to be three preliminary questions.

First, is the AI technology in question subject to the 'study, development, acquisition or adoption' by a state party to AP 1? An affirmative answer to this question will arguably engage the state's AP 1 obligation. However, the answer may not be clear. For example, a state may sponsor the study and development of new applications of AI technology by the defence industry and academic institutions without an immediate intention to adopt or acquire the technology. In such a case, is the state sponsorship of defence industry or academic institutions' research sufficient to trigger the legal review obligation? Nasu suggests that 'companies engaging in research and development of AI independently of military funding programs or procurement are not subject to government regulation requiring legal review'.[50] There may, however, be export control regulation that is relevant to the export of military or dual-use technologies. If, however, the industry study and development of weapon technology is funded by the AP 1 state, even indirectly through non-state organisations designed to facilitate such research (e.g., DARPA or TASDCRC), the legal review obligation arguably exists as contemplated by the use of the terms 'study,

48 M Verbruggen, 'The Role of Civilian Innovation in the Development of Lethal Autonomous Weapon Systems' (2019) 10(3) *Global Policy* 338, 338 <https://onlinelibrary.wiley.com/doi/pdf/10.1111/1758-5899.12663>.

49 A Letendre, 'Lethal Autonomous Weapon Systems: Translating Legal Jargon for Engineers' in *2016 International Conference on Unmanned Aircraft Systems* (2016) 795, 795.

50 Nasu (n 46) 11.

development' in art 36 (see Chapter 4). Alternatively, the question may be concisely reframed as whether state-sponsored research engages state responsibility as contemplated by art 4 of the Draft Articles of State Responsibility as an 'organ of the State'.[51] This issue ought to be the subject of a separate study and is not considered further in this book.

The second question is whether the specific military application falls within the state definition of 'new weapon, means and method of warfare'. The scope of this phrase was addressed in Chapter 4. It is possible that an AI technology, particularly one that enhances an existing weapon, will be assessed as a 'means of warfare' and therefore be subject to the art 36 obligation.

The final question is whether the military technology is ultimately adopted or acquired by the sponsoring state and whether this is necessary to enliven the art 36 obligation. As a matter of legal interpretation, the use of the conjunctive 'or' in the phrase 'study, development, or adoption' suggests that the obligation is not cumulative.[52]

There is no clear reference in the publicly available national legal review documents regarding study and development completed outside the military weapon acquisition process. This leaves open the questions of whether state practice accurately reflects the full extent of the art 36 legal review obligation, whether the obligation must be interpreted by reference to the state practice that there is and whether the development of AWS alters this analysis.

2.3 *Should a Legal Review Continue during an AWS' In-Service Life?*

As demonstrated in Chapter 5, the art 36 legal review obligation clearly exists prior to the fielding of the weapon in armed conflict. However, it is less clear whether the obligation continues following a weapon's introduction into service. Both art 36 and the ICRC Commentary are silent on whether the legal review obligation exists during the life of the weapon.

It may be argued that the development of autonomy in weapons places increasing importance on the ongoing art 36 legal determination of legality during the weapon's in-service life. The ICRC Guide does not address the issue directly but identifies the need to review existing weapons that have undergone technical or field modifications. They cite, for example, the Australian Instruction, which directs that:

---

51 Draft Articles of State Responsibility (n 1) art 4.

52 D Copeland, 'Legal Review of New Technology Weapons' in H Nasu and R McLaughlin (eds), *New Technologies and the Law of Armed Conflict* (TMC Asser Press, 2014) 148.

> [a]ny proposal to make field modifications to weapons shall be vetted in accordance with this instruction.[53]

A field modification may be a physical or software change to the weapon itself. It does not address a change to the weapon's use. The ICRC Guide briefly contemplates the review after the procurement process by stating that a review is required if:

> new evidence comes to light on the operational performance or effects of the weapon both during and after the procurement process.[54]

However, this does not address a change to the method of use of a weapon, either by way of field expedient or through a change in tactics. Wexler argues that the art 36 legal review obligation should be changed to an ongoing duty to review. He states that:

> it can be agreed that there is an effective requirement to reassess weapons if further information comes to light that should suggest that the previous review is no longer correct.[55]

The key is in the art 36 use of the word 'new'. A material change such as a physical modification, a software update or a change to its method of use may be regarded as 'new' for the purpose of art 36. There is little evidence of state practice of further review where there is a change in the method of use of an in-service weapon. This is unsurprising given the emphasis of the legal review is the legality of the weapon per se rather than the legality of its use on any occasion, which is linked to the obligation under art 82 of AP I. However, this does not mean that art 36 does not require a further review where a method of use is identified that is materially different from that considered by the original review.

An example of such a requirement would be where an anti-material munition, such as the Raufoss Mk 211, were used in an anti-personnel role. The Raufoss Mk 211 is an explosive and incendiary munition designed as a multipurpose

53 ICRC, *A Guide to the Weapons Review of New Weapons, Means and Methods of Warfare: Measures to Implement Article 36 of Additional Protocol I of 1977* (2006) 24, fn 82 ('ICRC Guide').

54 Ibid.

55 L Wexler, 'Limiting the Precautionary Principle: Weapons Regulation in the Face of Scientific Uncertainty' (2006) 39 *UC Davis L* 459.

round able to target military aircraft, light vehicles and tanks.[56] If a state proposed a new normal or expected use that included attacking combatants, this would arguably require a further legal review of this new use. In conducting a legal review, the state may identify the 1868 St. Petersburg Declaration (prohibiting explosive rounds below 400 grams)[57] and the general prohibition against weapons that cause superfluous injury or unnecessary suffering[58] as relevant to a determination of legality. It is likely that such a review would determine the anti-personnel use of the Raufoss Mk 211 as prohibited.

It follows that an AWS capable of machine learning was designed to attack enemy material targets using the Raufoss Mk 211 it may be capable of passing a legal review. However, if the AWS' machine learning decided to adopt a new method of warfare that involved targeting enemy combatants, it may require a further legal review. In anticipation of this possibility, the reviewing state may require the AWS design or programming to act as an 'IHL governor' to prevent machine learning from enacting new methods of warfare until a further legal review has been undertaken. While the content of a further legal review is a matter for the reviewing state, it may only be necessary to build upon the content of an earlier review and therefore only addresses the new method of warfare.

The requirement for further review may also arise in other circumstances particular to AWS. For example, an AWS equipped with a convolutional neural network (CNN) designed to recognise and classify military objectives in a specific operating environment will likely have to be trained and tested using data specific to that environment. If, however, the AWS is designed for a specific environment, such as a maritime environment, but was deployed to an urban environment, its use is likely to require further review to ensure that the initial determination of legality remains valid.

Similarly, if the context in which the AWS was deployed changed from that considered by the art 36 legal review, a further review may also be necessary. For example, for an AWS designed for use in conventional operations against a conventional adversary, one where enemy combatants and military objectives are clearly distinguished from civilians and civilian objects, to one of

56 Nammo Ammunition Handbook, ed 5, (2018), Raufoss Mk 211, 61. <https://www.nammo.com/wp-content/uploads/2020/05/nammo_ammo_handbook_aw_screen_updated.pdf>.

57 *Declaration Renouncing the Use, in Time of War, of Explosive Projectiles under 400 Grammes Weight*, opened for signature 29 November 1868 (entered into force 11 December 1868) ('St. Petersburg Declaration').

58 AP I (n 11).

counterinsurgency against an unconventional adversary who is not clearly distinguished, the AWS programming may need updating to reflect the different characteristics of the persons and objects in the operating environment.

3 Conclusions Arising from the Interpretive and Methodological Questions

This chapter has identified several interpretive and methodological questions raised by autonomy in weapons. It argues that states may need to consider these challenges in order determine their national approaches to determining the legality of their AWS.

There are questions as to whether the traditional interpretations of art 36's operative terms, which determine how a state conducts a legal review, remain appropriate for the legal review of AWS. These interpretive issues arise in the preliminary step of a traditional legal review and inform both the application and scope of the national art 36 obligation. These interpretive questions are:

a) During a legal review of an AWS, can the weapon reviewer presume that the weapon operator will use the weapon lawfully? This question highlights the dichotomy in the traditional legal review analysis between weapons law and targeting law. If an AWS is designed to perform a function regulated by targeting law, for example complete precautions in attack, it is argued that the presumption that the AWS will do so in compliance with art 57 of API cannot be relied upon and that the relevant targeting law must be analysed in the context of the AWS' normal or expected use during the legal review.

b) Does a legal review of an AWS need to consider how humans will retain legal responsibility for the use of the AWS? This analysis is not part of a traditional legal review as IHL and international law hold states and their agents responsible for violations of international law. As AWS are not legal entities responsible under the law, there is a need to mitigate the risk of accountability gaps by states considering clear lines of human accountability during the legal review of an AWS.

c) What are the legal standards a legal review will apply in making a determination of whether the AWS can perform its functions in compliance with IHL? These standards will be determined by individual states and may be based on human standards. Standards applied to specific IHL rules are likely to be influenced by policy, technical, operational and environmental factors and are unlikely to be binary.

This chapter also identifies questions regarding the method of conducting a legal review of an AWS. While the traditional legal review steps remain relevant to the AWS there is a need to consider whether they are sufficient to determine the legality of AWS. This may require states to review their legal review methodologies to consider:

a) Should the legal review occur prior to and after to the 'study, development, acquisition or adoption' of an AWS. This question recognises that much of the important design and development of AWS occurs in private industry or research organisations outside the state military acquisition process. This early design and development should be informed by the state's art 36 requirements rather than considering them at a later, more mature, stage of an AWS' development.

b) Should a legal review continue during the in-service life of an AWS? There is an ongoing requirement to determine the legality of AWS to ensure that it is capable of lawful use. This is particularly where the AWS can change its normal or expected use through machine learning.

Chapters 7 and 8 will address these interpretive and methodological questions by proposing an additional legal review step and an expanded framework for the legal review of AWS respectively. Drawing on the interpretive questions and the argued need to analyse an AWS ability to operate in compliance with targeting law, Chapter 7 proposes, in addition to the traditional legal review steps discussed in Chapter 5, a new 'functional review' step to identify and determine an AWS ability to operate in compliance with specific IHL rules regulating its methods of warfare. The proposed functional review step also considers issues specific to AWS including standards of compliance, appropriate levels of human control over AWS use, environmental context, approaches to legal risk and the relevance of trust.

To address the methodological questions raised in this chapter, Chapter 8 argues the need for national legal review methodologies to expand from a determination of legality during the military capability acquisition process to incorporate early engagement with defence industry and ongoing governance during the in-service life of the AWS. Defence industry is becoming increasingly responsible for the research and development of new technologies that enable AWS, and so they must be informed of the state's legal review obligations so as to incorporate these requirements into the AWS design. This expansion should also extend beyond the introduction into the service of an AWS to include measures designed to identify changes that trigger the requirement to review the earlier determination of legality.

CHAPTER 7

An Additional 'Functional' Legal Review Step to Address Autonomy in Weapons

To enable a legal review to determine an AWS's ability to perform targeting functions lawfully this chapter proposes an additional step to the traditional legal review process. This additional step, referred to as a 'functional review' step, is intended to allow a legal review to identify the IHL targeting rules that govern the AWS functions and determine whether the AWS can perform these functions in compliance with the reviewing state's international law obligations. The step also includes consideration of national AWS policy addressing legal risk mitigation, human control, reliability, predictability and explainability.

To introduce a functional review step in the national legal review process, a state will require domestic policy that describes how the additional step is undertaken in addition to the traditional steps described in Chapter 5. The policy must articulate the need to identify the relevant targeting law and the standards of compliance required by the reviewing state. This chapter concludes that an additional step in an expanded legal review methodology will require a state to consider a range of legal and policy requirements that will not only determine the legality of AWS but inform their study, development and use. This chapter will inform the argument for an expanded framework for the legal review of AWS in Chapter 8.

To illustrate how the functional review analysis will occur, this chapter will consider a hypothetical AWS called an Uncrewed Ground Vehicle – Combat (UGV-C) loosely based on the GaardTech's Jaeger-C uncrewed ground vehicle.[1] The UGV-C is designed to track, identify, classify and attack enemy tanks by navigating to a position where it can detonate its explosive payload and destroy the tank's tracks and running gear, rendering it immobile. The UGV-C is capable of autonomous navigation and uses its sensors to identify preprogrammed indicia including size, shape, acoustics signature and heat signature to identify enemy tanks. Once activated by its human operator, the UGV-C can operate autonomously in a geo-fenced area for 6 days or until it is recalled

1 The Defence Post, 'Australia to Acquire Bulletproof Jaeger-C Swarming Attach Robots' (online, 5 November 2021).

 | DOI:10.1163/9789004707047_010

or deactivated. A human operator can also direct it to a specific location to attack tanks identified by other surveillance assets.

1 Adding a Functional Review Step to the Traditional Legal Review Methodology

In addition to the traditional legal review steps, it is argued that the legal review of an AWS must consider international law regulating the use of weapons, i.e., targeting law. Where the AWS functionality, for example identifying targets, is regulated by IHL, the legal review must also determine the AWS ability to perform those functions lawfully.

As noted earlier, the feature that distinguishes an AWS from a conventional, human-operated weapon is the ability for the weapon to interpret and interact with its environment and make decisions or recommendations that are governed by IHL. This distinguishes the art 36 legal review of an AWS from that of a conventional weapon which relies on the presumption that a weapon will be used lawfully.

The traditional legal review process, consisting of four common steps identified in Chapter 5, focuses primarily on the legality of a weapon *per se*. Boothby explains that the focus of a traditional legal review is on the 'construction, design, control mechanisms, destructive characteristics, intended circumstances of use and intended military effect'.[2] However, these traditional steps are not sufficient to determine the legality of AWS as they do not analyse its ability to perform autonomous functions in compliance with IHL targeting rules. This is the basis for arguing the need for an additional 'functional review' step in the legal review process to address the characteristics of autonomy in weapons and the risks that autonomy generates.

2 Describing the Elements of the 'Functional Review' Step

The focus of the functional review step is the AWS AI and software that interprets data and enables its autonomous functionality. Given the importance of the AWS AI and software to the lawful operation of the weapon, the functional review may precede the traditional legal review steps which focus on the weapon itself. Alternatively, in the case of an existing weapon enhanced by AI,

2 W Boothby, *Weapons and the Law of Armed Conflict* (Cambridge University, 2009) 343.

the functional review will be the primary focus of the legal review, which will rely on the recommendations of the legal review completed when the weapon was originally acquired.

There are eight elements of the proposed functional review step. For each AWS function that engages IHL rules, the functional review step will:

a. Element 1 – identify the IHL rules that govern the function;
b. Element 2 – identify the standards of legal compliance required to determine legality for that function;
c. Element 3 – identify the operational context in which the AWS will perform the function;
d. Element 4 – obtain the AWS' technical, functional and performance data relevant to the function;
e. Element 5 – conduct a legal risk analysis for the function in light of the intended use in the different operational contexts;
f. Element 6 – determine the appropriate level of human control over the AWS to ensure legality;
g. Element 7 – confirm lines of human responsibility; and
h. Element 8 – trust from reliability, predictability and explainability.

Accordingly, for each autonomous function, the functional review step will analyse the AWS' ability to perform specific functions in compliance with the relevant IHL rules in different operational and environmental context. For example, the UCV-C is designed to identify enemy tanks on the battlefield as targets of attack, the functional review step should consider its ability to distinguish between lawful and unlawful targets as required by the rule of distinction in art 48. This requires the UGV-C to understand and apply the IHL definitions that are relevant to the distinction rule including the definitions of civilian objects and military objectives.[3] Such analysis is likely to be complicated and may include ascertaining whether those responsible for the UGV-C development and programming understand these rules, definitions and their

3 *Protocol Additional to the Geneva Conventions of 12 August 1949, and relating to the Protection of Victims of International Armed Conflicts (Protocol I)*, opened for signature 8 June 1977, 1125 UNTS 3 (entered into force 7 December 1978) ('AP 1') defines a civilian is any person who does belong to the categories of persons referred to in arts 4A(1), (2), (3) and (6) of the Geneva Conventions and art 43 of AP 1. The civilian population comprises all persons who are civilians. Where there is doubt whether a person is civilian, they must be considered civilian. Civilian objects are all objects that are not military objectives. Combatants are those categories of persons described in art 43 of AP 1. Military objectives are defined by art 52(2) as 'those objects which by their nature, location, purpose or use make an effective contribution to military action and whose total or partial destruction, capture, or neutralization offers a definite military advantage'.

application so as to enable them to accurately translate them into code. In addition, the art 36 legal review may consider the data used to train the UGV-C's neural network to identify objects and determine which objects are tanks and which are protected by IHL. This includes analysing the data used to train the neural network.

To analyse how the UGV-C will perform its functions in specific operational circumstances, a functional review will require a series of hypothetical use cases or scenarios that are consistent with the UGV-C's normal or expected use. These scenarios will reflect realistic situations and include variations in terrain, weather and tactical situations that will affect the UGV-C's sensors and data. This may reveal that it can perform a specific function lawfully in one situation but not in another.

The conduct of a functional review is a departure from the traditional art 36 legal review methodology as it will consider those IHL rules that regulate the conduct of an attack beyond the prohibitions against weapons that cause unnecessary suffering or are by nature indiscriminate. The focus of the functional review will be the AWS' operating system and its ability to interpret data from its environment and perform its intended functions in compliance with IHL. The functional review will by informed by state policy that may elaborate on what functions the reviewing state will permit an AWS to perform autonomously.

2.1 *Functional Review (Element 1/8) – Identifying the IHL Rules Governing the AWS' Normal or Expected Use*

This section discusses the need for the legal review to analyse each AWS function and identify the IHL rules and principles that govern that function. The outcome of this analysis is a record of each IHL rule directly or indirectly relevant to the AWS' normal or expected use in its anticipated operating environment. For each rule, an important task is to plot or map the rule against the AWS normal or expected use across a range of scenarios, operating environments and data inputs. One approach is to create a record that enables each AWS function and the relevant IHL rules to be assessed and recorded across the various human, environmental and operational conditions and data inputs.

In the case of the UGV-C, the autonomous function of 'identify enemy tanks' would require consideration of the IHL basic rule of distinction. The ability of the UGV-C to distinguish enemy tanks from other objects would be analysed using difference use cases or scenarios that reflect a range of anticipated environmental conditions (including light, obscuration, distance between the sensor and the identified object, presence of civilians and civilian objects) and tactical scenarios (including enemy movements, enemy attack and obstacles).

When conducted early in the UGV-C's study and development, such an approach would inform both the UGV-C's study and development by enabling the AI engineers to design, program and train the system to be capable of performing specific roles to meet the specific performance standards in different contexts. It permits the legal review to identify which AWS tasks are capable of being lawfully performed and in what circumstances. Shortfalls in the AWS performance standards would be recorded and either further researched and developed, or the AWS's ability to perform that task could be restricted or prohibited.

A record of the functional review is important for several reasons. From a practical perspective, this allows the legal reviewer to focus the legal review analysis on only those AWS functions governed by IHL or other international law rules. If the AWS is in its early stage of design and development, it also enables the legal reviewer to advise those responsible for the development of the AWS of the application and requirements of IHL rules and what standard the AWS will need to meet to be determined lawful. It is important that those responsible for the programming software that controls an AWS' functions understand not only the existing rule of the IHL and other rules that govern an AWS' function but also their application.

An example of such a record is called an 'IHL matrix' (see Table 7.1). This spreadsheet-based record provides a simple system for recording the AWS functions, corresponding IHL rules, operational circumstances and legal risk. The legal risk may be visually represented in a traffic light system that corresponds with the assessed risk to legality and identifies risk mitigation options. There would be a single line identifying, for each AWS function, the specific IHL rule governing that function. In practice, an AWS such as the UGV-C would have dozens of lines representing the different environmental and operational effects for each AWS function and IHL rule, each resulting in different levels of legal risk and requiring different legal risk mitigations.

Table 7.1 shows how, for the UGV-C function of distinguish military objectives (enemy tanks), the relevant IHL rule is identified (art 48) and the specific environmental and operational effects would influence the assessment of legal risk and method of mitigation. This same AWS function and IHL rule would be subject to a series of variations of environmental and operational effects. These would inform the legal review and its recommendations regarding the circumstances in which the UGV-C can be used autonomously and when it will require human control to mitigate legal risk.

TABLE 7.1 Example IHL matrix – UGV-C – Art 48

AWS function	IHL rule	Nature of autonomy	Autonomous function(s)	Environmental effects	Operation effects	Legal risk	Legal risk mitigation
Distinguish military objectives – Enemy tanks	Art 48	Full autonomy,	Locate, identify, classify enemy tanks	Land environment obscuration (dust, terrain, weather, day/night)	Risk of civilians in target location	High collateral damage risk	Human operator to confirm civilian presence using an independent information source

2.1.1 Limiting AWS Functions That Engage Certain IHL Rules?

By identifying the IHL rules that govern an AWS function, a reviewing state may decide, as national policy, to limit AWS functionality that engages certain legal obligations. From example, a state may limit AWS functions that pose significant legal risks or are inconsistent with national policy that gives effect to international political undertakings. For example, states party to the CCW have agreed by consensus to Guiding Principles, which include an affirmation that 'human responsibility for decisions on the use of weapons systems must be retained since accountability cannot be transferred to machines'.[4] This may be reflected in state policy describing the requirement for human control.[5] States may also express requirements regarding the use of AWS. For example, an issue of international concern is the use of AWS to target human beings. On 12 May 2021, the ICRC released the *Position on Autonomous Weapon Systems*, which recommended states adopt new international law, which, among other things, rules out the use of AWS to target human beings.[6]

National policy concerning the development and use of AWS may also address ethical concerns. As discussed in Chapter 5, ethical considerations are likely to play a role in state legal review processes. For example, in February 2021, the Australia Defence Science and Technology Group released a report titled *A Method for Ethical AI in Defence*, which identified five ethical facets relevant to the development of AWS in the ADF: responsibility, governance, trust, law and traceability.[7] The report includes a method for identifying ethical risks, measuring the risks against these ethical facets, and proposing mitigating measures. For example, if a state identified during the development of an AWS that an autonomous function regulated by IHL was difficult to trace

4 *Guiding Principles affirmed by the Group of Governmental Experts on Emerging Technologies in the Area of Lethal Autonomous Weapons System*, Annex III to the Final Report of the Meeting of the High Contracting Parties to the Convention on Prohibitions or Restrictions on the Use of Certain Conventional Weapons Which May be Deemed to be Excessively Injurious or to Have Indiscriminate Effects, UN Doc CCW/MSP/2019/9 (13 December 2019) ('UN GGE Guiding Principles').

5 See US Department of Defense, Directive Number 3000.09 *Autonomy in Weapon Systems* (21 November 2012, updated Jan 25, 2023) 13–14 ('US Directive 3000.09'), which requires, 'Autonomous and semi-autonomous weapon systems shall be designed to allow commanders and operators to exercise appropriate levels of human judgment over the use of force'.

6 ICRC, 'ICRC Position on Autonomous Weapon Systems: ICRC Position and Background Paper' (2020) *International Review of the Red Cross* 102 (915), 1 <https://www.icrc.org/en/document/icrc-position-autonomous-weapon-systems>.

7 SK Devitt et al, *A Method for Ethical AI in Defence* (DSTG-TR-3786, Defence Science and Technology Group, February 2021) ('MEAID') <https://tasdcrc.com.au/a-method-for-ethical-ai-in-defence/>.

or explain, it may create a policy requiring restrictions or measures to ensure accountability for that autonomous function being maintained.

To illustrate this point, a hypothetic state acquiring the UGV-C may determine, as a matter of national policy, not to permit the UGV-C to be operate autonomously in environments where civilians and civilian objects are present. Alternatively, the state may require direct human control or authorisation for the UGV-C to conduct an attack in such environments.

2.2 *Function Review (Element 2/8) – Identify the Standards of Legal Compliance Required to Determine Legality for That Function*

International humanitarian law does not specify legal or technical standards required to determine the legality of weapons in compliance with art 36 of AP 1. As noted in Chapter 4, a legal review 'is not intended to create a subjective standard. Determination by any state that the employment of a weapon is prohibited or permitted is not binding internationally'.[8] Further, as identified in Chapter 6, there are no internationally recognised standards for an AWS to be considered lawful. Consistent with the internal nature of national legal review processes, the onus is on states to develop their own legal standards and tests to assess legality of AWS against.

The standards applied in a functional review can be approached in several ways. Primarily, a legal review is concerned with the legal standards necessary to determine that the state's possession and use of an AWS comply with their international law obligations. Second, a state is likely to develop national policy and internal directives addressing its use of AWS. This policy may describe the legal risks to be identified and mitigated or minimum of compliance for AWS functions relating to the use of force.

The tests applied by a legal reviewer to determine the legality of a weapon are broad. A reviewing state may determine that the use of a particular weapon is lawful in some specific circumstances but unlawful in others. For example, UGV-C is designed to track, identify and destroy enemy tanks. It identifies its target by detecting and assessing a range of indicia including size, shape, noise and heat. While this may technically be a very accurate method of identifying enemy tanks which have these unique characteristics, the UGV-C is not capable of identifying the presence of civilians or civilian objects in the vicinity of the enemy tanks. Accordingly, the legal review may determine that the UGV-C may be used lawfully where there is no risk of collateral damage however

8 Y Sandoz, C Swinarski and B Zimmerman (eds), *Commentary on the Additional Protocols of 8 June 1977 to the Geneva Conventions of 12 August 1949* (ICRC and Martinus Nijhoff, Geneva, 1987) [1469] ('ICRC Commentary').

where there is a risk that the expected collateral damage it must not be used in full-autonomous mode as it cannot complete precautions in attack.[9]

2.3 *Functional Review (Element 3/8) – Identify the Operational Context in Which the AWS Will Perform the Function*

At a foundational level, autonomy is concerned with an artificial agent acting in its environment.[10] The ability of an AWS to interpret and act within its environment is fundamental to the lawful use of AWS. An AWS will interpret environmental data obtained through its sensors using software. As the environment is likely to affect the operation of an AWS it is important for the legal review to consider the legal risks that the environment presents. As a general proposition, it is likely that the more complex the AWS operating environment, the greater the legal risk to the reviewing state. To mitigate legal risks, a legal review may recommend safeguards, including increased levels of human control and 'restrictive engagement parameters, such as limiting the area of operation or nature of the target'.[11]

A legal review will consider both the effect of the weapon on the environment and the effect of the environment on the weapon. The former is addressed in the traditional review process, which will analyse the harm caused by the AWS to the natural environment and if the AWS normal or expected use includes the hostile use of the environment. This analysis focuses on the IHL prohibitions against weapons intended to cause widespread, long-term and severe damage in arts 35(3) and 55 of AP 1[12] and the Convention on the Prohibition of Military or Any Other Hostile Use of Environmental Modifications Techniques.[13] In contrast, the functional review will assess how the operating environment affects the ability of the AWS to operate in compliance with IHL rules governing methods of warfare.

The AWS operating environment contains two distinct aspects that are relevant to compliance with IHL rules. The first aspect relates to the natural environment, and it affects the AWS ability to sense and perceive its environment.

---

9 AP 1 (n 3) art 57(2)(a)(iii).

10 H Abbass, J Scholz and D Reid (eds), *Foundations of Trusted Autonomy* (Springer Open Press, 2018) 1.

11 M Sassòli, 'Autonomous Weapons and International Humanitarian Law: Advantages, Open Technical Questions and Legal Issues to be Clarified' (2014) 91 *International Law Studies* 308, 312.

12 AP 1 (n 3) arts 35(2), 55.

13 *Convention on the Prohibition of Military or Any Hostile Use of Environmental Modification Techniques*, opened for signature 10 December 1976, 1108 UNTS 151 (entered into force 5 October 1978) ('ENMOD Convention').

For example, an AWS sensor may be able to accurately detect objects in daylight but be unable to do so reliably at night. Similarly, the effects of rain, wind, dust and fog are relevant to an AWS functionality and standards of performance. A legal review must determine whether the AWS can reliably and lawfully perform its autonomous functions in the various environmental conditions.

The second aspect of the operational environment are those elements that have legal significance, including the presence of civilian persons and objects, the presence and actions of the enemy and operational limitations or restraints imposed by rules of engagement or tactical directives. An AWS may be capable of identifying certain categories of military objectives in areas without the presence of civilians but is unable to do so in complex urban environments.[14]

To perform its programmed functions, an AWS must 'perceive the world, reason and learn about it, and propose actions that meet the agent's goals'.[15] It must sense and interpret both the natural and operational environments and respond in a reliable and predictable way. This is not a simple task, as most operating environments are likely to be contested by enemy forces and subject to unexpected changes. In comparison, a human decision-maker will consider a range of inputs, including information from their own senses, intelligence information on enemy locations and actions, environmental conditions, the presence or absence of persons and objects in a target area, the tactical situation and personal military knowledge and experience.[16] An AWS must be capable of performing its functions lawfully in complex, unpredictable and dynamic environments. Those unable to do so must be restricted or require greater human control to mitigate the legal risks.

An assessment of the environment within a legal review will require the input of experts from a range of disciplines.[17] The effect of the weapon on the natural environment will require advice from environmental specialists and munitions technicians. Similarly, the expertise of computer scientists,

14 Michael Schmitt, 'Regulating Autonomous Weapons Might be Smarter Than Banning Them', *Just Security* (10 August 15) <https://www.justsecurity.org/25333/regulating-autonomous-weapons-smarter-banning/>.

15 Alexander Kott, 'The Artificial Becomes Real: A Back-and-Forth Interplay of Government and Commercial Funding and Research has Brought AI to the Edge of a Breakthrough', *Army Acquisition Logistics and Technology Magazine* (January-March 2018) 90–5.

16 Alan Schuller, 'At the Crossroads of Control: The Intersection of Artificial Intelligence in Autonomous Weapon Systems with International Humanitarian Law' (2017) 8 *Harvard National Security Journal* 379, 395.

17 K Lawand, 'Reviewing the Legality of New Weapons, Means and Methods of Warfare' (2006) 88 (863) *International Review of the Red Cross* 925, 945.

engineers and military commanders is needed to understand the effect of the operating environment on the AWS.

The legal review analyses of the environmental effects on AWS performance must be informed by independent testing. This is necessary to confirm performance claims by a weapon manufacturer and to ensure that the AWS performs to the standards required by the reviewing state.[18] Accordingly, having identified which AWS functions are regulated by IHL rules, it will be necessary to analyse and test the performance in the anticipated environmental settings to identify and analyse those that present legal risks.

An outcome of a legal review may be a recommendation to restrict the use of a weapon in circumstances of elevated legal risk. For example, the hypothetical UGV-C relies on video, heat and acoustic sensors to detect and identify an enemy tank. If testing data shows that certain environmental conditions, such as smoke or heavy rain, degrade the video sensor then the legal review will need to consider whether this reduces the ability of the UGV-C to identify enemy tanks in compliance with art 48 of AP 1. This may result in a legal review recommendation against using the UGV-C in certain environmental conditions or requiring human operators to determine whether a detected object is in fact an enemy tank.

2.4 *Functional Review (Element 4/8) – Obtain AWS Functional, Technical and Performance Information*

The technical and performance information necessary to undertake a legal review of an AWS will broadly fall into two categories. First, the information required for the traditional legal review is discussed in Chapter 4. This includes information describing weapon design and construction and its destructive mechanism, reliability and accuracy.[19] In contrast, the functional review will require information relating to the AWS autonomous functionality.

An AWS design will likely incorporate a range of subsystems. Each subsystem may be subject to technical testing and evaluation processes before undergoing system testing. Such testing will be undertaken by multidisciplinary experts who will seek to provide an objective measure of whether a system or a component of a system, will perform reliably to a performance specification.[20]

---

18 Ibid 951.

19 A Letendre, 'Lethal Autonomous Weapon Systems: Translating Legal Jargon for Engineers' in *2016 International Conference on Unmanned Aircraft Systems* (2016) 798.

20 A Backstrom and I Henderson, 'New Capabilities in Warfare: An Overview of Contemporary Technological Developments and the Associated Legal and Engineering Issues in Article 36 Weapons Reviews' (2012) 94 (886) *International Review of the Red Cross* 483, 508.

The testing information should be provided to those undertaking the legal review.

The person undertaking the legal review will need sufficient knowledge of the underlying AWS technology to understand how the AWS' design and operation are relevant to the legal review analysis. For example, the hypothetical UGV-C is designed to autonomously detect and classify an object as an enemy tank. As such, the legal reviewer will consider the test and evaluation data to determine how accurately and reliably the AWS is able to perform this function. This data should include results gained from testing across a range of expected operational scenarios and environmental contexts. If the performance standards vary, there will need to be a process of analysis to identify the technical, operational or environmental causes that effect the UGV-C's performance and its ability to meet the performance standard determined to be lawful. This may require a program of progressive tests during the development of the UGV-C. This testing may reveal that UGV-C's sensors are inadequate or there are faults in the programming or AI that result in performance variation or unpredictability. If this were the case, the legal review may recommend a review of the design or systems used to perform the UGV-C's normal or expected use.

2.5 *Functional Review (Element 5/8) – Conduct a Legal Risk Analysis of Each AWS Function Governed by IHL*

Risk assessments and mitigation measures should be part of the design, development, testing and deployment cycle of emerging technologies in any weapons systems.[21]

Having established a record of the AWS functions and the applicable IHL rules, such as an IHL matrix, the legal review should undertake a legal risk analysis of each AWS function identified as being regulated by IHL. This risk analysis will identify those functions where the risk of unlawful actions exists and propose methods to mitigate the legal risk. Methods of risk mitigation may include increasing the level of human control, improving the human-machine interface, limiting the AWS autonomous function in certain operational scenarios, or preventing the AWS from performing that function without human control.

---

21 See <https://documents.unoda.org/wp-content/uploads/2020/07/20200626-Germany.pdf>.

TABLE 7.2 Risk likelihood[a]

Level	Descriptor	Description
1	Rare	May occur only in exceptional circumstances
2	Unlikely	Could occur at some time
3	Possible	Might occur at some time
4	Likely	Will probably occur in most circumstances
5	Almost certain	Is expected to occur in most circumstances

a Based on the University of New South Wales legal risk matrix template <https://www.legal.unsw.edu.au/commercial/Risk_Assessment_Template.doc>.

2.5.1 Legal Risks

Legal risk can be quantified in terms of likelihood and consequences.[22] For example, the likelihood may range from 1 (rare) to 5 (almost certain) (see Table 7.2).

Similarly, the consequences can be described using a scale ranging from 1 (insignificant) to 5 (catastrophic). The levels of risks may be described in terms of the likely consequences (see Table 7.3).

The likelihood and consequences of risks can be combined in a legal risk matrix designed to represent levels of risk. For example, Table 7.4 describes levels of risks ranging from low to extreme.

The legal risks are closely linked to ethical risks. However, legal risks arise from the reviewing state's international and domestic law obligations, while ethical risks are a product of national policy. The reviewing state may establish national policy that describes the legal risks and the corresponding level of human control required to mitigate the legal risks. For example, an AWS functionality assessed as low legal risk may be permitted more autonomous operation. Similarly, autonomous functionality assessed as medium risk may require direct human oversight or reprogramming. A high or extreme legal risk may preclude a state from allowing the AWS to perform a particular function autonomously and require direct human control.

22 AS/NZS 4360-2004 *Risk Management* (2004) <https://www.standards.org.au/standards-catalogue/sa-snz/publicsafety/ob-007/as-slash-nzs--4360-2004>.

TABLE 7.3 Risk consequences[a]

Level	Descriptor	Example detail description
1	Insignificant	No injuries to civilians or damage to civilian objects
2	Minor	First aid treatment required; small damage to civilian objects
3	Moderate	Medical treatment required; serious damage to civilian objects
4	Major	Extensive injuries to civilians; major damage to civilian objects
5	Catastrophic	Death; huge effects on civilian objects

a Ibid.

TABLE 7.4 Levels of legal risk

Likelihood	Consequences				
	1 Insignificant	2 Minor	3 Moderate	4 Major	5 Catastrophic
1 (Rare)	Low	Low	Medium	High	High
2 (Unlikely)	Low	Low	Medium	High	Extreme
3 (Moderate)	Low	Medium	High	Extreme	Extreme
4 (Likely)	Medium	High	High	Extreme	Extreme
5 (Almost certain)	High	High	Extreme	Extreme	Extreme

This risk-based approach is consistent with the approach taken by different industries and organisations to ascribe levels of automation. In the automotive car industry, there are five levels of driving automation that are intended to indicate how capable a vehicle is of performing without human control.[23] These levels are:

23 See <https://www.iotforall.com/5-autonomous-driving-levels-explained>.

1) *Driver assistance* – The vehicle assists the driver with some functions (e.g., autonomous braking), but the driver is primarily responsible for all vehicle functions such as accelerating, braking, and monitoring the surrounding environment.
2) *Partial automation* – The vehicle can assist with steering and acceleration functions and enable the driver to disengage from some of the tasks. The driver must, however, be always ready to take over the control of the vehicle and is still responsible for most safety-critical functions and monitoring the environment.
3) *Conditional automation* – The vehicle is responsible for monitoring the environment. While the driver's attention is still required to maintain attention on driving, they can disengage from safety-critical functions such as braking.
4) *High automation* – In a self-determined safe environment, the driver can activate the automation to allow the vehicle to steer and brake, monitor the vehicle and road conditions, respond to events and determine when to change lanes, turn and use signals. It cannot determine more dynamic situations, such as traffic congestion and merging onto a highway.
5) *Complete automation* – There is no human attention required. The vehicle is completely responsible for driving and, therefore, there are no controls (e.g., steering wheel or brake pedal) to enable human control.[24]

Similarly, in April 2022 the International Maritime Authority began work on the Maritime Autonomous Surface Ships (MASS) code which contains the following four degrees of autonomy:

1) *Degree one:* Ship with automated processes and decision support: Seafarers are on board to operate and control shipboard systems and functions. Some operations may be automated and at times be unsupervised but with seafarers on board ready to take control.
2) *Degree two:* Remotely controlled ship with seafarers on board: The ship is controlled and operated from another location. Seafarers are available on board to take control and to operate the shipboard systems and functions.
3) *Degree three*: Remotely controlled ship without seafarers on board: The ship is controlled and operated from another location. There are no seafarers on board.

24 Ibid.

4) *Degree four*: Fully autonomous ship: The operating system of the ship is able to make decisions and determine actions by itself.[25]

These levels of human control or degrees of autonomy may be adapted to mitigate risk in the use of AWS by requiring certain levels of human control over AWS in different risk scenarios. This is discussed further in the next Functional Review Step below.

2.6 *Functional Review (Element 6/8) – Determine the Appropriate Level of Human Control*

Human control over AWS functions is likely to be a primary method of mitigating legal risk with the use of AWS. The required level of human control will likely depend on the operational context and the characteristics and capabilities of a weapons system determined to be acceptable by the reviewing state. Human control can be ensured by an appropriate design, by a sufficient degree of predictability (ensured through a set of given parameters within which the system must be operating as well as rigid testing and review) and by a commander's and operator's sufficient understanding of the weapons system, including its autonomous functions, which enable the commander and operator to predict (prospective focus) and explain (retrospective) the behaviour of the weapons system. Temporal and spatial restrictions or limits need to be applied to the operation of any such weapons system.[26]

The appropriate type and level of human–machine interaction will be determined by the characteristics and capabilities of the system in question, vis-a-vis the operational circumstances and the mission's requirements. In other words, there is no 'one-fits-all' set of requirements that every weapon system needs to meet, but rather, these requirements may be adapted appropriately. Accordingly, for example, temporal and spatial restrictions may be applied to the operation of the system – during its development, deployment or before specific uses (depending on the case) – as necessary to ensure lawful use in the intended circumstances of use.[27]

Several states have publicly endorsed the concept of meaningful human control.[28] The concept of meaningful, appropriate or effective human control was first expressed by non-government organisation Article 36.com, during the

25 International Maritime Organisation, Media Centre, *Autonomous Shipping* (Website) https://www.imo.org/en/MediaCentre/HotTopics/Pages/Autonomous-shipping.aspx.

26 See <https://documents.unoda.org/wp-content/uploads/2020/07/20200626-Germany.pdf>.

27 See <https://documents.unoda.org/wp-content/uploads/2020/09/20200831-Israel.pdf>.

28 Germany, Argentina, Australia, Canada, Croatia, Czech Republic, Denmark, Greece, Poland, South Africa and Zimbabwe.

2014 Experts Meeting on LAWS.[29] Despite its argued importance, neither states nor civil society have agreed upon an authoritative definition of meaningful human control or consensus as to what is required. In support of meaningful human control, the ICRC argues that meaningful human control should be exercised over the 'critical functions' of a weapon system, including 'selecting and attacking targets'.[30] The components of these critical functions include searching for, detecting, identifying, track and selecting targets and using force to neutralise, damage and destroy.[31]

What constitutes meaningful human control is an ongoing discussion. Moyes and Roff suggest that 'a human simply pressing a "fire" button in response to indications from a computer, without cognitive clarity or awareness, is not sufficient to be considered "human control" in a substantive sense'.[32] The Centre for a New American Security build upon this argument by suggesting that there are three essential components to meaningful human control:

1. Human operators are making informed, conscious decisions about the use of weapons.
2. Human operators have sufficient information to ensure the lawfulness of the action they are taking, given what they know about the target, the weapon, and the context for action.
3. The weapon is designed and tested, and human operators are properly trained, to ensure effective control over the use of the weapon.[33]

These components are pre-conditions to the application of existing IHL rules rather than additional IHL norms. The extent and nature of human control over a weapon system is difficult to define in the absence of context. Ekelhof

29 Article36, *Key Areas for Debate on Autonomous Weapon Systems* (Briefing Paper, May 2014) 2 <https://www.article36.org/wp-content/uploads/2014/05/A36-CCW-May-2014.pdf>.

30 ICRC, *International Law and the Challenges of Contemporary Armed Conflicts* (32IC/15/11, October 2015) 44 <https://www.icrc.org/en/document/international-humanitarian-law-and-challenges-contemporary-armed-conflicts>.

31 Ibid.

32 H Roff and R Moyes, 'Meaningful Human Control, Artificial Intelligence and Autonomous Weapons'. Briefing paper prepared for the Informal Meeting of Experts on Lethal Autonomous Weapons Systems, UN Convention on Certain Conventional Weapons (April 2016) 1 <https://article36.org/wp-content/uploads/2016/04/MHC-AI-and-AWS-FINAL.pdf>.

33 Michael C Horowitz and Paul Scharre, *Meaningful Human Control in Weapon Systems: A Primer* (16 March 2015) 14–25 <https://www.cnas.org/publications/reports/meaningful-human-control-in-weapon-systems-a-primer>.

contends that an important question is: 'does the human operator have sufficient information to make informed as well as conscious decisions about the use of weapons?'[34] Until the concept is formulated into an international treaty, the nature and context of human control in their use of AI-enhanced or autonomous weapons remains an issue for states to determine through national policy mechanisms.

An important question is how temporal the human control must be to the performance of the AWS' intended role. Is the primary concern the time between the human decision to activate the AWS and the conduct of an attack on a military objective? Practically speaking, the longer the time between the human decision to deploy an AWS and the effect, the higher the risk that changes in the environmental and operational circumstances will affect the AWS performance. Will a computer program designed to enable an AWS to accurately identify and attack pre-selected, lawful targets be sufficient, or must there be ongoing human control to ensure that a human can cancel an attack if circumstances change? To determine the appropriate level of human control, Goussac argues that:

> A reviewer will need to be satisfied that the proposed AI design and its method of use will not prevent the operator or commander from exercising the judgments required by IHL.[35]

There are likely to be multiple factors a reviewing state will consider in identifying the appropriate level of human control. These factors may include:

a) the state's interpretation of the IHL requirement for human control over specific methods of warfare;
b) national policy, including ethical requirements;
c) an AWS function and technical ability; and
d) legal risk.

The hypothetical UGV-C is programmed to operate without direct human control. Once activated, it can identify an enemy tank and attack it. As noted earlier, the UGV-C's sensors are not capable of identifying the presence of other

34 Merel Ekelhof, 'Moving Beyond Semantics on Autonomous Weapons: Meaningful Human Control in Operation' (2019) 10(3) *Global Policy* 343 <https://onlinelibrary.wiley.com/doi/full/10.1111/1758-5899.12665>.

35 N Goussac, 'Safety Net or Tangled Web: Weapons Reviews of AI in Weapons and War-Fighting', *International Committee of the Red Cross Humanitarian Law & Policy Blog* (Blog Post, 18 April 2019) <https://blogs.icrc.org/law-and-policy/2019/04/18/safety-net-tangled-web-legal-reviews-ai-weapons-war-fighting>.

civilians or civilian objects. If the UGV-C was permitted to operate in an environment where civilians were present, there is a high risk that it may cause collateral damage. The reviewing state may mitigate this risk by either restricting the use of the UGV-C to environments where there are no civilians or civilian objects present or requiring direct human control to enable a human operator to assess the risk of collateral damage.

2.6.1 Is Human Control an IHL Obligation?

It is generally accepted that the application of IHL rules, particularly rules regulating methods of warfare, require the exercise of human judgement.[36] The question is whether the law requires a certain degree, quality or timeliness of human judgement in the performance of certain methods of warfare. States such as Switzerland and Venezuela, 'consider that the criteria underlying the principles of distinction, proportionality and precautions necessarily demand evaluative decisions and value judgments by humans'.[37] While it may be technically possible to program IHL compliance into deterministic AWS software, effectively applying human decisions in advance, the text of some IHL rules clearly contemplate the application of distinctly human cognition such as 'recognise' and 'doubt'. In such cases, a state may require, as a matter of law, that all AWS functions governed by such rules are performed or directly controlled by humans. This issue requires significant research and this book will only provide a limited survey.

The need for human control may be considered in the context of an AWS designed to attack military objectives. To do so, the AWS must act consistently with the distinction rule found in art 48 of AP 1 by distinguishing between 'the civilian population and combatants and between civilian objects and military objectives'.[38] While an AWS' sensors and software may be technically capable of distinguishing persons and objects in certain circumstances, numerous delegations to the UN CCW debate on LAWS have argued that human judgement was necessary to assess the fundamental principles of proportionality,

36 United Nations, *Report of the 2017 Group of Governmental Experts on 'Lethal Autonomous Weapon Systems' (LAWS)*, UN Doc CCW/GGE.1/2017/CRP.1 (20 November 2017) 7 <https://docs-library.unoda.org/Convention_on_Certain_Conventional_Weapons_-_Meeting_of_High_Contracting_Parties_(2017)/2017_CCW_GGE.1_2017_CRP.1_Advanced_%2Bcorrected.pdf>; US Directive 3000.09 (n 5).

37 V Boulanin, L Bruun, N Goussac, *Autonomous Weapon Systems and International Humanitarian Law: Identifying Limits and the Required Type and Degree of Human-Machine Interaction* (June 2021) Stockholm International Peace Research Institute, 19.

38 AP 1 (n 3) art 48.

distinction and precautions in attack.[39] A state may, therefore, prevent AWS from performing functions that are governed by IHL rules that require the application of distinctly human cognition or judgement. For example, the protection afforded to civilian objects in art 52(3) of AP 1 relies on the absent of 'doubt'. The rule requires a presumption of civilian status to be applied to objects normally used for civilian purposes when there is doubt as to its use.[40] A state may require an AWS designed to distinguish objects to require human input where a threshold of certainty is not met.

The concept of meaningful human control appears to be sufficiently imprecise to enable broad application.[41] This also brings a degree of legal imprecision. The exercise of judgement may be seen as the product of the information available to the decision-maker at the relevant time as well as their experience, training and knowledge. Where there are gaps in information, a human may rely on intuition based on experience and an intangible 'sense' of what is right in a particular circumstance. In the conduct of a legal review, a reviewing state may therefore determine, as a matter of law, certain AWS' functions that are governed by IHL rules requiring the exercise of judgement must be performed or controlled by humans.

2.6.2 National Policy on Human Control

A state may not interpret all IHL as requiring human control over all actions but recognise the need for human control over AWS functions governed by certain IHL rules e.g., only those rules regulating an attack. It is therefore open to a state to outline their national requirements for human control over AWS in national policy directives. An advantage of establishing a policy basis for human control is that may be readily adjusted to accommodate developments in AWS technology.

National policy will influence the study and development of AI-enhanced and autonomous weapons. The first example of national policy stating requirements for human control was released by the US Department of Defence in

39 *Draft Report of the 2016 Informal Meeting of Experts on Lethal Autonomous Weapons* (*LAWS*), submitted by the Chairperson of the Informal Meeting of Experts, 44 <https://docs-library.unoda.org/Convention_on_Certain_Conventional_Weapons_-_Informal_Meeting_of_Experts_(2016)/ReportLAWS_2016_AdvancedVersion.pdf>.

40 AP 1 (n 3) art 52(3): 'In cases of doubt whether an object which is normally dedicated to civilian purpose, such as a place of worship, a house or other dwelling or a school, is being used to make an effective contribution to military action, it shall be presumed not to be so used'.

41 Rebecca Crootof, 'A Meaningful Floor for "Meaningful Human Control"' (2015) 30 *Temple International & Comparative Law Journal* 3.

2012. Directive 3000.09 *Autonomy in Weapon Systems* applies to the 'design, development, acquisition, testing and fielding, and employment of autonomous and semi-autonomous weapons systems, including guided munitions that can independently select and discriminate targets'.[42] While the directive was released prior to the debate on meaningful human control, the directive states:

> Autonomous and semi-autonomous weapon systems shall be designed to allow commanders and operators to exercise appropriate levels of human judgment over the use of force.[43]

Other examples of national policy broadly describing their requirements for human control over AWS include the ADF *Concept for Robotic and Autonomous Systems*, which states:

> Defence will enhance its combat capability within planned resources by employing RAS in human commanded teams to improve efficiency, increase mass and achieve decision superiority while decreasing risk to personnel.[44]

A state may include specific requirements for human control in their legal review policy. Many states that undertake formal legal reviews have policies within their respective departments or ministries of defence directing responsibilities and processes for legal reviews. While there is no evidence of a state creating or amending an existing legal review policy to address the requirements for the legal review of AWS, this may occur.

It follows that a reviewing state with such policies addressing the national requirements for human control of AWS should consider and identify the appropriate levels of human control. This requires analysis of the intended relationship between human commanders and weapon operators and ensure that the human control exists over the AWS operation.

The levels or degrees of autonomy designed to mitigate risk in the autonomous vehicle and maritime industries (identified in Functional Review Step 5 above) may be modified and applied to AWS to provide a basis for mitigating legal risk through a national policy on the minimum level of human control. To

42 US Directive 3000.09 (n 5).

43 Ibid 2.

44 Australian Government, Australia Defence Force, *Concept for Robotic and Autonomous Systems*, Version 1 (25 November 2020) 28 ('ADF RASAI Concept') 8.

illustrate this, a state may create a policy describing AWS human control levels (HCLs) in the following way:

1) *HCL 1 – for low-risk AWS functions.* Humans will be responsible for tasking, activating and condition setting and be able to cancel an AWS task at any time but humans will not have direct oversight of AWS actions while it is performing the assigned task.
2) *HCL 2 – for medium-risk AWS functions.* Humans will be responsible for tasking, activating, condition setting and maintaining oversight of the AWS actions in performing the assigned task. A human operator will be able to cancel an AWS task at any time.
3) *HCL 3 – for intermediate-risk AWS functions.* Humans will be responsible for tasking, activating, and condition setting and be primarily responsible for the AWS actions in performing the assigned task. The AWS may recommend actions for a human operator to approve. A human operator will be able to cancel an AWS task at any time.
4) *HCL 4 – for high-risk AWS functions.* Humans will be responsible for tasking, activating and condition setting and be directly responsible for the AWS actions in performing the assigned task. A human operator will be able to cancel an AWS task at any time.

As a component of a national policy on AWS governance a state may determine that decisions relating to certain functions or targets will always be made by humans. In that case, HCL 4 will be applied to such decisions. Alternatively, the political or operational nature of a military operation may require additional precautions. For example, if the hypothetical UGV-C is employed in an armed conflict where the risk of civilian casualties is high, a state may indicate in their rules of engagement that the UGV-C are to only operate at HCL 4 with direct human control. Alternatively, if an UGV-C is employed in an armed conflict where civilians and civilian objects are not present, it may be authorised to operate at HCL 1 or 2.

2.6.3 National HLCs Applied to an AWS Targeting Process

It is widely recognised that the legal risks associated with AWS are most evident in the context of targeting. It is useful to consider what IHL decisions those who plan or decide upon an attack are required to make. These decisions are incorporated in the art 57 of AP 1 rule requiring 'precautions in attack'.[45]

Where the legal review of an AWS identifies functions governed by IHL targeting rules, the reviewing state should consider how such risks can be

45 AP 1 (n 3) art 57(2).

mitigated. If there are no technical solutions (e.g., replacing an inaccurate sensor with an accurate one), a state may require higher levels of human control over the AWS function to reduce the risk to an acceptable level.

Where an AWS is designed to attack specific military objectives, T&E may demonstrate that the AI is susceptible to false positive classifications in particular circumstances. A false positive classification may result in an unlawful attack on civilians or civilian objects. One area of legal risk is in the classification of persons as combatants and where the protected status of a combatant changes due to becoming *hors de combat* as regulated by art 41(2) of AP 1.[46] A combatant is protected from attack when recognised as being *hors de combat*, including where 'he clearly expresses an intention to surrender'.[47] If the AWS is unable to reliably recognise this change in protected status, then human control may be necessary to compensate for the legal risk.[48]

Sensor technology will affect the risk analysis. An AWS may employ biometric sensors to identify or differentiate between individuals.[49] Such technology may obtain data from an individual's fingerprints or DNA or employing facial recognition and use this to inform distinction decisions. In doing so there may be a reduction of legal risk in certain circumstances in contrast to AWS without such sensor technology.

Alternatively, a state may also consider the legal risks associated with errors in human judgement. There may be circumstances where an AWS can perform a function more effectively than a human. This may be where the speed and accuracy of a decision may be critical to the legality and effectiveness of a decision. In such a case, the legal risk may be increased by the human operator and, therefore, the appropriate mitigation is to reduce the human control. This may be demonstrated by reference to the IHL obligation to take precautions in attack.

The ADF applies a targeting process called the '6-Step Targeting Process'.[50] The process was designed to give effect to the art 57 of AP 1 obligation to take 'precautions in attack'. If an AWS is designed to perform some or all the steps in the 6-Step Targeting Process, the risks associated with each step performed autonomously may be mitigated by applying a suitable HCL.

---

46 Ibid art 41(2).

47 Ibid art 41(2)(b).

48 Boulanin et al (n 39) 19.

49 W Boothby, 'Biometrics' in *New Technologies and the Law in War and Peace* (Cambridge University Press, 2018) 392–420.

50 I Henderson, *The Contemporary Law of Targeting* (Martinus Nijhoff Publishers, 2009) 246–7.

The 6-Step Targeting Process consists of four planning steps (1–4) and two executive steps (5–6).[51] The following discussion considers each of these steps in turn:

Step 1 – Locate and observe the potential target and its surrounding area.

This first step is intended to ensure there is sufficient information for a human operator or AWS to make an effective targeting decision. This step equates to the 'observe' and 'orientation' stages of Boyd's OODA loop decision cycle.[52] The identification of potential targets requires consideration of IHL rules. Accordingly, the risks associated with accountability and responsibility may be assessed as low until the decision is acted upon in later steps. A risk analysis may assess the likelihood and consequences of an error in Step 1 as low, enabling a state to permit a high or complete level of automation (e.g., HCL 1 described above). Alternatively, if there are concerns with the reliability of the AWS's ability to locate potential targets in certain environments or operational circumstances, a higher risk level may require a higher level of human control (e.g., HCL 3). In the case of the UGV-C, its inability to detect civilians and civilian objects may require its use to be limited to a minimum of HCL 3 where there is a risk of collateral damage.

Step 2 – Assess the target is a valid military objective and that it is not otherwise protected from attack by IHL.

This step requires categorisation of the person or object identified as a potential target in Step 1. A risk analysis will consider the likelihood and consequences of a distinction error. An AWS designed to identify a narrow range of military objectives, based on discrete indicia (e.g., ground radars based on specific radar emissions), may have a lower likelihood of error and, therefore, permit less human control. In contrast, a system that is designed to distinguish a broader range of civilians and civilian objects from combatants and military objectives will generate higher levels of legal risk. The consequences of error may also increase where the anticipated operating environment has a high likelihood of civilians and civilian objects in the target area. Similarly, where testing suggests that the system is unreliable or unpredictable in certain operational or environmental circumstances, a lower level of automation and greater human control is appropriate. T&E may demonstrate that the HCL level for each AWS function may vary depending on the target and operational environment. In such a case, the

51 Ibid.

52 J Boyd, *A Discourse on Winning and Losing* (Air University Press, 2018) 383.

operating procedures for the AWS may describe different levels of human control for different AWS tasks.

Step 3 – Take all feasible precautions to minimise collateral damage.

The third step gives effect to the art 57(2) requirement to take 'all feasible precautions in the choice of means and methods of attack with a view to avoiding, and in any event to minimising' collateral damage.[53] There are a range of feasible precautions that may be available to an attack in a particular circumstance, including weapon selection (including precision or low yield weapons); type of munitions (penetrator or delayed fuse to minimise fragmentation); attacking at a time of day or night where civilian presence is reduced; and attacking from a direction that avoids collateral effects in the direction of civilian objects.[54] Where consideration of such mitigations is beyond the capability of the AWS or can only be made in a limited way, feasible precautions must be taken by human weapon operators. If humans are responsible for such decisions (e.g., HCL 4), the risk assessment is likely to be low. In such a case, the human operator will need to ensure that the time between the deployment of the AWS and it attacking its target is minimised to avoid the tactical environment changing in a way that alters the initial precautionary measures.

Step 4 – Assess whether any expected collateral damage is proportional (i.e., not excessive) to the anticipated military advantage to be gained from the attack.

Step 4 is the final planning step in the targeting process. As discussed in Chapter 6, a proportionality assessment requires the comparison of unlike values, namely collateral damage to civilians and civilian objects, with an anticipated military advantage. This assessment is largely subjective and it is only when the resulting collateral damage is 'excessive' in relation to the military advantage that an attack is prohibited by IHL. The subjective nature of this assessment may not be easily programmed unless it is reduced to the simplest equations using pre-determined proportionality ratios or assessments assessed as low risk.[55] For example, an enemy tank may always be designated with high military advantage with low collateral risk where there is an absence of civilians and civilian objects and the AWS uses precision munitions. However, it is likely that most proportionality assessments will

53 AP I (n 3) art 57(2).

54 Backstrom and Henderson (n 20) 171.

55 Michael Schmitt, 'Regulating Autonomous Weapons Might be Smarter Than Banning Them', *Just Security* (10 August 15) <https://www.justsecurity.org/25333/regulating-autonomous-weapons-smarter-banning/>.

be complex and require human decisions and, therefore, will be assessed as HCL 4.
Step 5 – Authorise the attack.
Art 57(2) allocates responsibility for taking precautions in attack to those who 'plan or decide upon the attack'. The attacking state may employ ROE or targeting directives which limit this authority to 'decide' upon an attack to one or more military commanders responsible for the precautionary planning Steps 1–4. This enables an informed decision as to whether sufficient 'precautions in attack' have been taken (e.g. confirming that the intended target is lawful and not protected, that the collateral damage is proportionate to the anticipated military advantage, where possible advance warning is given if the attack will affect the civilian population and ensuring the method of attack is in one which will cause the least harm to civilians and civilian objects). This decision making is likely to be informed by advice from a legal advisor assigned for that purpose under art 82. In many cases where collateral damage is likely, this deliberate targeting process involves complex decision making and high risks and consequently will require direct human involvement (i.e. HCL 4). In other cases, such as attacks in self-defence or in the absence of civilians or civilian objects, those responsible for planning or deciding upon an attack may set the parameters in which a decision is made and then permit the AWS to perform targeting functions within those parameters (i.e. HCL 2). A common factor in these two scenarios is that there is a commander who authorises the attack and then the AWS performs the authorised attack with human control commensurate with the legal risk.
Step 6 – Cancel or suspend the attack if the assessment in steps 1–4 is incorrect or change.
The final step requires an attack to be cancelled or suspended where it becomes apparent that the determinations made during Steps 1–4 are incorrect e.g. the target is not a military objective or is otherwise protected or the collateral damage will be excessive in relation to the anticipated military advantage. The decision to cancel or suspend an attack, particularly one that has already commenced, will require rapid decision making to avoid a high risk of an unlawful attack. This is likely to require direct human control (HCL 4) or be triggered by an AWS detecting new or previously undetected civilian persons or objects in the target area.

The proposed HCL may be a useful tool not only for mitigating legal risk but also ensuring that the risk of gaps in legal accountability are reduced.

2.7 *Functional Review (Element 7/8) – Identify Lines of Human Responsibility*

As discussed in Chapter 6, the use of AWS in armed conflict presents the risk of a legal accountability gap.[56] While states are the legally responsible for violations of IHL in armed conflict[57] specific persons, such as military commanders and those who 'decide or plan an attack', are also held responsible for compliance with IHL rules in armed conflict.[58]

The immediate question is, who will be accountable and responsible for harm or damage caused by AWS in armed conflict?[59] There are a range of views, with some suggesting that the use of AWS will risk IHL violations being unattributable to either a state or persons.[60] Alternatively, others suggest that concerns of an accountability gap are based on a false premise as humans will always decide how to program and when to launch an AWS.[61]

Human control is argued as an implicit IHL requirement and necessary to avoid the risk of an accountability gap.[62] Regardless of which view a state supports, those responsible for the development of AWS should ensure that they consider how human accountability and responsibility can be maintained in the design and development of AWS.

A potential advantage of AWS is the ability to record human input and decisions. This may assist states to ascertain responsibility for violations associated with AWS use by identifying what information was available and relevant at the time of an incident. This may be supported by AWS design that requires a human operator to manually over-ride an AWS program in certain circumstances e.g., if an AWS is programmed to not attack an object displaying a protected emblem.

---

56 T McFarland and T McCormack, 'Mind the Gap: Can Developers of Autonomous Weapon Systems be Liable for War Crimes?' 90 *International Law Studies* 361 (2014) 361.

57 Sassòli (n 11) 323.

58 Relief Web, *Towards Limits on Autonomy in Weapon Systems* (Web Page, 9 April 2018) <https://reliefweb.int/report/world/towards-limits-autonomy-weapon-systems>.

59 International Human Rights Clinic and Human Rights Watch, *Losing Humanity: The Case Against Killer Robots* (IHRC and HRW, 2012) 52 ('Losing Humanity').

60 Human Rights Watch and the International Human Rights Clinic, *Mind the Gap: The Lack of Accountability for Killer Robots* (Human Rights Watch, 2015).

61 M Schmitt and J Thurnher (2013) '"Out of the Loop": Autonomous Weapon Systems and the Law of Armed Conflict' (2013) 4(2) *Harvard National Security Journal* 231, 277.

62 Human Rights Watch and the International Human Rights Clinic (n 62); Article 36, *Remarks Prepared for the CCW Debate on Lethal Autonomous Weapons Systems* (13 November 2015) <https://unoda-documents-library.s3.amazonaws.com/Convention_on_Certain_Conventional_Weapons_-_Meeting_of_High_Contracting_Parties_(2015)/2015_CCWMSP_LAWS_Article%2B36.pdf>.

Military decisions concerned with the use of force in armed conflict are distributed across different levels of responsibility and authority. For example, in a deliberate 'joint targeting process', decisions are dispersed between government, strategic, operational and tactical levels.[63] Some decisions are informed by computer software designed to predict weapon effects on buildings or structures.[64] Ultimately, the responsibility for a particular attack falls to the commander with the authority to approve it. This authority is determined by the level of military command and described in directives from a higher commander.

Human accountability and responsibility are contingent upon the existence of human control. Human control may be achieved through the decisions of software engineers programming the AWS, the decisions by a state to acquire the AWS for use in armed conflict and the decisions of its military commanders responsible for deploying an AWS on a specific task. As is the case for any weapon, a commander will be responsible for harm resulting from a decision to use an AWS in circumstances beyond known technical limitations.

The latter point reinforces the need for a legal review to identify the circumstances in which the use of an AWS raises IHL compliance risks. These circumstances must be clearly articulated in the AWS operating instructions, and those responsible for their use must be sufficiently trained and aware of the AWS use and limitations. This is, however, dependent on the weapon performing its expected role in a reliable and predictable way.

2.8 *Functional Review (Element 8/8) – Trust from Reliability, Predictability and Explainability*

For an AWS to be effective the procuring state and its military operators must trust its ability to perform its normal or expected use reliably, predictably and in a way that can be explained. Trust is not an IHL or international law obligation but is a 'firm belief in the reliability, truth or ability of someone or something'.[65] For an AWS to be trusted, it must be reliable, predictable and explainable. A state and its military who are responsible for the use of an AWS need to trust that the AWS can perform its functions in armed conflict in compliance with IHL.

63 See Australian Government, Department of Defence, ADDP 03.14 *Targeting* (2 February 2009) <https://iihl.org/wp-content/uploads/2022/08/ADDP_3_14_Targeting.pdf>.

64 ICRC, IHL in Action, *Iraq, Computer Modelling in Collateral Damage Estimates and Choice of Weapons* (Web Page) <https://ihl-in-action.icrc.org/case-study/iraq-computer-modelling-collateral-damage-estimates-and-choice-weapons>.

65 ADF RASAI Concept (n 46) 24.

Trust also a risk. While humans must be able to trust the AWS' ability to perform its role lawfully, they are also susceptible to over trusting it.[66] An appropriate level of human control will be influenced by the balance between the necessary level of trust to use an AWS in armed conflict and a level of dis-trust in it to avoid over trusting. The less an operator can trust an AWS, the greater the need for human control over its use.

A positive legal review of an AWS may contribute to a level of trust by determining its ability to be used in compliance with IHL. A combatant is entitled to trust that a weapon issued by the military is lawful and that their responsibility is to use the weapon lawfully. However, trust will be not easy to achieve. While autonomous technology is becoming more sophisticated, autonomous capabilities are known for their 'brittleness'.[67] This means that they may not easily adapt to an unexpected or non-structured environment and can easily break down.[68] Autonomous systems are most reliable in environments that are known, predictable and understood.[69] The legal risks of AWS malfunction resulting from hardware faults, programming errors or sensor failures must be considered during the functional review. Equally, the risk that an AWS will function in an unintended manner requires thorough T&E. This must identify the AWS limitations to enable their use to be limited to those circumstances where it can be trusted to perform reliably and predictably. Moreover, the AWS must be capable of being understood by its operators and, therefore, it should be explainable.

2.8.1 Reliability

Reliability is an objective measure of performance based on the results of successive trials.[70] There are several performance measures that may contribute to how a state assesses the overall reliability of its AWS. These include the performance of the AWS human–machine interface, the technical performance of AWS subsystems, including integrated and remote sensors, software and the system's ability to operate in different, unpredictable environments.

---

66 M Verbruggen, *The Question of Swarms Control: Challenges to Ensuring Human Control over Military Swarms* (No 65, EU Non-Proliferation and Disarmament Consortium, December 2019) 5 <https://www.nonproliferation.eu/wp-content/uploads/2019/12/EUNPDC_no-65_031219.pdf>.

67 P Scharre, *Army of None: Autonomous Weapons and the Future of War* (Norton & Company, 2018) 145.

68 ICRC, *Report on the ICRC Expert Meeting on Autonomous Weapon Systems: Technical, Military, Legal and Humanitarian Aspects*, 26–28 March 2014, Geneva (9 May 2014) 5.

69 Ibid 40.

70 Ibid 5.

The reliability of the AWS will be tested in a range of operational scenarios designed to identify reliability risks.

For the weapon component of the AWS, e.g. the gun or projectile, reliability may be expressed as a failure rate or percentage of cases where the munition fails to explode or strike its target.[71] States will accept reliability rates for conventional munitions between 95 and 99 per cent.[72] Reliability may also include a measure of a weapon's accuracy in terms of its ability to strike within a certain distance of the intended target.

Reliability will affect the determination of legality in several ways. First, a munition with a high failure rate creates risks of civilian harm from explosive remnants of war. States party to Protocol V to the CCW are required to 'strive to achieve the highest reliability rates'.[73] Second, the ability of the AWS to accurately hit its intended target is relevant to the principle of distinction. A reviewing state is likely to determine that a weapon that is unable to reliably hit its intended target is indiscriminate by nature and unlawful per se. Alternatively, a reviewing state may determine that a munition that is unable to reliably strike its intended target is inaccurate and therefore place restrictions on its use of avoid the risk of indiscriminate uses, e.g. prohibit its use in environments where civilians and civilian objects are present. The technical threshold for such a determination is a matter of state policy.

Reliability will also be a measure of how often an AWS can perform its intended functions in compliance with IHL. While all complex systems, including weapons, are susceptible to malfunction, an AWS will be expected to operate in its intended environment reliably. Where reliability falls below the state-determined performance standard, measured in levels of certainty or statistical probability, a legal review will recommend a restriction on the use of the AWS in those circumstances.

Finally, reliability also raises a risk of automation complacency or overreliance on AWS decisions.[74] This is particularly so where human operators are required to multitask by controlling several systems at once. Overreliance is a concern where the AWS performs a function incorrectly; however, this is

---

71 Defence Science Board Task Force, *Report on Munitions Systems Reliability* (US Department of Defense, September 2005) 14 <https://permanent.fdlp.gov/lps72288/ADA441959.pdf>.

72 Ibid 15.

73 *Protocol V on Explosive Remnants of War to the Convention on Prohibitions or Restrictions on the Use of Certain Conventional Weapons Which May be Deemed to be Excessively Injurious or to Have Indiscriminate Effects*, opened for signature 28 November 2003, 2399 UNTS 126 (entered into force 12 November 2006).

74 V Boulanin et al, *Limits on Autonomy in Weapon Systems: Identifying Practical Elements of Human Control* (Stockholm International Peace Research Institute, 2020) 19.

neither detected or questioned by a human operator. This risk requires states to develop the training of human operators to ensure they are aware of the risk and to create human–machine processes to mitigate against automation bias.

2.8.2 Predictability

Reliability and predictability are closely related terms. Where reliability is a measure of past performance, predictability is a probability of future performance based on past testing. Put differently, predictability is a measure of an AWS' ability to perform its functions in armed conflict as it did in testing.[75] AWS predictability may require uniformity of data inputs and environmental conditions in both testing and operational use.

Unpredictable AWS performance raises operational and legal risks. From an operational perspective, military commanders and operators need to anticipate how the AWS will function to be able to plan their use in armed conflict. A military commander must be able to trust that the AWS will perform in an expected manner and be able to anticipate how it will achieve an assigned task once it has been deployed. An AWS that acts in unreliable is of little military utility and a significant legal risk. Unpredictable behaviour may lead to unintended or unforeseen injury or harm to individuals otherwise protected by IHL.[76]

The application of AI and machine learning to AWS will increase the risk of unpredictable AWS behaviour. While a military commander authorising the deployment of an AWS in armed conflict may not need to know the specific method by which an AWS will achieve its directed task (e.g., the route it may take to the target or the time it will strike), the commander should understand the capabilities and methods that an AWS may use. This is important for a range of reasons, including enabling the coordination of military assets on the battlefield and ensuring the AWS is capable and has appropriate means of warfare to conduct the attack.

Unpredictability may reduce the ability of those who plan or decide upon an attack to take the appropriate precautions in attack.[77] This includes 'taking all feasible precautions in the choice of means and methods of attack with a view to avoiding, and in any event to minimising, incidental loss of civilian

---

75 A Tattersall and D Copeland, 'Reviewing Autonomous Cyber Capabilities' in R Liivoja and A Väljataga (eds), *Autonomous Cyber Capabilities Under International Law* (NATO CCDOE Publications, 2021) 230.

76 R Liivoja and A Väljataga (eds), *Autonomous Cyber Capabilities Under International Law* (NATO CCDOE Publications, 2021) 8.

77 AP 1 (n 3) art 57.

life, injury to civilians and damage to civilian objects'[78] and ensuring that the AWS attack will be proportionate. If an AWS with machine learning performs its directed task in an unpredictable way, the risks of unintended and unlawful consequences are elevated. Moreover, an unpredictable AWS may act too quickly to allow effective human oversight and control.

Predictability also raises issues for states in fulfilling their legal review obligation. As noted in Chapter 5, a legal review determination of legality is based on a weapon's normal or expected use at the time of the review. If it is not possible to predict the behaviour of an AWS, it is difficult to identify which normal or expected behaviour is the subject of the legal review at any time. Moreover, an AWS capable of changing its method of operation potentially triggers the state obligation to conduct a further legal review for each new method of warfare that was not considered by an earlier review.[79] This is a basis for an ongoing legal review process addressed in Chapter 8.

2.8.3 Explainability

The final element of AWS trust is explainability. As the roles and relationship between humans and AWS evolve, it will become increasingly important for humans to understand, and for AWS to explain, certain decisions.[80] This is a difficult task. An AWS may employ deep neural networks that can learn to complete increasingly complex tasks without specific programming. In doing so, they become increasingly difficult to understand. Some of the most competent AI algorithms are the least able to explain their actions.[81] This is because many neural networks rely on statistical algorithms[82] and, therefore, are unable to explain their decisions except in a statistical way.[83] This opacity is commonly referred to as the 'black box' problem'.[84]

---

78 Ibid.

79 M Schmitt (ed), *Tallinn Manual 2.0 on the International Law Applicable to Cyber Operations* (Cambridge University Press, 2nd ed, 2017) ('Tallinn Manual 2.0') 466.

80 G Moy et al, *Technical Report: Recent Advances in Artificial Intelligence and their Impact on Defence* (Defence Science and Technology Group, May 2020) 20 ('DSTG Report').

81 J Scholz and J Galliott, *AI in Weapons: The Moral Imperative for Minimally-Just Autonomy* (Defence Science and Technology Group, 2019) <https://www.dst.defence.gov.au/sites/default/files/basic_pages/documents/ICSILP18Wed1600_Scholz_et_al-AI_in_Weapons.pdf>.

82 See DSTG Report (n 82) 9. Statistical algorithms are designed to take raw data (sometimes with human-defined labels) and attempt to extract statistical patterns with increasingly complex concepts emerging at each layer.

83 DSTG Report (n 82) 28.

84 S Ritter et al, 'Cognitive Psychology for Deep Neural Networks: A Shape Bias Case Study' (Conference Paper, 34th International Conference on Machine Learning, 29 June 2017) <https://arxiv.org/pdf/1706.08606.pdf>.

To address this problem, research organisations like DARPA are researching explainable AI ('XAI') to develop machine learning techniques that produce explainable models and use explanation interfaces intended to enable a human user to understand the rationale for AI decisions, recommendations or actions.[85] An AWS that is unable to explain its decisions is unlikely to be trusted and is likely to present operational and legal risks. As the need for human–machine teaming increases, it will become increasingly important for AWS to explain themselves in a way that humans can understand.

Explainable AI will also enable transparency of AWS actions.[86] This will enable a legal review, particularly where an AWS employs a deep neural network. Where an AWS is designed to make decisions in application of IHL rules, the legal reviewer will seek to analyse the basis for the decision. Where the AWS is unable to explain the basis of its reasoning, particularly in the event of unexpected decisions, the legal review may be unable to make an accurate determination of legality. The question then is whether a reviewing state will accept the legal risk associated with the unexplainable AWS function or whether it will impose a limitation on this function to mitigate the legal risk.

Not all AWS decisions will, however, need to be explained. To minimise the risk of information overload for human operators, a balance must be found between explainability and efficient performance of AWS functionality.[87] An AWS operator will need to understand tactical implications of AWS decisions to enable operational planning. Similarly, a legal reviewer must analyse those AWS decisions that enable a determination of the AWS ability to perform in compliance with IHL rules or principles. The most important AWS decisions will be those that apply qualitative judgements, such as distinguishing between a civilian and a civilian taking a direct part in hostilities. The latter may be categorised based on abstract indicia, such as perceived intention, likely actions and behaviour inconsistent with that expected of a civilian. Such decision-making must be explainable to mitigate legal risk and be trusted by AWS operators and military commanders who are required to approve AWS operations.

A functional review will require data from an independent operational test and verification process. This data should include information describing the performance of the AWS function, the effect and the neural network's explanation or reasoning for those decisions necessary to perform. This process may

85 M Turek, *Explainable Artificial Intelligence* (XAI) (Defence Advanced Research Projects Agency, 2016) <https://www.darpa.mil/program/explainable-artificial-intelligence>.

86 Ibid 30.

87 MEAID (n 7) 15.

require multiple iterations to consider the AWS performance in divergent operational circumstances. A legal reviewer may apply a reasonableness standard to determine the legality of the AWS decisions or recommendations.

2.8.3.1 *Good Data: Addressing the Data Risks*

A final issue that is central to the legality of AWS is data. While IHL does not address the use or quality of data, ensuring sufficient or accurate data may be relevant to the obligation to take precautions in attack as an element of 'doing everything feasible'.[88] Over the past decade, a combination of greater computational power and availability of larger datasets have allowed deep learning algorithms to solve more real-world problems.[89] Neural networks use multiple layers, with each layer designed to progressively extract increasingly higher level features from the previous layers.[90] Neural networks take raw data, sometimes with human-defined labels, and attempt to identify statistical patterns.[91] However, it takes tens of millions of images to train a neural network to recognise images.[92] If the human-labelled data contain inherent biases, there is a risk that the neural network's outputs will be biased and inaccurate. The expression 'garbage-in, garbage-out' recognises that a neural network will simply process the data that it is inputting.[93] The quality of the output is closely related to the quality of the input. Data preparation is essential for any neural network designed to learn through supervised learning.[94] Lowrance contends that:

> data is the precursor and an essential ingredient to building an AI/ML classification or prediction model. The more opportunities we take to collect good, realistic data, the more effective our systems will be in identifying and classifying similar objects in the future.[95]

---

88 AP 1 (n 3) art 57(2)(a)(i).

89 DSTG Report (n 82) 29.

90 Ibid 9.

91 Ibid.

92 Ibid.

93 Ciklum, *Garbage in, Garbage Out: How to Prepare Your Date Set for Machine Learning* (Blog Post, 11 January 2019) <https://www.ciklum.com/blog/garbage-in-garbage-out-how-to-prepare-your-data-set-for-machine-learning/>.

94 HP Bunaes, 'Bad Data Can Kill Good AI', *Global Banking and Finance Review* (Web Page) <https://www.globalbankingandfinance.com/bad-data-can-kill-good-ai/>.

95 P Ferraris, *Aided Detection on the Future Battlefield* (US Army, 5 February 2020) <https://www.army.mil/article/232074>.

This is particularly the case where the AI will inform decisions concerning the use of force in armed conflict. Open-source civilian datasets, while readily available, may not be suitable for military purposes as they may contain inherent biases (e.g., through inaccurate labelling) and risk developing biased AWS decisions.[96] States developing or acquiring AWS will need to consider creating a policy and processes for AWS-specific datasets that are appropriately labelled (e.g., identifying military features of interest),[97] designed for operational environments, and tested and certified as good data to enable independent training and testing.

On 4 August 2021, the Australian Government released its Defence Data Strategy 2021–23.[98] Relevantly, this policy recognises that:

> Emerging technologies, highly dependent on data, are being rapidly translated into weapons systems. Technologies such as artificial intelligence, machine learning and autonomous unmanned weaponry, are shrinking decision time and improving weapon precision and lethality.[99]

This strategy provides a policy framework for Australian defence data management that is built upon five pillars (govern, trust, discover, use and share). Importantly, the trust pillar is concerned with the quality of defence data, which is managed by three levels of certification and assurance:

a. Gold: thoroughly examined and considered fit for general release and re-use, including public and government-level release.
b. Silver: considered fit for purpose for a specific business use case and for specific user requirements, but generally not to be re-used or released publicly.
c. Bronze: discoverable and has assigned custodianship, but with only a basic assessment of its quality.[100]

The strategy does not describe which of these categories of data will be required for use in the development and use of AWS; however, it is likely to be at least in the silver category.

96 DSTG Report (n 82) 9–23.

97 Ibid 26.

98 Australian Government, Department of Defence, *Defence Data Strategy 2021–2023* (4 August 2021) <https://www.defence.gov.au/sites/default/files/2021-08/Defence%20data%20strategy.pdf>.

99 Ibid 12.

100 Ibid 31.

States developing AI systems for AWS are likely to require specific datasets to be security classified. For security reasons, a state will not want an adversary to know that an AWS is designed to target specific military objectives. Such knowledge may allow an adversary to understand how an AWS identifies its intended target and, in response, design its own equipment or tactics to disrupt or confuse an AWS.

Data bias has an effect on artificial decision-making. While there is no doubt that human decisions in armed conflict are affected by bias (e.g., classifying males of a certain age as 'fighting aged males' and, therefore, potential threats),[101] there is a risk that human biases will be perpetuated in AWS using biased data in the training and testing of AI deep neural networks. Bad data can result in bad outputs, which can lead to disastrous results in armed conflict.

The risks of race and gender bias in AI algorithms are well known. For example, in the civilian law enforcement context, investigations have raised concerns with AI-based risk assessment programs used by police and courts to assist with parole decisions.[102] In other AI applications, such as video conferencing, AI bias is evident in the design of video backgrounds intended to enhance privacy. The recent increase in reliance on video conferencing in response to COVID-19 lockdown measures has amplified an issue referred to as 'cropping bias' where the video conferencing algorithm would crop or obscure the head of people with dark complexions.[103] While there are no reported cases of AWS bias, these examples demonstrate the risk that underlying bias in training data for statistical techniques is likely to result in inaccuracies or introduce bias into learning algorithms.[104]

In addition to biased data, bias may be deliberately or unknowingly programmed into algorithms. Algorithmic or machine bias in AI decision-making software often results in unfair decisions.[105] These can arise in many ways,

---

101 See C Friedersdorf, 'Under Obama, Men Killed by Drones are Presumed to be Terrorists 2012', *The Atlantic* (website, 30 May 2012) <https://www.theatlantic.com/politics/archive/2012/05/under-obama-men-killed-by-drones-are-presumed-to-be-terrorists/257749/>.

102 L Lewis, 'Killer Robots Reconsidered: Could AI Weapons Actually Cut Collateral Damage', *Bulletin of Atomic Scientists* (online, 10 January 2020) <https://thebulletin.org/2020/01/killer-robots-reconsidered-could-ai-weapons-actually-cut-collateral-damage/>.

103 M Dickey, *Twitter and Zoom's Algorithmic Bias Issues* (Web Page, 22 September 2020) <https://techcrunch.com/2020/09/21/twitter-and-zoom-algorithmic-bias-issues/>.

104 DST Report (n 82) 28.

105 J Angwin et al, *Machine Bias: There's Software Used Across the Country to Predict Future Criminals. And it's Biased Against Blacks* (ProPublica, 23 May 2016) <https://www.propublica.org/article/machine-bias-risk-assessments-in-criminal-sentencing>.

including issues with the design of the AI-powered decision-making tool.[106] These can lead to erroneous and unlawful decisions with significant implications in the context of targeting, which may unlawfully target persons based on gender, ethnicity, age or other social indicia.[107]

Consideration of bias in training data is also important. The quality and appropriateness of training datasets should be considered when AI with machine learning is used to enable target selection and engagement. This is because data bias, or the way the algorithm interprets the data, will substantially affect the predictability and reliability of the weapon system.[108]

Consequently, a legal review of an AWS must consider the quality of data and the risks of data bias to ensure the AWS is capable of lawful decision-making. As bias in AWS algorithms may result in incorrect and unlawful AWS decisions or recommendations, legal reviewers will require the advice of defence data scientists or other experts responsible for developing and certifying the AWS datasets to advise on the quality of the data used to develop and use AWS. The reviewing state's legal review policy should include the requirements for data assurance during the weapons development and review process.

3 Conclusion

This chapter identifies an addition functional review step to the traditional legal review process to address weapon autonomy. This step is intended to address the unique legal, national policy and practical challenges raised by AWS performing functions that are governed by IHL rules. The function review consists of eight elements which are intended to enable a legal review to identify and mitigate legal risks for each AWS function by recommending levels of human control.

The first element of the functional review identifies those AWS functions that specifically engage IHL targeting rules or national policy considerations.

---

106 Australian Human Rights Commission, *Using Artificial Intelligence to Make Decisions: Addressing the Problem of Algorithmic Bias* (24 November 2020) <https://humanrights.gov.au/our-work/rights-and-freedoms/publications/using-artificial-intelligence-make-decisions-addressing>.

107 *Report of the 2021 Session of the Group of Governmental Experts on Emerging Technologies in the Area of Lethal Autonomous Weapons Systems*, UN Doc CCW/GGE.1/2021/CRP.1 (8 December 2021) Annex III, 13.

108 See <https://documents.unoda.org/wp-content/uploads/2020/07/20200626-Germany.pdf>.

This is followed by elements 2, 3 and 4 which identify the legal standards against which to measure the AWS performance, the circumstances in which the AWS will perform the functions and the data that enables the legal analysis. Element 5 involves a legal risk analysis designed to categorise the likelihood and consequence of the AWS performing a certain function in a particular circumstance.

The risk analysis enables the weapon reviewer in element 6 to consider the relationship between legal risk, human control and human responsibility. To address legal risk element 6 identifies the necessary level of human control to mitigate the risk. This links closely with the risk of an accountability gap and so element 7 identifies of lines of human responsibility.

Finally, element 8 considers the characteristics of reliability, predictability and explainability as they contribute to commander and operator trust in the AWS. This is particularly important for an AWS that employs neural networks to perform its functions. While these characteristics are not IHL requirements, they are nonetheless relevant to the ability of an AWS to operate in compliance with IHL and so it is argued necessary for a legal review of an AWS to consider them. Similarly, it is necessary to for a legal review to seek expert advice on the quality of data used to both train and operate an AWS.

The function review step is argued as a necessary addition to the traditional legal review process for AWS. However, the challenges raised by AWS are not static, unlike the traditional legal review process, it is not possible to make a singular determination of legality prior to a weapon's use in armed conflict. The use of complex neural networks, capable of adapting their programming and therefore use, raises the need for an ongoing legal review process. It is argued in Chapter 8 that this process should extend throughout an AWS' lifecycle to ensure their continued use in compliance with IHL and international law.

CHAPTER 8

Proposal to Expand the Legal Review throughout the AWS' Lifecycle

To determine the legality of AWS, this chapter argues that a reviewing state should expand the legal review process beyond a singular determination of legality during the AWS acquisition process. An expanded process would enable an ongoing determination of legality across the entire AWS lifecycle from its initial design and development, during its procurement and, finally, during its use in armed conflict. This is a fundamental change from the traditional legal review process.

An expanded approach the legal review of AWS would consist of three broad stages, each designed to achieve a different legal review outcome. The first stage, described in Section 2, is the informative stage which recognises that the design and development of AWS is likely to occur outside the state by defence industry, academia and research organisations. As such, much of the critical development occurs before an AWS enters a defence acquisition process and may be done in ignorance of a state's legal review or international law obligations. The informative stage seeks to inform those designing or developing AWS of the national legal review process and its requirements through a process of self-assessment designed to identify legal risks. Section 3 then describes a determinative stage which focusses on the military acquisition process and the determination of an AWS's legality prior to its introduction into service and use in armed conflict. The determinative stage includes the traditional legal review process and the additional functional review step proposed in Chapter 7. Finally, Section 4 introduces the governance stage which recognises that an AWS' functions are unlikely to be fixed and may be influenced by factors including machine learning, environmental conditions and operational circumstances. The governance stage recognises the need for ongoing governance of the AWS during its in-service life to ensure its use remains in compliance with the state's IHL and international law obligations. The governance stage emphasises the relationship between art 36 and art 82 of AP 1, the need for environmental certification to ensure the AWS can perform its normal or expected use in new operational environments, and the need for a functional re-review where there is a material change to the AWS use, either through updates to software or programming changes resulting from machine learning.

 | DOI:10.1163/9789004707047_011

1 Stage 1 – Informative Stage

In Chapter 4 it was identified that the art 36 legal review obligation arises when a reviewing state decides to study, develop, acquire or adopt a new weapon, means or method of warfare. Chapter 5 noted that, in practice, the traditional legal review process generally coincides with the national defence capability acquisition process and informs decisions made during this process. Historically, this approach is appropriate to the static nature of a conventional weapon. The traditional legal review process does not reflect the increasing role of the defence industry in the development of AWS.[1] The Australian Government's *Defence Industrial Capability Plan* observes the close relationship between Australia's defence industry and the ADF's AI capabilities. In its recent update to the government's Sovereign Industry Capability Priorities, it included robotics, AI and autonomous systems.[2] The prominence of the defence industry in Australia is demonstrated by the range of new AWS projects being considered, including Athena AI's targeting decision support tool,[3] Boeing Defence Australia's Loyal Wingman,[4] DefendTex's Drone40 munition[5] and GaardTech's Jaeger-C uncrewed ground vehicle.[6]

The challenge is that defence industry, academia or research organisations are generally unaware of either the legal review obligation or how IHL regulates means and methods of warfare. The consequence is that they potentially develop AI technologies underpinning AWS functionality that is governed by international law without being aware of what the law requires.[7] This raises the risk that a state will study, develop, acquire or adopt an AWS capability that

1 M Verbruggen, *The Question of Swarms Control: Challenges to Ensuring Human Control over Military Swarms* (No 65, EU Non-Proliferation and Disarmament Consortium, December 2019) 5 <https://www.nonproliferation.eu/wp-content/uploads/2019/12/EUNPDC_no-65_031219.pdf>.

2 Australian Government, *Morrison Government supporting Australia' Sovereign Defence Industrial Capabilities* (Web Page, 26 August 2021) <https://www.minister.defence.gov.au/media-releases/2021-08-26/morrison-government-supporting-australia-sovereign-defence-industrial-capabilities>.

3 Athena AI Defence, *Trusted AI Decision Support* (Website) <https://athenadefence.ai/>.

4 H Dowling, 'Loyal Wingman Program Hits New Milestone with Two New Test Flights', *Australian Aviation* (online, 4 November 2021) <https://australianaviation.com.au/2021/11/loyal-wingman-program-hits-new-milestone-with-two-new-test-flights/>.

5 DefendTex's, *Unmanned Systems – Air* (Web Page) <https://www.defendtex.com/uav/>.

6 D Hambling, 'Australian Army Getting Bulletproof Swarming Attack Robots', *Forbes* (online, 4 November 2021) <https://www.forbes.com/sites/davidhambling/2021/11/04/australian-army-gets-bulletproof-attack-robots/?sh=7b44d129463b>.

7 Based on the author's personal experience with the Australian defence industry.

must be reprogrammed or redesigned to account for IHL rules and principles. This is potentially costly and time-consuming and may result in a legal review recommending that an AWS use is restricted to avoid IHL compliance risks.

A state may address this risk in two ways. First, as discussed in Chapter 4, where the state is sponsoring the research and development of an AWS the art 36 obligation exists as a matter of law. A state may provide the defence industry with training and advice on the IHL and international law obligations relevant to the capability. An example of such training is TASDCRC's Ethics Uplift Program, which provides art 36 awareness training for defence industry participating in their programs, which are developing autonomous systems for the ADF.[8]

Second, where defence industry research is not funded by the state, it is likely that the art 36 obligation does not arise as a matter of law. However, a state may still provide information and advice to defence small to medium enterprises (SMEs) as a matter of policy to ensure that the content and requirements of art 36 are understood. This information may be provided in several forms. For example, a state may develop a self-assessment mechanism to enable the defence industry to determine whether the subject of their research and development falls within the state's national definition of a 'new weapon, means or method of warfare'. This type of self-assessment is provided by the Australian Defence Export Control Office to enable defence industry or academia to self-assess whether a proposed export, supply, publishing or brokering activity is controlled by Australia's export control legislation.[9] In addition, where a particular technology or capability is dual-use or novel, a state may allow the defence industry to request a formal assessment of their technology to identify whether it is likely to be subject to a legal review.

1.1 *Early Legal Review Self-Assessment*

Defence industry may not understand when an art 36 legal review is required or the nature and scope of the legal review obligation. This is especially for those SMEs who seek to engage with a state's military acquisition for the first time. Consequently, many new capabilities are developed without an awareness of the potential client state's art 36 obligation or legal review requirements.

8 TASDCRC, *International Weapons Review delivering law for AI Basic Workshops part of TAS Ethics Uplift Program* (Web Page) <https://tasdcrc.com.au/international-weapons-review-delivering-law-for-ai-basics-workshops-part-of-the-tas-ethics-uplift-program/>. (Note: this training was not requested or endorsed by the Australian Department of Defence).

9 See Australian Government, Department of Defence, *Online DSGL Tool* (Website) <https://dsgl.defence.gov.au/pages/home.aspx>.

Unlike the development of new conventional weapons (e.g., a new rifle or munition), the engineers responsible for the design and programming of the AI will need to have a good understanding of the IHL rules and principles that regulate the new weapon's normal or expected use. They will need to anticipate the context in which an AWS may perform its functions. For example, if an AWS is designed to classify persons and objects on the battlefield, the AI programmers will need to understand the categories of persons and objects protected by IHL and the circumstances in which their status may change. It is, therefore, more important that the study and development be informed by the legal review requirements in the early stages of development. This differs from the traditional legal review.

There is arguably an increased need for awareness and communication between defence and defence industry SMEs conducting the research and development of military AWS technology. Austria has previously noted that:

> [a] detailed insight into legal reviews is provided, if ever, only years after a particular weapon system was considered for development. In the light of emerging technologies advancing at an unprecedented pace, such insights would be possibly shared at a stage when the information exchange might be too late to influence policy decisions in other states.[10]

1.1.1 Article 36 Self-Assessment

A self-assessment tool may assist SMEs, research or academic organisations undertaking research or developing military capabilities to (a) identify the need for, and (b) anticipate the requirements of a legal review in accordance with IHL. This includes dual-use technologies that may be modified by the military to assist or augment human decisions relating to the use of force in armed conflict.

The self-assessment tool should provide background information explaining why countries complete legal reviews during their capability acquisition processes and that a weapon is required to pass a legal review prior to being authorised for use in armed conflict. A weapon that does not pass a legal review will either not be procured or its use will be restricted.

The self-assessment tool may be in two parts. Part 1 should contain preliminary questions designed to determine whether the object falls within the

10 Austria, *Statement to the UN CCW Group of Governmental Experts re Guiding Principles* (1 September 2020) <https://documents.unoda.org/wp-content/uploads/2020/09/20200901-Austria.pdf>.

reviewing state's definition of a new weapon, means or method of warfare. For example, the self-assessment questions may include:

a. Is the capability designed to cause harm (including temporary pain), injury or death to persons in armed conflict (e.g., enemy soldiers)?
b. Is the capability designed to cause damage or destruction to or to neutralize objects in armed conflict, including by cyber means?
c. Is the capability designed to augment the operation of a weapon, including by aiding human decisions regarding the use of the weapon?
d. Is the capability an existing weapon that is being procured by a country for the first time?
e. Is the capability an existing weapon that has already been procured by a country but its use or effect has been modified?

A positive answer to any of these questions may indicate the need for a legal review in Part 2 that consists of a series of questions that focus on the legal issues covered in a legal review. For example, the following questions may be included in Part 2 of an on-line assessment tool:

a. What is the capability's normal or expected use? This is assessed at the time of review and is described by stating the design purpose and how it is planned to be used in accordance with military doctrine.
b. How does the capability achieve its intended effect(s)? The effects may be caused by inter alia: the transfer of kinetic or chemical energy (i.e., explosion, directed energy, cyber means or chemical).
c. What is the intended effect (e.g., to injure or kill a person, damage or destroy an object)?
d. Are any of the functions enabling the capability to achieve its intended effect autonomous or AI-enhanced?
e. Does the weapon employ any of the following harm mechanisms: poison, explosive projectiles under 400 grams, asphyxiating, poisonous or other gases, bullets that expand or flatten easily in the human body, biological or bacteriological methods of warfare, environmental modification techniques; non-detectable fragments; anti-personnel mines or booby traps; incendiary effects; blinding lasers; chemical weapons; anti-personnel mines; cluster munitions?
f. Is the capability of a nature to cause unnecessary suffering or superfluous injury to combatants?
g. Does the capability have indiscriminate effects (i.e., the weapon cannot be directed at a specific military target and so is of a nature to strike military targets and civilians and civilian objects without distinction) and/or its effects cannot be limited?

h. Does the capability cause widespread, long-term and severe damage to the natural environment?
i. Does the capability use decision support tools, including artificial intelligence? If it utilizes AI, what are the lines of legal accountability for the object's use? How is the object controlled? How is trust in the object achieved? What are the ongoing governance requirements and mechanisms?

A positive answer to any of these questions may help identify legal review issues and prompt an organisation researching or developing an AWS, or AWS technology, to consider the need mitigate a legal risk in their design or seek advice on the nature of the risk.

1.1.2 Legal Risk Identification and Mitigation Process

An alternate approach is to require SMEs developing an AWS or AWS technology for a state to undertake a risk-based assessment of IHL and international law obligations. One example is the risk-based approach proposed by the DSTG report titled *A Method for Ethical AI* (MEAID).[11]

MEAID introduces the concept of 'facets' of ethical AI in defence, consisting of responsibility, trust, governance, law and traceability, and provides corresponding questions for the defence industry to address in relation to each facet. This provides a broad framework for defining legal and ethical requirements by AI stakeholders.[12] It is designed to enable ethical risks associated with AI capabilities to be mitigated through industry-led system development, design and deployment. The facets are complemented by three tools:

d) ethical AI for defence checklist
e) ethical AI risk matrix
f) Legal and Ethical Assurance Program Plan (LEAPP).[13]

These risk assessment tools were designed to provide a pragmatic approach to legal and ethical risk identification and management. Importantly, the tools emphasise the important role of the defence industry in addressing legal and ethical risks in their design and development of any AWS capabilities before they enter the ADF's capability life cycle. They enable defence to assess and validate defence industry consideration of ethical risks. Where the AWS capability is higher risk the defence industry is required to identify strategies for

---

11 SK Devitt et al, *A Method for Ethical AI in Defence* (DSTG-TR-3786, Defence Science and Technology Group, February 2021) ('MEAID') <https://tasdcrc.com.au/a-method-for-ethical-ai-in-defence/>.

12 Ibid ii.

13 Ibid iii.

mitigating ethical risk in the form of a LEAPP to inform defence acquisition decisions and assessment.[14]

The DSTG approach enables SMEs to self-identify and mitigate legal risks relevant to art 36. The significance of this approach is that it enables defence to require a new AWS to be capable of art 36 compliance as a contractual prerequisite. This places the onus on developing organisations to understand the legal risks and identify design or functional measures to address the risks. This is prior to a new capability entering a defence capability acquisition process, which is when the traditional legal review obligation is often recognised to commence.

The reviewing state may create a legal review policy that it makes publicly available to enable SMEs seeking to contract with defence. This may be complemented by the creation of publicly funded corporate entities, such as the TASDCRC, to engage with and inform SMEs of defence's legal and ethical requirements.[15]

1.1.3 Legal Review Requirements as Design Criteria

An AWS designed to cause damage or harm should be capable of being legally reviewed. If some or all of an AWS' functionality is unable to be appropriately analysed during a legal review, its use is likely to be either limited or prohibited as the reviewing state is unable to ensure it can be used consistently with its IHL obligations. This will require that the effects of the AWS are sufficiently predictable or capable of being limited. As discussed in Chapter 7, aspects of the AWS design and function may also need to be identifiable, measurable and explainable/understandable to permit a legal review assessment of compliance with IHL.[16]

To this end, a state may include in a statement in the performance requirements for design that it be capable of legal review and use in compliance with IHL and international law. While this is arguably implicit, the legal review obligation may become a design criterion.

---

14 Ibid.

15 See Trusted Autonomous Systems Defence Cooperative Research Centre <https://tasdcrc.com.au/>.

16 A Michel, *The Black Box, Unlocked: Predictability and Understandability in Military AI* (UNIDIR, 2020) 9 <https://unidir.org/publication/black-box-unlocked>.

2 Stage 2 – Determinative Stage

The determinative stage reflects the traditional legal review process described in Chapter 5 in that it commences when a new weapon formally enters a defence capability acquisition process. This may be for the purpose of trialling a new capability[17] or to enable testing as part of an acquisition process. The purpose of the determinative stage is to fulfil the reviewing state's art 36 requirement of assessing and determining the legality of a new weapon, means or method of warfare before its use in armed conflict. The determinative stage will also include the functional review step proposed in Chapter 7. The determinative stage concludes with the introduction into service of the new weapon capability.

The traditional and functional reviews may be conducted in sequence or in parallel to one another. If the weapon component of the AWS was an existing weapon (e.g., a machine gun), the traditional legal review process is unlikely to be complicated. In contrast, depending on the proposed AWS' normal or expected use, the complexity of the anticipated operating environment and the level of human control over its operation, the functional review may require significant analysis.

This analysis may be informed by the information provided by the SME during the informative stage. If the reviewing state's defence acquisition contract requires art 36 risks to be identified and addressed by the SME as part of its tender proposal, the legal review process will consider this during the legal review analysis.

2.1 *Test and Evaluation during the Determinative Stage*

A test and evaluation process may be undertaken in progressive stages during the life of an AWS, commencing with an initial design, capability acquisition and operational evaluation.[18] However, the critical stage for testing and evaluation is the determinative stage as this will determine the legality of an AWS before its acquisition and use in armed conflict.

---

17 See, eg, The Defence Post, 'Australia to Acquire Bulletproof Jaeger-C Swarming Attach Robots' (online, 5 November 2021) <https://www.thedefensepost.com/2021/11/05/australia-jaeger-attack-robot/>.

18 A Backstrom and I Henderson, 'New Capabilities in Warfare: An Overview of Contemporary Technological Developments and the Associated Legal and Engineering Issues in Article 36 Weapons Reviews' (2012) 94 (886) *International Review of the Red Cross* 483, 509.

The requirements of a national test and evaluation may vary between states however their aim will be to confirm, independently of the manufacturer, the weapon meets the required performance and compliance standards. National policies may require specific testing regimes. For example, US Directive 3000.09 states that AWS 'will go through rigorous hardware and software V&V [verification and validation] and realistic system developmental and operational T&E [testing and evaluation], including analysis of unanticipated emergent behaviour resulting from the effects of complex operational environments'.[19]

There are a range of test and evaluation methods for autonomous systems that are designed for both individual subsystems and systems. For example, the University of York has developed a process called Assurance for Machine Learning for use in Autonomous Systems (AMLAS) that seeks to integrate safety assurance into the development of machine learning components.[20] This methodology involves a multi-stage, iterative process focusing on a safety case for each machine learning component. While focused expressly on safety, this process may be a basis for determining the legality of machine learning components. The AMLAS methodology follows the machine learning lifecycle stages through safety assurance scoping, safety requirements elicitation, data management, model learning, model verification and model redeployment.[21]

An alternate approach, focused on IHL compliance rather than safety cases has been proposed elsewhere by Reynoldson and myself.[22] Similar to AMLAS, this IHL 'testing and learning' loop approach focuses on individual AWS use cases or models centred on AWS functions that are governed by IHL. It involves an iterative process that includes a progression from an initial code review, to virtual or simulated testing and finally live or physical testing. This process is intended to enable the legal review both to inform the development of the AWS but also determine its ability to perform its autonomous functions in compliance with IHL. It is intended to enable 'the early identification of the limitations in the capabilities' LOAC decision-implementation ability, necessitating a modification of 'normal or expected use' or supporting the imposition of operational limitations if required.[23]

19 US Department of Defense, Directive Number 3000.09 *Autonomy in Weapon Systems* (21 November 2012, updated Jan 25, 2023) 4(a)(1) ('US Directive 3000.09').

20 See <https://www.york.ac.uk/assuring-autonomy/guidance/amlas/>.

21 Ibid.

22 D Copeland and L Reynoldson, 'How to Avoid "Summoning the Demon": The Weapons Review of Weapons with Artificial Intelligence' (2017) *Pandora's Box 97, 106*–8.

23 A Tattersall and D Copeland, 'Reviewing Autonomous Cyber Capabilities' in R Liivoja and A Väljataga (eds), *Autonomous Cyber Capabilities Under International Law* (NATO CCDOE Publications, 2021) 239–40.

This IHL 'testing and learning' loop approach has multiple aims: to identify IHL risks, elicit their requirements and assess the AWS' functions. Noting the high costs of live testing, AWS performance can be initially analysed through synthetic or virtual environment test scenarios designed to evaluate the weapon's ability to perform the aspects of its normal or expected use that are regulated by IHL rules. For example, if the weapon's AI is designed to classify persons and objects on the battlefield, the testing and learning loop would involve a series of virtual scenarios that would, for each IHL rule or principle, test the AWS' performance across a range of expected operating environments (open terrain, urban or forest) with different sensors (based on existing UAS platforms), from different operating profiles (near, far, high or low), in varying environmental conditions (day, night, rain, fog or smoke) with varying complicating factors (movement or concealment). There would be a series of scenarios to test each AWS weapon function that engages an IHL rule or principle across the technical, operational and environmental variations. This process primarily tests the AWS but could be used to train a human operator, using a human-machine interface, to properly control the AWS.

A series of IHL scenarios developed in a virtual environment will be necessary to assess the AWS' ability to perform lawfully and ethically its normal or expected use. Each scenario could include progressively more complex variations designed to test different operational, technical and environmental complexities. This could range from a baseline scenario to confirm that the AI can identify various categories of persons and objectives without variations to more complex, edge-case scenarios based on actual events in armed conflict or fictional situations.

There may be different purposes for the IHL AI Scenarios. An important purpose is to enable the test and assessment of an AWS' ability to lawfully perform its functions. This test and assessment process would, if conducted during the initial study and development of an AI system, enable AI engineers to identify performance issues and work to refine them. IHL scenarios may also be used to demonstrate the utility of an AWS (e.g., by recreating IHL incidents involving human error and demonstrating how an AWS system may have helped to avert the error); train human operators in the system and familiarise them with its capabilities; certify an AI system for progression through various stages of the capability life cycle; assess the ability of the AI system to operate on different weapon platforms; and retest an AI system that has changed its method of operation from that originally tested.

3 Stage 3 – Governance Stage

The governance stage commences following a legal review determination of legality and introduction into military service of an AWS. This stage recognises that, where an AWS uses neural networks capable of machine learning, the legal review determination is unlikely to remain reliable throughout the weapon's in-service life and that there is an ongoing requirement to determine the legality of an AWS.

As discussed in Chapters 4 and 6, a trigger for a further legal review during a weapon's in-service life may arise when there is material change to the weapon or to its method of use that was either not contemplated during the original legal review or that renders the weapon 'new' for the purpose of art 36 of AP 1. An AWS may be assessed as new because of a modification to the AWS' methods of use, either by its human operators or by the AWS itself (e.g., through machine learning); changes to the operating environment; or unexpected or unexplainable AWS actions, including system failures.

3.1 *Relationship between Article 36 and Article 82 of AP 1*

The potential for AWS with machine learning to act in new and unforeseen ways underlines the need for states to develop a system of ongoing legal reviews. This potential raises the need for both technical restraints preventing novel AWS actions and developing a complementary relationship between weapon reviews under art 36 and legal advice by legal officers deployed under art 82 of AP 1.

Article 82 requires:

> The High Contracting Parties at all times, and the Parties to the conflict in time of armed conflict, shall ensure that legal advisers are available, when necessary, to advise military commanders at the appropriate level on the application of the Conventions and this Protocol and on the appropriate instruction to be given to the armed forces on this subject.[24]

An important role of the legal adviser deployed under art 82 is to advise commanders, or 'those who plan or decide upon an attack', on the appropriate choice of weapons as a legal requirement when taking precautions in attack.[25]

24 *Protocol Additional to the Geneva Conventions of 12 August 1949, and relating to the Protection of Victims of International Armed Conflicts (Protocol I)*, opened for signature 8 June 1977, 1125 UNTS 3 (entered into force 7 December 1978) ('AP 1') art 82.

25 Ibid art 57(2)(a).

The legal advice includes whether a weapon is appropriate, 'with a view to avoiding, and in any event to minimizing incidental loss of civilian life, injury to civilians or damage to civilian objects'.[26] This nature of the advice is distinct from that given in compliance with art 36. Jevglevskaja observes that while, 'Article 36 is concerned with a generic legal review of a certain weapon system, article 82 covers operational legal advice on the use of that system in particular circumstances'.[27]

To give advice concerning the legality of an AWS, the legal adviser deployed in compliance with art 82 must be aware of the basis upon which a weapon passed a legal review, including any restrictions that were placed on its use.[28] This information will reside in a legal review report and be reflected in the weapon manual and training. To enable a further legal review, an AWS may be designed to restrict new, self-determined methods of use and alert its operators of the need for a further legal assessment. In the absence of such self-reporting, the weapon operator must be aware of the need to identify material changes to the method of use and seek further legal review analysis.

The development of AWS that autonomously perform targeting functions will require those who program and train the AI to anticipate the contextual use of the AWS. This will require the legal review to consider the AWS's ability to perform lawfully in these contextual circumstances. This arguably blurs the line between the determinations of legality under art 36 during the study, development, acquisition or adoption, and those under art 82 in armed conflict. To fulfil each obligation, legal advisers will need to assess the legality of AWS in a range of operational scenarios.

Additionally, an AWS deployed to new operating environments may require a process of operational certification to confirm its ability to operate in that environment. For example, an AWS designed to operate in an uncluttered environment such as an open field may be deployed to a complex operating environment such as a city. Similarly, an AWS trained to distinguish categories of persons using data from one environment may be deployed to an environment where the data differs from that in the new operating environment. For example, data used to train an AWS to recognise civilian objects common in one continent may differ dramatically from that used to recognise civilian objects in another continent. A reviewing state may require the legal adviser deployed in compliance with art 82 to certify an AWS for use in new operating

26 Ibid art 57(2)(a)(ii).

27 N Jevglevskaja, *International Law and Weapons Review: Emerging Military Technology under the Laws of Armed Conflict* (Cambridge University Press, 2021) 134.

28 Ibid 199.

environments or circumstances.[29] This requirement is likely to be an extension of the art 36 obligation to re-review a weapon that is subject to a material modification and, therefore, is 'new' for the purpose of art 36.

The governance stage of an AWS legal review will require legal advisers deployed under art 82 of AP 1 to participate in the legal review process. As noted in Chapter 6, a legal adviser deployed under art 82 will need to be familiar with the legal review of the AWS to understand how the determination of legality was made. This includes understanding the autonomous functions and relevant IHL, the required standard of legal compliance, the required level of human control, the anticipated operating environment(s), the legal risks identified in its use and lines of human accountability. The legal adviser should also know whether the legal review recommended any restrictions on the AWS use.

This knowledge will enable the legal adviser to perform several important legal review governance roles. These roles include certifying the AWS for use in new operating environments; monitoring the AWS for ongoing use in compliance with IHL; and identifying circumstances where further legal review is required, either locally or at the strategic level by legal reviewers under art 36.

3.2 *Environmental and Operational Certification*

Unlike a conventional weapon, an AWS may require in-service T&E to ensure that it can perform lawfully within a new operating environment, for example, if a military force deploys to a new region or environment for the first time. This may be for technical or software reasons such as:

a. An AWS' neural network is programmed and trained to distinguish persons using data representing a particular cultural group that differs from that of the persons in a new operating environment.
b. The AWS is designed to target military objectives in a conflict against a conventional adversary with unique military equipment (e.g., tanks and artillery) but is deployed to a conflict environment against an unconventional adversary which utilises civilian objects.
c. An AWS is deployed in a coalition environment that utilises different sensors to those normally deployed with the AWS.

It will be good practice for a state to certify an AWS as capable of lawful use in each new operating environment. An initial environmental certification may be complemented by periodic tests and evaluations during the deployment or following specific events such as software upgrades or following unexpected AWS actions. The certification process may be completed in conjunction

29 Tattersall and Copeland (n 23) 256.

with military training or rehearsals and require input from multidisciplinary experts.

The result of the certification may reflect the outcomes of a legal review, including restrictions on the AWS functions or use. Where legal risks are identified, a legal adviser deployed under art 82 of AP 1 may recommend to the military commander that the use of the AWS is restricted to those which can be confidently assessed as lawful. Alternatively, the legal adviser may recommend that the level of human control be increased for specific AWS functions. This may mitigate legal risks associated with AWS functions governed by IHL.

3.3 *Functional Re-review*

Where there is change to either the use or operation of an in-service AWS, a legal adviser may recommend a re-review of the AWS on the basis that the change renders the AWS 'new' for the purpose of art 36 of AP 1. The re-review will enable a formal assessment of whether the change alters the original determination of legality, including the ongoing relevance of control measures or restrictions.

The re-review may be undertaken locally by the art 82 legal adviser or by those responsible for legal reviews at the national level. The subject of the re-review will determine the appropriate level to complete the re-review. If a minor change to the AWS method of use is proposed, an art 82 legal adviser may complete the re-review and advise the art 36 legal advisers of the outcome of the review. Alternatively, if a new machine learning initiated method of use is identified, either because the AWS self-identified the change in its operations or because the change was observed by the AWS' operators, a strategic-level review and technical inquiry will be necessary to inform further legal analysis.

The starting point for the re-review will be the existing legal review report. This must be made available to allow a review of the report's findings and recommendations. If the original legal review report contains recommendations against the new use, the basis for this recommendation must be reconsidered. If technical limitations existed at the time of the original report that precluded certain methods of use, they may have been resolved by a technical advancement. The re-review will likely focus only on those aspects of the report that relate to the AWS changes. The focus of the re-review will be the rules governing IHL methods of warfare, which will require consideration of the elements of the functional review.

While a re-review is being completed, an art 82 legal adviser may assess the legal risk of the AWS performing the new method of use and, if necessary, recommend to the commander that such use is restricted until the review is completed. Alternatively, the legal adviser may recommend that the level of human control over the AWS performing the new capability is raised to reduce the legal risk of an AWS error.

4 Conclusion

The challenges and risks raised by the use of AWS in armed conflict will require additional national governance measures. The art 36 legal review obligation is an important component of a national governance framework that can be adapted to meet legal challenges and national policy requirements. These are not static issues and so this chapter proposed an expanded approach to the traditional legal review process to determine lawful use of AWS throughout its lifecycle.

An expanded legal review process is intended to inform the early development, to determine the legality prior to use and the govern the ongoing lawful use of AWS in armed conflict. The first stage is intended to be an informative stage to ensure those primarily undertaking the research and development of AWS, namely defence industry, academia and research organisations, understand a state's art 36 obligation or international law obligations. The informative stage includes a process of self-assessment to help identify whether the research and development is likely to fall within the art 36 obligation and identify initial legal risks. It enables those responsible for early design and development to understand a state's legal obligations and identify legal and other risks that AWS may raise. The determinative stage commences when a new AWS formally enters a military acquisition process and includes the traditional legal review process and the new functional review step (as proposed in this book) to provide government decision makers with a determination of an AWS legality prior to its introduction into service and use in armed conflict. Finally, the governance stage recognises the need to maintain a process of ongoing governance to ensure that machine learning, environmental conditions and operational circumstances do not affect the AWS' ability to perform its functions in compliance with IHL. The governance stage emphasises the relationship between art 36 and art 82 of AP I and includes a process of environmental certification to ensure the AWS can lawfully perform its normal or expected use in new operational environments. It also includes a functional re-review where there a material changes to the AWS are identified, either through updates to software or programming changes resulting from machine learning.

CHAPTER 9

Conclusions and Findings

The use of AWS in armed conflict is no longer a remote possibility. As evidenced by the UN Report of Experts on Libya[1] and by the ongoing conflicts in Ukraine[2] and Gaza[3] their use is now a reality. Beyond these conflicts, states including the US,[4] Russia,[5] Israel,[6] South Korea[7] and Turkey[8] all possess weapons with varying degrees of autonomy, while Australia, the UK and China are heavily investing in AWS development.[9]

Against this background, the prospects for new international law regulating the use of AWS are difficult to predict.[10] Consensus among states party to the CCW on the need for new law remains elusive and progress in this forum is likely to remain limited while Russia's invasion of Ukraine continues.[11] Although the

---

1 United Nations, *Final Report of the Panel of Experts on Libya Established Pursuant to Security Council Resolution 1972*, UN Doc S/2021/229 (2011) [63] ('UN Report on Libya').

2 G Allen, *Russia Probably Has Not Used AI-Enabled Weapons in Ukraine, But That Could Change* (Web Page, Centre for Strategic & International Studies, 26 May 2022) <https://www.csis.org/analysis/russia-probably-has-not-used-ai-enabled-weapons-ukraine-could-change>.

3 A Safadi, *Israel's AI can produce 100 bombing targets a day in Gaza. Is this the future of war?* (8 December 2023, The Conversation Website), https://theconversation.com/israels-ai-can-produce-100-bombing-targets-a-day-in-gaza-is-this-the-future-of-war-219302>.

4 Raytheon Missiles and Defence, *Phalanx Close In Weapon System* (Web Page) <https://www.raytheonmissilesanddefense.com/capabilities/products/phalanx-close-in-weapon-system>.

5 Y Tadjdeh, 'Algorithmic Warfare: Russia Expanding Fleet of AI-Enabled Weapons', *National Defense* (online, 20 July 2020) <https://www.nationaldefensemagazine.org/articles/2021/7/20/russia-expanding-fleet-of-ai-enabled-weapons>.

6 IAI, *IAI Harpy* (Website) <https://www.iai.co.il/p/harpy>.

7 A Velez-Green, 'The Foreign Policy Essay: The South Korean Sentry – A "Killer Robot" to Prevent War', *Lawfare Blog* (Blog Post, 1 March 2015) <https://www.lawfareblog.com/foreign-policy-essay-south-korean-sentry%E2%80%94-killer-robot-prevent-war>.

8 STM, *Kargu, Combat Proven Rotary Wing Loitering System* (Web Page) <https://www.stm.com.tr/en/kargu-autonomous-tactical-multi-rotor-attack-uav>.

9 Human Rights Watch, *Stopping Killer Robots: Country Positions on Banning Fully Autonomous Weapon Systems and Retaining Human Control* (10 August 2020) <https://www.hrw.org/report/2020/08/10/stopping-killer-robots/country-positions-banning-fully-autonomous-weapons-and#_ftn10>.

10 F Sauer, 'Stepping Back from the Brink: Why Multilateral Regulation of Autonomy in Weapon Systems is Difficult, Imperative and Feasible' (2020) 102(913) *International Review of the Red Cross* 235, 236.

11 A Saliba and L Barbosa, '"Like a Dog Chasing Its Tail": Group of Governmental Experts on Lethal Autonomous Weapons', *International Law Agendas* (Blog Post, 25 March 2022) <http://ila-brasil.org.br/blog/like-a-dog-chasing-its-tail/>.

 | DOI:10.1163/9789004707047_012

UN GGE Guiding Principles[12] provide a useful framework and clarification of the application of existing IHL principles, they are non-binding and, therefore, do not create new legal obligations beyond the existing rules of IHL.

Legal reviews play an important role in ensuring that states determine whether their use of AWS in armed conflict is in compliance with their international law obligations. The characteristics of AWS, however, raises numerous challenges for states to address in practice.

The aim of this book was to analyse how a state party to AP 1 can fulfil its art 36 legal review obligation to determine the legality of AWS. To achieve this aim, the book considered two broad questions. First, Part 1 addressed the fundamental question of whether the traditional legal review process is sufficient to determine the legality of AWS? Second, having concluded that the traditional legal review is not sufficient, Part 2 proposed how a state may conduct a legal review to determine the legality of an AWS?

The key conclusions of this book are as follows: First, there is limited academic discourse or evidence of state practice relating to the legal review of AWS. Chapter 2 analysed academic literature and state policy across three broad periods. The initial period, referred to as the ICRC Period, focused on the ICRC's efforts to encourage states to undertake legal reviews. This period produced several important scholarly works that were influential in defining the scope of the legal review obligation including the ICRC Guide.[13] Some of the interpretations of art 36 however are opaque and challengeable, as explained in Chapter 4. The second period, referred to the LAWS Period, coincided with the informal meetings of states party to the CCW in the UN. This period was characterised by the increased recognition of the importance of legal reviews and a recognition of the challenges that autonomy in weapons present to the conduct of legal review. Non-government organisation including SIPRI[14] and

12 *Guiding Principles affirmed by the Group of Governmental Experts on Emerging Technologies in the Area of Lethal Autonomous Weapons System*, Annex III to the Final Report of the Meeting of the High Contracting Parties to the Convention on Prohibitions or Restrictions on the Use of Certain Conventional Weapons Which May be Deemed to be Excessively Injurious or to Have Indiscriminate Effects, UN Doc CCW/MSP/2019/9 (13 December 2019) ('UN GGE Guiding Principles').

13 ICRC, *A Guide to the Weapons Review of New Weapons, Means and Methods of Warfare: Measures to Implement Article 36 of Additional Protocol I of 1977* (2006) 24, fn 82 ('ICRC Guide').

14 See V Boulanin, 'Implementing Article 36 Weapons Reviews in the Light of Increasing Autonomy in Weapon Systems' (November 2015) *SIPRI Insights on Peace and Security* 2015/1 ('2015 Report'); V Boulanin and M Verbruggen, 'Article 36: Dealing with the Challenges Posed by Emerging Technologies' (December 2017), *Stockholm International Peace and Research Institute* ('SIPRI 2017 Report').

the ICRC played an important role in informing the debate; however it did not extend it beyond identifying the challenges. Finally, the CCW GGE Period saw in increase in scholarly work by Liivoja and Väljataga[15] and Jevglevskaja[16] on the legal review of AWS and the identification of 11 Guiding Principles[17] by states party to the CCW. The literature review demonstrates that, while commentary recognises the importance and challenges associated with the legal review of AWS, it does not assess whether the traditional legal review process is sufficient to determine the legality of AWS or address how a state can determine the legality of AWS. This gap in knowledge is an underlying reason for this book.

The second key conclusion is that, in the absence of international law specifically regulating AWS, IHL rules governing the lawful use of a weapon are critical to determining the legality of AWS. Chapter 3 analyses how international law regulates a state's possession and use of AWS. It identifies the range of political and humanitarian objectives the law, referred to as 'weapons law' seeks to achieve in both peace time and during armed conflict. A survey of the specific and general international law prohibitions and restrictions reveals how weapons law primarily determines the legality of weapons *per se* and less concerned with the legality of a specific weapon use. Chapter 3 also emphasises that weapons law does not expressly prohibit or restrict autonomy in weapons. This highlights the importance of legal reviews to ensure the development and use of AWS is in compliance with a state's international law obligations. The chapter also argues that the most significant risk in the legality of AWS relates to its use. Much of the law governing the lawful use of weapons resides in the body of IHL referred to as 'targeting law' which, while consistent with, is distinct from, weapons law and is found predominately in Part IV of AP I.

The third key conclusion is that, in addition to legal challenges, AWS raise ethical, moral and operational challenges that states may address through national policy and consider during a legal review. Chapter 3 also identified the Martens clause and its role in considering national AWS policy in the conduct of a legal review. While the Martens clause is not determinative of legality, it invites consideration of existing law in the context of 'the principles of humanity' and 'dictates of public conscience'. A state may include consideration of national policy addressing quasi-legal requirement including the level

15 R Liivoja and A Väljataga (eds), *Autonomous Cyber Capabilities Under International Law* (NATO CCDOE Publications, 2021).

16 N Jevglevskaja, *International Law and Weapons Review: Emerging Military Technology under the Laws of Armed Conflict* (Cambridge University Press, 2021).

17 UN GGE Guiding Principles (n 12).

of human control, standards of trust, reliability, predictability and explainability and the influence of soft law.

The fourth key conclusion is that the traditional interpretations of the art 36 obligation are challenged by the use of autonomy in weapons. In analysing the operative terms of art 36 of AP 1, Chapter 4 observes that several traditional interpretations are identified that define the scope and content of the traditional legal review process. These interpretations originate from the ICRC's Commentary on AP 1 and the academic literature identified in Chapter 2. These interpretations of the art 36's operative terms including 'study, development, acquisition or adoption', 'new' and 'in some or all circumstances' are challenged in the context of AWS. The traditional interpretations may be regarded as too narrow in application and so require re-interpretation to allow a state to consider the increased role of defence industry and research organisations, the potential for AWS capable of machine learning to change method of use and therefore become 'new', and finally the possibility of AWS performing normal or expected uses in unpredictable and unintended ways.

The fifth key conclusion is that there is a dichotomy in the traditional legal review analysis between weapons law, concerned with the legality of a weapon per se, and targeting law which is concerned with the lawful use of weapons in specific circumstances. Chapter 5 analyses what is referred to as the 'traditional legal review' process. It notes that, while states are not required to adopt a particular process, it is possible to identify the content of the traditional legal review process and its application in four common steps. The traditional legal review analysis focusses primarily on a weapon's compliance with weapons law and does not consider compliance with targeting law. This legal review dichotomy between weapons law and targeting law supports the argument that the traditional legal review process is insufficient to determine the legality of AWS as it presumes, rather than determines, that the weapon will be used lawfully in armed conflict. If an AWS is designed to perform functions that are governed by IHL the AWS' ability to perform these functions in compliance with targeting law must be determined during a legal review.

The sixth key finding is that the legal review of AWS raises interpretive and methodological challenges that need to be addressed via a revised legal review process. Chapter 6 identifies unique challenges raised by autonomy in weapons. This includes whether the legal review needs to identify lines of human responsibility and what are the appropriate standards to determine the legality of AWS. These interpretative challenges are parallel to methodological challenges relating to when and how a legal review needs to be conducted. As much of the technology enabling AWS is developed by private industry and research organisations, the legal review needs to take this into account to ensure early development considers states' art 36 and international law obligations. Furthermore, the prospect of AWS being capable of machine learning means that the legal review obligation must enable ongoing consideration of legality during the AWS in-service life. Together, these findings suggest a legal review of an AWS must expand beyond the traditional process so occur on an ongoing basis during the AWS lifecycle.

The seventh conclusion and first key recommendation advocated by this book is that an additional 'functional review' step is required in the legal review of AWS to determine the AWS' ability to operate in compliance with IHL, including targeting law. Chapter 7 proposes the functional review step for AWS to complement the four steps of the traditional legal review process and requires additional elements designed to identify the specific IHL rules governing the AWS functions and assess its ability to lawfully perform its functions in a range of operational and environmental circumstances. The functional step also considers the application of national policies addressing the issues of human control, lines of human responsibility and trust in the AWS.

The final conclusion and second key recommended solution advocated by this book is that the legal review process for an AWS should be expanded beyond the military acquisition process to include informing early study and development, determining the legality prior to acquisition and governing its ongoing legality during its in-service use. Chapter 8 finalises the book by proposing an expanded legal review process for AWS that occurs over the entire lifecycle. It argues that an expanded approach is necessary to address the different risks and challenges that arise during the AWS lifecycle. The expanded process will consist of three stages: first, an informative stage, commencing during early AWS research and development, providing those responsible for the design and development of AWS with necessary IHL and art 36 information. This will include defence industry and is intended to ensure that early AWS development, particularly the design, programming and training of its AI, considers the state's IHL obligations and ensures the AWS is capable of being the subject of a legal review. The second stage is a determinative stage, coinciding with a state's capability acquisition process, during which the legality of the AWS is assessed through both the traditional legal review process and the functional review step. These may occur separately or in parallel. The outcome of the determinative stage is a legal review advice determining the legality of the AWS and making recommendations concerning its use in armed conflict. Finally, a new governance stage must commence when the AWS is introduced into service and continues until its decommissioning. This stage links the art 36 obligation with the role of legal advisers deployed to advise military commanders under art 82 of AP 1. The purpose of the governance stage is to maintain ongoing legal review oversight of the AWS legality, including the environmental and operational certification of AWS on deployment into new theatres.

The ultimate conclusion of this book is that the traditional legal review process is not sufficient to determine the legality of AWS as it does not determine the legality of AWS functions governed by IHL or consider the other quasi-legal issues raised by AWS. In light of this conclusion the book proposes an expanded approach to the legal review of AWS. This expanded approach consists of a functional review step in addition to the traditional legal review process, and an expanded scope of the legal review process that spans the entire lifecycle of the weapon.

The development and use of AWS are still relatively new. There remains a clear need for states to consider the creation of specific treaty law prohibiting or regulating the possession and use of AWS. Regardless of the existence of new law, however legal reviews play an important role in ensuring their lawful use. As AWS technology develops, so will the legal review process.

Bibliography

Articles, Books, Reports

Abbass, H, J Scholz and D Reid (eds), *Foundations of Trusted Autonomy* (Springer Open Press, 2018).

Anderson, K, D Reisner and M Waxman, 'Adapting the Law of Armed Conflict to Autonomous Weapon Systems' (2014) 90 *International Law Studies* 386.

Backstrom, A and I Henderson, 'New Capabilities in Warfare: An Overview of Contemporary Technological Developments and the Associated Legal and Engineering Issues in Article 36 Legal reviews' (2012) 94 (886) *International Review of the Red Cross* 483.

Bellinger, JB and WJ Hayes, 'A US Government Response to the International Committee of the Red Cross Study on Customary International Humanitarian Law' (2007) 89 *International Review of the Red Cross* 443.

Biller, J and M Schmitt, 'Classification of Cyber Capabilities and Operations as Weapons, Means or Methods of Warfare' (2019) 95 *International Law Studies* 179.

Biontino, M, *Summary of Technical Issues, CCW Expert Meeting Lethal Autonomous Weapons Systems* (13–16 May 2014).

Blake, D and J Imburgia, '"Bloodless Weapons"? The Need to Conduct Legal reviews of Certain Capabilities and the Implications of Defining them as "Weapons" (2010) 66 The Air Force Law Review 157, 166.

Blix, H, 'Means and Methods of Combat' in UNESCO (ed), *International Dimensions of Humanitarian Law* (Henry Dunant Institute, 1988).

Boothby, W, 'Biometrics' in W Boothby (ed), *New Technologies and the Law in War and Peace* (Cambridge University Press, 2018).

Boothby, W, *Conflict Law: The Influence of New Weapons Technology, Human Rights and Emerging Actors* (T.M.C. Asser Press, 2014).

Boothby, W, *Weapons and the Law of Armed Conflict* (Oxford University Press, 2009).

Boothby, W, *Weapons and the Law of Armed Conflict* (Oxford University Press, 2nd ed, 2016).

Bothe, M, K Partsch and W Solf, *New Rules for Victims of Armed Conflicts: Commentary on the Two 1977 Protocols Additional to the Geneva Conventions of 1949* (Martinus Nijhoff Publishers, 1982).

Boulanin, V and M Verbruggen, *Article 36: Dealing with the Challenges Posed by Emerging Technologies* (Stockholm International Peace and Research Institute, 2017).

Boulanin, V et al, *Limits on Autonomy in Weapon Systems: Identifying Practical Elements of Human Control* (Stockholm International Peace Research Institute, 2020).

Boulanin, V, 'Implementing Article 36 Legal reviews in the Light of Increasing Autonomy in Weapon Systems' (November 2015) *SIPRI Insights on Peace and Security* 2015/1.

Boulanin, V, L Bruun and N Goussac, *Autonomous Weapon Systems and International Humanitarian Law: Identifying Limits and the Required Type and Degree of Human–Machine Interaction* (Stockholm International Peace Research Institute, 2021).

Boyd, J, *A Discourse on Winning and Losing* (Air University Press, 2018).

Casey-Maslen, S (ed), *Weapons Under International Human Rights Law* (Cambridge University Press, 2014).

Cassese, A, 'Weapons Causing Unnecessary Suffering: Are They Prohibited?' (1975) 58 *Rivista di Diritto Internazionale* 12.

Clapham, A and P Gaeta (eds), *The Oxford Handbook of International Law in Armed Conflict* (Oxford University Press, 2018).

Copeland, D and L Reynoldson, 'How to Avoid "Summoning the Demon": The Legal review of Weapons with Artificial Intelligence' (2017) *Pandora's Box* 97.

Copeland, D, 'Legal Review of New Technology Weapons' in Hitoshi Nasu and Robert McLaughlin (eds), *New Technologies and the Law of Armed Conflict* (Springer, 2014).

Copeland, D, R Liivoja and L Sanders, 'The Utility of Legal reviews in Addressing Concerns Raised by Autonomous Weapon Systems' *Journal of Conflict and Security Law*.

Corn, G, 'Mixing Apples and Hand Grenades: The Logical Limit of Applying Human Rights Norms to Armed Conflict' (2010) 1(1) *Journal of International Humanitarian Legal Studies* 52.

Crawford, E, *Non-Binding Norms in International Humanitarian Law* (Oxford University Press, 2021).

Cronan, P et al, 'Operations Bastille and Falconer: Legal Support to Commanders' (2011) 184 *Australian Defence Force Journal* 33.

Crootof, Rebecca, 'A Meaningful Floor for "Meaningful Human Control"' (2015) 30 *Temple International & Comparative Law Journal* 3.

Daoust, I, R Coupland and R Ishoey, 'New Wars, New Weapons? The Obligation of States to Assess the Legality of Means and Methods of Warfare' (2002) 84(846) *International Review of the Red Cross* 345.

Defence Advanced Research Projects Agency, *Creating Technology Breakthroughs and New Capabilities for National Security* (August 2019) <https://www.darpa.mil/attachments/DARPA-2019-framework.pdf>.

Defence Science Board Task Force, *Report on Munitions Systems Reliability* (US Department of Defense, September 2005) <https://permanent.fdlp.gov/lps72288/ADA441959.pdf>.

Devitt, SK and D Copeland, 'Australia's Approach to AI Governance in Security and Defence' in M Raska, Z Stanley-Lockman and R Bitzinger (eds), *AI Governance for National Security and Defence: Assessing Military AI Strategic Perspectives* (Routledge, 2022).

Devitt, SK et al, *A Method for Ethical AI in Defence* (DSTG-TR-3786, Defence Science and Technology Group, February 2021).

Dinstein, Y, *The Conduct of Hostilities under the Law of International Armed Conflict* (Cambridge University Press, 2nd ed, 2010).

Doswald-Beck, L, *San Remo Manual on International Law Applicable to Armed Conflicts at Sea* (Cambridge University Press, 1995).

Dunant, H, *A Memory of Solferino* (ICRC Geneva, 2002).

Ekelhof, Merel, 'Moving Beyond Semantics on Autonomous Weapons: Meaningful Human Control in Operation' (2019) 10(3) *Global Policy* 343

Farrant, J and Ford, C, 'Autonomous Weapons and Legal reviews: The UK Second International Legal review Forum' (2017) 93 *International Law Studies* 389 <https://digital-commons.usnwc.edu/cgi/viewcontent.cgi?article=1710&context=ils>.

Fry, J, 'Contextualised Legal reviews for Means and Methods of Warfare: Cave Combat and IHL' (2006) 44 *Columbia Journal of Transnational Law* 453.

Galliott, J, JD Ohlin and D MacIntosh (eds), *Lethal Autonomous Weapons: Re-Examining the Law and Ethics of Robotic Warfare* (Oxford University Press, 2021).

Garner, J, *International Law and the World War* (Longmans, Green and Co, 1920).

Goussac, N, N Jevglevskaja, R Liivoja, and L Sanders, (2023). *Enhancing the Legal Review of Autonomous Weapon Systems: Report of an Expert Meeting.* Brisbane, QLD Australia: Law and the Future of War Research Group, TC Beirne School of Law, The University of Queensland <https://espace.library.uq.edu.au/view/UQ:2bbfd31>.

Greenwood, C, 'The Law of Weaponry at the Start of the New Millennium' in Michael N Schmitt and Leslie C Green (eds), *The Law of Armed Conflict: Into the New Millennium* (U.S. Naval War College, 1999).

Hagstrom, M, 'Complex Critical Systems: Can LAWS be Fielded?' in Robin Geiss and Henning Lahman (eds), *Lethal Autonomous Weapon Systems: Technology, Definition, Ethics, Law & Security* (Federal Foreign Office, 2016).

Haines, S, 'The Developing Law of Weapons: Humanity, Distinction, and Precautions in Attack' in Andrew Clapham and Paola Gaeta (eds), *The Oxford Handbook of International Law in Armed Conflict* (Oxford University Press, 2018).

Hays Parks, W, 'Conventional Weapons and Legal reviews' (2005) 8 *Yearbook of International Humanitarian Law* 55.

Hays Parks, W, 'Joint Service Combat Shotgun Program' (1997) 10 *Army Law Review* 16.

Hays Parks, W, 'Means and Methods of Warfare, Symposium in Honour of Edward R Cummings' (2006) 38 *George Washington International Law Review* 511.

Henckaerts, JM and L Doswald-Becks, *Customary International Humanitarian Law* (Cambridge University Press, 2005).

Henderson, I, *The Contemporary Law of Targeting* (Martinus Nijhoff Publishers, 2009).

Heyns, C, *Report of the Special Rapporteur on Extrajudicial, Summary or Arbitrary Executions*, UN General Assembly, Human Rights Council, A/HRC/23/47 (9 April 2013).

Human Rights Watch and the International Human Rights Clinic, *Mind the Gap: The Lack of Accountability for Killer Robots* (Human Rights Watch, 2015).

Human Rights Watch, *Making the Case: The Dangers of Killer Robots and the Need for a Preemptive Ban* (2016).

Human Rights Watch, *Making the Case: The Dangers of Killer Robots and the Need for a Preemptive Ban* (2016).

Human Rights Watch, *Stopping Killer Robots: Country Positions on Banning Fully Autonomous Weapon Systems and Retaining Human Control* (10 August 2020) <https://www.hrw.org/report/2020/08/10/stopping-killer-robots/country-positions-banning-fully-autonomous-weapons-and#_ftn10>.

International Committee of the Red Cross, 'ICRC Expert Meeting on Legal reviews of Weapons and the SIrUS Project' (2001) 83(842) *International Review of the Red Cross* 539, <https://international-review.icrc.org/sites/default/files/S156077550010584Xa.pdf>.

International Committee of the Red Cross, *A Guide to the Legal review of New Weapon Means and Methods of Warfare: Measures to Implement Article 36 of Additional Protocol I of 1977* (ICRC, January 2006).

International Committee of the Red Cross, *Report on the ICRC Expert Meeting on Autonomous Weapon Systems: Technical, Military, Legal and Humanitarian Aspects*, 26–28 March 2014, Geneva (9 May 2014) <https://www.icrc.org/en/document/report-icrc-meeting-autonomous-weapon-systems-26-28-march-2014>.

International Human Rights Clinic and Human Rights Watch, *Losing Humanity: The Case Against Killer Robots* (IHRC and HRW, 2012) <https://www.hrw.org/report/2012/11/19/losing-humanity/case-against-killer-robots>.

International Law Commission, 'Draft Articles on State Responsibility' in *Report of the International Law Commission on the Work of its 52nd Session*, UN Doc A/55/10 (2000).

Jensen, E, 'The (Erroneous) Requirement for Human Judgment (and Error) in the Law of Armed Conflict' (2020) 96 *International Law Studies* 26.

Jevglevskaja, N, 'Legal review Obligation Under Customary International Law' (2018) 94 *International Laws Studies* 186.

Jevglevskaja, N, *International Law and Legal review: Emerging Military Technology under the Laws of Armed Conflict* (Cambridge University Press, 2021).

Kraska, J and Pedrozo, R. A. *Disruptive Technology and the Law of Naval Warfare* (2022) Oxford University Press.

Kruppy, Tetyana, 'Of Souls, Spirits and Ghosts: Transporting the Application of the Rules of Targeting to Lethal Autonomous Robots' (2015) 16 *Melbourne Journal of International Law* 1.

Lawand, K, 'Reviewing the Legality of New Weapons, Means and Methods of Warfare' (2006) 88(864) *International Review of the Red Cross* 925.

Letendre, Lindell A, 'Lethal Autonomous Weapon Systems: Translating Legal Jargon for Engineers' in *2016 International Conference on Unmanned Aircraft Systems* (2016).

Lewis, L, *Redefining Human Control: Lessons from the Battlefield for Autonomous Weapons* (Centre for Autonomy and AI, 2018).

Liivoja, R and A Väljataga (eds), *Autonomous Cyber Capabilities Under International Law* (NATO CCDOE Publications, 2021) <https://ccdcoe.org/uploads/2021/05/Autonomous_Cyber_Capabilities_210525.pdf>.

Liivoja, R and L Chircop, 'Enhanced Warfighters, Weapons, Means or Methods of Warfare?' (2018) 94 *International Law Studies* 161.

Liivoja, R, 'Protecting Warfighters from Superfluous Injury and Unnecessary Suffering' in Matt Killingsworth (ed), *Who Do the Laws of War Protect? Civility, Barbarity and the Evolution of International Humanitarian Law* (Cambridge University Press, forthcoming).

Massingham, E and A McConnachie (eds), *Ensuring Respect for International Humanitarian Law* (Routledge Press, 2020).

Mauri, Diego, *Autonomous Weapon Systems and the Protection of the Human Person: An International Law Analysis* (Edward Elgar Publishing, 2022).

McClelland, J, 'The Legal review of Weapons under Article 36 of Additional Protocol 1' (2003) 850 *International Review of the Red Cross* 397.

McFarland, T and T McCormack, 'Mind the Gap: Can Developers of Autonomous Weapon Systems be Liable for War Crimes?' (2014) 90 *International Law Studies* 361.

McFarland, T, *Autonomous Weapon Systems and the Law of Armed Conflict: Compatibility with International Humanitarian Law* (Cambridge University Press, 2020).

Meier, M.W. 'Lethal Autonomous Weapons Systems (LAWS): Conducting a Comprehensive Legal review (2016) 30, *Temple International and Comparative Law Journal* 1, 119–132.

Michel, A, *The Black Box, Unlocked: Predictability and Understandability in Military AI* (UNIDIR, 2020) <https://unidir.org/publication/black-box-unlocked>.

Moy, G, et al, *Technical Report: Recent Advances in Artificial Intelligence and Their Impact on Defence* (Defence Science and Technology Group, May 2020) <https://www.dst.defence.gov.au/publication/recent-advances-artificial-intelligence-and-their-impact-defence>.

Nasu, H and R McLaughlin (eds), *New Technologies and the Law of Armed Conflict* (TMC Asser Press, 2014).

Nasu, H, 'Artificial Intelligence and the Obligation to Respect and to Ensure Respect for International Humanitarian Law' in Eve Massingham and Annabel McConnachie (eds), *Ensuring Respect for International Humanitarian Law* (Routledge Press, 2020).

NATO, *Arms Control, Disarmament and Non-proliferation in NATO* (6 April 2022).

NSW Coroner, *Report into the Inquest into the Deaths Arising from the Lindt Café Siege* (24 May 2017) <https://www.lindtinquest.justice.nsw.gov.au/Pages/Findings.aspx>.

Oswald, B and R. McLaughlin, 'Wilful Killing During Armed Conflict: Is There a Defence of Proportionality in Australia?' (2007) *University of Melbourne Legal Studies Research Paper No. 267*, Vol. 18, No. 1, 1–41.

Pictet, J, 'The New Geneva Conventions for the Protection of War Victims' (1951) 45(3) *The American Journal of International Law* 462.

Pilloud, C, et al (eds), *Commentary on the Additional Protocols of 8 June 1977 to the Geneva Conventions of 12 August 1949* (Martinus Nijhoff, 1987).

Poitras, R, 'Article 36 Legal review & Autonomous Weapons Systems: Supporting an International Review Standard' (2018) 34(2) *American University International Law Review*.

Program on Humanitarian Policy and Conflict Research at Harvard University, *HPRC Manual on International Law Applicable to Air and Missile Warfare* (Program on Humanitarian Policy and Conflict Research, 2010).

Puscas, I, *Human–Machine Interfaces in Autonomous Weapon Systems: Considerations for Human Control* (United Nations Institute for Disarmament Research, 2022).

Ritter, S et al, 'Cognitive Psychology for Deep Neural Networks: A Shape Bias Case Study' (Conference Paper, 34th International Conference on Machine Learning, 29 June 2017) <https://arxiv.org/pdf/1706.08606.pdf>.

Robblee, PA, 'The Legitimacy of Modern Conventional Weaponry' (1976) 71 *Military Law Review* 95.

Roberts, A and R Guelff (eds), *Documents on the Laws of War* (Oxford University Press, 3rd ed, 2000).

Sanders, L and D Copeland, 'Developing an Approach to the Legal Review of Autonomous Weapon Systems', *International Law Association Reporter* (27 November 2020) <https://ilareporter.org.au/2020/11/developing-an-approach-to-the-legal-review-of-autonomous-weapon-systems-lauren-sanders-and-damian-copeland/>.

Sandoz, Y, C Swinarski and B Zimmerman (eds), *Commentary on the Additional Protocols of 8 June 1977 to the Geneva Conventions of 12 August 1949* (ICRC and Martinus Nijhoff, Geneva, 1987).

Sassòli, M, 'Autonomous Weapons and International Humanitarian Law: Advantages, Open Technical Questions and Legal Issues to be Clarified' (2014) 90 *International Law Studies* 308.

Sassòli, M, 'The Role of Human Rights and International Humanitarian Law in New Types of Armed Conflicts' in Orna Ben-Naftali (ed), *International Human Rights and Humanitarian Law* (Oxford University Press, 2011).

Sauer, F, 'Stepping Back from the Brink: Why Multilateral Regulation of Autonomy in Weapon Systems is Difficult, Imperative and Feasible' (2020) 102(913) *International Review of the Red Cross* 235.

Scharre, P, *Army of None: Autonomous Weapons and the Future of War* (Norton & Company, 2018).

Schmitt, M (ed), *Tallinn Manual 2.0 on the International Law Applicable to Cyber Operations* (Cambridge University Press, 2017).

Schmitt, M and J Thurnher, '"Out of the Loop": Autonomous Weapon Systems and the Law of Armed Conflict' (2013) 4(2) *Harvard National Security Journal* 231.

Schmitt, M and L Green (eds), *The Law of Armed Conflict: Into the New Millennium* (Naval War College Newport, 1999).

Schmitt, M, 'Autonomous Weapon Systems and International Humanitarian Law: A Reply to the Critics' (2013) *Harvard National Security Journal Features* 8.

Schmitt, M, 'Military Necessity and Humanity in International Humanitarian Law: Preserving the Delicate Balance' (2010) 50(4) *Virginia Journal of International Law* 795.

Schmitt, M, 'Precision Attack and International Humanitarian Law' (2005) 87 *International Review of the Red Cross* 445.

Schmitt, M, 'Regulating Autonomous Weapons Might be Smarter Than Banning Them', *Just Security* (10 August 2015) <https://www.justsecurity.org/25333/regulating-autonomous-weapons-smarter-banning/>.

Schmitt, M, 'The Principle of Distinction in 21 Century Warfare' (1999) 2 *Yale Human Rights and Development Law Journal* 144.

Schmitt, W, 'War, Technology, and International Humanitarian Law' (HPCR Occasional Paper Series No 4, 2005).

Scholz, J and Galliott, J, *AI in Weapons: The Moral Imperative for Minimally-Just Autonomy* (Defence Science and Technology Group, 2019).

Schuller, Alan 'At the Crossroads of Control: The Intersection of Artificial Intelligence in Autonomous Weapon Systems with International Humanitarian Law' (2017) 8 *Harvard National Security Journal* 379.

Stanley-Lockman, Z, *Responsible and Ethical Military AI: Allies and Allied Perspectives* (Centre for Security and Emerging Technology, August 2021).

Steinberger, H, 'Sovereignty' in Max Planck Institute for Comparative Public Law and International Law, *Encyclopaedia for Public International Law* (Vol 10, 1987).

Tattersall, A and D Copeland, 'Reviewing Autonomous Cyber Capabilities' in Rain Liivoja and Anne Väljataga (eds), *Autonomous Cyber Capabilities Under International*

Law (NATO CCDOE Publications, 2021) <https://ccdcoe.org/uploads/2021/05/Autonomous_Cyber_Capabilities_210525.pdf>.

Ticehurst, R, 'The Martens Clause and the Laws of Armed Conflict' (1997) 317 *International Review of the Red Cross* 125.

Tsagourias, N and G Biggio, 'The Regulation of Cyber Weapons' in Eric Myer and Thilo Marauhn (eds), *Research Handbook on Arms Control Law* (Edward Elgar Publishing, 2021).

Turek, M, *Explainable Artificial Intelligence* (*XAI*) (Defence Advanced Research Projects Agency, 2016).

Turns, D, 'Weapons in the ICRC Study on Customary International Humanitarian Law' (2006) 11(2) *Journal of Conflict and Security Law* 201.

United Kingdom Government, *Guidance: Ethics, Transparency and Accountability Framework for Automated Decision-Making* (13 March 2021) <https://www.gov.uk/government/publications/ethics-transparency-and-accountability-framework-for-automated-decision-making/ethics-transparency-and-accountability-framework-for-automated-decision-making>.

United Kingdom Government, Ministry of Defence, *Ambitious, Safe, Responsible: Our Approach to the Delivery of AI-enabled Capability in Defence* (June 2022).

United Nations Institute for Disarmament Research, *Unintentional Risk and Accidents in the Weaponization of Increasingly Autonomous Technologies* (UNIDIR Resources No 5, 2016) <https://www.unidir.org/files/publications/pdfs/safety-unintentional-risk-and-accidents-en-668.pdf>.

United Nations, *Final Report of the Panel of Experts on Libya Established Pursuant to Security Council Resolution 1972*, UN Doc S/2021/229 (2011).

Verbruggen, M, 'The Role of Civilian Innovation in the Development of Lethal Autonomous Weapon Systems' (2019) 10(3) *Global Policy* 338 <https://onlinelibrary.wiley.com/doi/pdf/10.1111/1758-5899.12663>.

Verbruggen, M, *The Question of Swarms Control: Challenges to Ensuring Human Control over Military Swarms* (No 65, EU Non-Proliferation and Disarmament Consortium, December 2019) <https://www.nonproliferation.eu/wp-content/uploads/2019/12/EUNPDC_no-65_031219.pdf>.

Vestner, T, and A Rossi, 'Legal Reviews of War Algorithms' (2021) 97 *International Law Studies* 509.

Villani, C, *Towards a French and European Strategy* (French Government, 2018).

Wexler, L, 'Limiting the Precautionary Principle: Weapons Regulation in the Face of Scientific Uncertainty' (2006) 39 *UC Davis L* 459.

Wezeman, P, A Kuimova and S Wezeman, *Trends in International Arms Transfers, 2021* (SIPRI, March 2022) <https://www.sipri.org/publications/2022/sipri-fact-sheets/trends-international-arms-transfers-2021>.

Cases

'*United States of America v Krupp von Bohen and Halbak*' in Hershc Lauterpacht (ed), *Annual Digest and Reports of Public International Law Cases: Being a Selection from the Decisions of Inte*rnational Courts and Tribunals and Military Courts during the Year 1948 (1953)

Legality of the Threat or Use of Nuclear Weapons (Advisory Opinion) [1996] ICJ Rep 226

Prosecutor v Galić (Judgement and Opinion) (International Criminal Tribunal for the Former Yugoslavia, Trial Chamber I, Case No IT-98-29-T, 5 December 2003)

Prosecutor v Tadic (Jurisdiction), 105 LL.R. 419, 504–20 (1995), Appeals Chamber, Decision on the Defence Motion for Interlocutory Appeal on Jurisdiction, 2 October 1995, 105 ILR 419

The Trial of the German Major War Criminals, Proceedings of the International Military Tribunal (1946), Part 22, 467

USA v List et al, United States Military Tribunal, Nuremberg (1948) 11 *Nuremberg Military Tribunal* 1230

Treaties

Arms Trade Treaty, opened for signature 3 June 2013 (entered into force 24 December 2014)

Charter of the United Nations

Convention on Cluster Munitions, opened for signature 30 May 2008, 2688 UNTS 39 (entered into force 1 August 2010)

Convention on Prohibitions or Restrictions on the Use of Certain Conventional Weapons Which May be Deemed to be Excessively Injurious or to Have Indiscriminate Effects (Geneva, 10 October 1980) and Amendment to Article 1 (21 December 2001) 1342 UNTS 137

Convention on the Prohibition of Military or Any Hostile Use of Environmental Modification Techniques, opened for signature 10 December 1976, 1108 UNTS 151 (entered into force 5 October 1978)

Convention on the Prohibition of the Development, Production and Stockpiling of Bacteriological (Biological) and Toxin Weapons and on Their Destruction, opened for signature 10 April 1972, 1015 UNTS 163 (entered into force 26 March 1975)

Convention on the Prohibition of the Development, Production, Stockpiling and Use of Chemical Weapons and on Their Destruction, opened for signature 13 January 1993, 1974 UNTS 45 (entered into force 29 April 1997)

Convention on the Prohibition of the Use, Stockpiling, Production and Transfer of Anti-Personnel Mines and on Their Destruction, signed 18 September 1997, 2056 UNTS 211 (entered into force 1 March 1999)

Declaration Renouncing the Use, in Time of War, of Explosive Projectiles under 400 Grammes Weight, opened for signature 29 November 1868 (entered into force 11 December 1868)

Declaration Respecting Maritime Law (entered into force 16 April 1856)

First Geneva Convention for the Amelioration of the Condition of the Wounded in Armies in the Field (entered into force 22 August 1864)

Hague Convention (IV) Respecting the Laws and Customs of War on Land, opened for signature 18 October 1899 (entered into force 26 January 1910)

Hague Convention (VIII) Relative to the Laying of Automatic Submarine Contact Mines (entered into force 26 January 1910)

Hague Convention IV Respecting the Laws and Customs of War on Land (18 October 1907)

Hague Declaration (IV,1), to Prohibit, for the Term of Five Years, the Launching of Projectiles and Explosives from Balloons, and Other Methods of Similar Nature, opened for signature 29 July 1899 (entered into force 4 September 1900)

Hague Declaration 2 Concerning Asphyxiating Gases (29 July 1899)

Hague Declaration 3 Concerning the Prohibition of Using Bullets which Expand or Flatten Easily in the Human Body (29 July 1899)

Project of an International Declaration Concerning the Laws and Customs of War, opened for signature 27 August 1874 (not in force)

Protocol Additional to the Geneva Conventions of 12 August 1949 and relating to the Protection of Victims of International Armed Conflicts, opened for signature 8 June 1977, 1125 UNTS 3 (entered into force 7 December 1978)

Protocol for the Prohibition of the Use in War of Asphyxiating, Poisonous or Other Gases, and of Bacteriological Methods of Warfare, opened for signature 17 June 1925 (entered into force 8 February 1928)

Protocol I on Non-Detectable Fragments, opened for signature 10 April 1981 (entered into force 2 December 1983)

Protocol II on Prohibitions or Restrictions on the Use of Mines, Booby Traps and Other Devices, opened for signature 10 April 1981 (entered into force 2 December 1983) as Amended on 3 May 1996 (Protocol II, as Amended on 3 May 1996)

Protocol III on Prohibitions or Restrictions on the Use of Incendiary Weapons, opened for signature 10 April 1981 (entered into force 2 December 1983)

Protocol IV on Blinding Laser Weapons, opened for signature 13 October 1995, 2024 UNTS 163 (entered into force 30 July 1998)

Protocol V on Explosive Remnants of War, opened for signature 28 November 2003, 2399 UNTS 126 (entered into force 12 November 2006)

Rome Statute of the International Criminal Court, opened for signature 17 July 1988, 2187 UNTS 90 (entered into force 1 July 2002)

Treaty between the United Kingdom of Great Britain and Northern Ireland and the French Republic for Defence and Security Co-operation (Treaty Series No 36, 1 July 2011)<https://assets.publishing.service.gov.uk/government/uploads/system/uploads/attachment_data/file/238153/8174.pdf>

Treaty on the Non-Proliferation of Nuclear Weapons, opened for signature on 1968 (entered into force 1970) <https://www.un.org/disarmament/wmd/nuclear/npt/>

Treaty on the Prohibition of Nuclear Weapons, UN GAOR, UN Doc A/CONF.229/2017/8 (7 July 2017) (entered into force 22 January 2021)

Treaty Relating to the Use of Submarines and Noxious Gases in Warfare, opened for signature 6 February 1922 (not in force)

Vienna Convention on the Law of Treaties, opened for signature 23 May 1969, 155 UNTS 331 (entered into force 27 January 1980)

Wassenaar Arrangement on Export Controls for Conventional Arms and Dual-Use Goods and Technologies <https://www.wassenaar.org/>

Other

Alcala, R, 'Afghanistan and Non-combatant Evacuation Operations', *Articles of War Blog* (Blog Post, 5 August 2021) <https://lieber.westpoint.edu/afghanistan-noncombatant-evacuation-operations/>.

Allen, G, *Russia Probably Has Not Used AI-Enabled Weapons in Ukraine, But That Could Change* (Web Page, Centre for Strategic & International Studies, 26 May 2022) <https://www.csis.org/analysis/russia-probably-has-not-used-ai-enabled-weapons-ukraine-could-change>.

Angwin, J et al *Machine Bias: There's Software Used Across the Country to Predict Future Criminals. And it's Biased Against Blacks* (ProPublica, 23 May 2016) <https://www.propublica.org/article/machine-bias-risk-assessments-in-criminal-sentencing>.

Argentinian Government, *Strengthening of the Review Mechanism of a New Weapon, Means or Methods of Warfare*, UN Doc CCW/GGE.1/2018/WP.2 (4 April 2018) <https://reachingcriticalwill.org/images/documents/Disarmament-fora/ccw/2018/gge/documents/GGE.1-WP2-English.pdf>.

Article 36, *Meaningful Human Control and AWS* (April 2016) <https://article36.org/wp-content/uploads/2016/04/MHC-AI-and-AWS-FINAL.pdf>.

Article 36, *Remarks Prepared for the CCW Debate on Lethal Autonomous Weapons Systems* (13 November 2015) <http://www.article36.org/wp-content/uploads/2015/11/A36- intervention-CCW-13-Nov-2015.pdf>.

Article36, Key *Areas for Debate on Autonomous Weapon Systems* (Briefing Paper, May 2014) <https://www.article36.org/wp-content/uploads/2014/05/A36-CCW-May-2014.pdf>.

Asia Pacific Institute for Law and Security, (2024) *Portal on the Legal Review of Weapons* (Website) <https://apils.org/>.

Australia, Canada, Japan, the Republic of Korea, the UK and the United States, 'Principles and Good Practices on Emerging Technologies in the Area of Lethal Autonomous Weapons Systems' (GGE LAWS, 7 March 2022) <https://reachingcriticalwill.org/images/documents/Disarmament-fora/ccw/2022/gge/documents/USgroup_March2022.pdf>.

Australian Declarations Made upon Ratification of Protocol Additional to the Geneva Conventions of 12 August 1949, and relating to the Protection of Victims of International Armed Conflicts (Protocol I), 1642 UNTS 473 (21 June 1991).

Australian Government, *2020 Defence Strategic Update* (1 July 2020).

Australian Government, Australian Defence Force, Australian Defence Doctrine Publication 06.4 *Law of Armed Conflict* (11 May 2006).

Australian Government, Australian Defence Force, *Defence Capability Manual*, Version 1.1 (4 April 2022) < https://www.defence.gov.au/business-industry/industry-governance/industry-regulations/defence-capability-manual >.

Australian Government, Australian Defence Force, *Concept for Robotics and Autonomous Systems*, Version 1 (25 November 2020).

Australian Government, Australian Defence Force, *Defence Article 36 Review of New Weapons Guide* (May 2020).

Australian Government, Australian Defence Force, Defence Instruction (General) Operations 44–1 *Legal review of New Weapons* (2 June 2005).

Australian Government, Department of Defence, ADDP 03.14 *Targeting* (2 February 2009) <https://iihl.org/wp-content/uploads/2022/08/ADDP_3_14_Targeting.>.

Australian Government, Department of Defence, *Defence Data Strategy 2021–2023* (4 August 2021).

Australian Government, Department of Defence, *Small Unmanned Aerial Systems (SUAS) Designed to 'Enhance 'Local' Situational Awareness and Increase Force Protection'* (Web Page, 2022) <https://www.dst.defence.gov.au/projects/small-unmanned-aerial-system-suas>.

Australian Government, *The Australian Article 36 Review Process*, UN Doc CCW/GGE.2/2018/WP.6 (20 August 2018).

Australian Human Rights Commission, *Using Artificial Intelligence to Make Decisions: Addressing the Problem of Algorithmic Bias* (24 November 2020) <https://humanrights.gov.au/our-work/rights-and-freedoms/publications/using-artificial-intelligence-make-decisions-addressing>.

Austria, *Statement to the UN CCW Group of Governmental Experts re Guiding Principles* (1 September 2020) <https://documents.unoda.org/wp-content/uploads/2020/09/20200901-Austria.pdf>.

Beschikking van de Minister van Defensie (Directive of the Minister of Defence) nr.458.614/A, 5 May 1978, establishing the *Adviescommissie Internationaal Recht en Conventioneel Wapengebruik* (Committee for International Law and the Use of Conventional Weapons).

Comments by Japan, *Commentary on the Operationalization of the Guiding Principles Affirmed by the Group of Government Experts on Emerging Technologies in the Area of Lethal Autonomous Weapons Systems at National Level* (28 August 2020) <https://documents.unoda.org/wp-content/uploads/2020/09/20200828-Japan.pdf>.

Copeland, D and L Sanders, 'Engaging with the Industry: Integrating IHL and into New Technologies in Urban Warfare', *International Committee of the Red Cross: Humanitarian Law and Policy Blog* (Blog Post, 7 October 2021) <https://blogs.icrc.org/law-and-policy/2021/10/07/industry-ihl-new-technologies/>.

Défense, Etat-Major de la Défense, *Ordre Général – J/836* (18 July 2002), establishing *La Commission d'Evaluation Juridique des nouvelles armes, des nouveaux moyens et des nouvelles méthodes de guerre* (Committee for the Legal review of New Weapons, New Means and New Methods of Warfare).

Department of National Defence of Canada, *The Department of National Defence and Canadian Armed Forces Data Strategy* (3 December 2019).

Department of the Air Force, Instruction 51–402 *Legal reviews of Weapons and Cyber Capabilities* (27 July 2011).

Department of the Army, *Review of Legality of Weapons Under International Law* (Regulation 27–53, 1 January 1979) <https://fas.org/irp/doddir/army/ar27-53.pdf>.

Dickey, M, *Twitter and Zoom's Algorithmic Bias Issues* (Web Page, 22 September 2020) <https://techcrunch.com/2020/09/21/twitter-and-zoom-algorithmic-bias-issues/>.

Direktiv om folkerettslig vurdering av vapen, krigforingsmetoder og krigforingsvirkemidler (Directive on the Legal review on Weapons, Methods and Means of Warfare), Ministry of Defence, 18 June 2003.

Dowling, H, 'Loyal Wingman Program Hits New Milestone with Two New Test Flights', *Australian Aviation* (online, 4 November 2021) <https://australianaviation.com.au/2021/11/loyal-wingman-program-hits-new-milestone-with-two-new-test-flights/>.

Draft Report of the 2016 Informal Meeting of Experts on Lethal Autonomous Weapons (*LAWS*), submitted by the Chairperson of the Informal Meeting of Experts.

Draft Report of the 2019 Session of the Group of Governmental Experts on Emerging Technologies in the Area of Lethal Autonomous Weapons Systems, UN Doc CCW/GGE.1/2019/CRP.1/Rev.2 (21 August 2019) <https://www.unog.ch/80256EDD006B8954/(httpAssets)/5497DF9B01E5D9CFC125845E00308E44/$file/CCW_GGE.1_2019_CRP.1_Rev2.pdf>.

Evans, G, 'Oral Statement of the Government of Australian', Legality of the Threat or Use of Nuclear Weapons (Advisory Opinion) [1996] *ICJ Pleadings* [15].

Ferraris, P, *Aided Detection on the Future Battlefield* (US Army, 5 February 2020) <https://www.army.mil/article/232074>.

Final Report of Meeting of the High Contracting Parties to the CCW, UN Doc CCW/MSP/2019/9 (13–15 November 2019) <https://undocs.org/CCW/MSP/2019/9>.

Förordning om folkrättslig granskning av vapenprojekt [Ordinance on the International Law Review of Arms Projects] SFS 2007:936 (15 November 2007).

France, *Non-Paper to the CCW Meeting of Experts on LAWS* (11–15 April 2016) <https://docs-library.unoda.org/Convention_on_Certain_Conventional_Weapons_-_Informal_Meeting_of_Experts_(2016)/2016_LAWSMX_CountryPaper_France%2BCharacterizationofaLAWS.pdf>.

Friedersdorf, C, Under Obama, 'Men Killed by Drones are Presumed to be Terrorists', *The Altantic* (online, 30 May 2012) <https://www.theatlantic.com/politics/archive/2012/05/under-obama-men-killed-by-drones-are-presumed-to-be-terrorists/257749/>.

Giacca, Gilles, *Notes CCW Meeting of Experts on LAWS: Challenges to International Humanitarian Law* (April 2016) 4.

Goussac, N, 'Safety Net or Tangled Web: Legal reviews of AI in Weapons and War-Fighting', *International Committee of the Red Cross Humanitarian Law & Policy Blog* (Blog Post, 18 April 2019) <https://blogs.icrc.org/law-and-policy/2019/04/18/safety-net-tangled-web-legal-reviews-ai-weapons-war-fighting>.

Hambling, D, 'Australian Army Getting Bulletproof Swarming Attack Robots', *Forbes* (online, 4 November 2021) <https://www.forbes.com/sites/davidhambling/2021/11/04/australian-army-gets-bulletproof-attack-robots/?sh=7b44d129463b>.

Horowitz, Michaeal C and P Scharre, *Meaningful Human Control in Weapon Systems: A Primer* (16 March 2015).

International Committee of the Red Cross, *Ethics and Autonomous Weapon Systems: An Ethical Basis for Human Control?* (April 2018).

International *Committee of the Red Cross, International Law and the Challenges of Contemporary Armed Conflicts* (32IC/15/11, October 2015) 44 <https://www.icrc.org/en/document/international-humanitarian-law-and-challenges-contemporary-armed-conflicts>.

International Committee of the Red Cross, *Protecting Civilians and Humanitarian Action Through the Arms Trade Treaty* (November 2013).

International Committee of the Red, 'ICRC Position on Autonomous Weapon Systems: ICRC Position and Background Paper' (2020) *International Review of the Red Cross* 102 (915), <https://www.icrc.org/en/document/icrc-position-autonomous-weapon-systems>.

International Law Commission, *Draft Articles on Responsibility of States for Intentionally Wrongful Acts* (2001) <https://legal.un.org/ilc/texts/instruments/english/commentaries/9_6_2001.pdf>.

Joint 'Commentary' on Guiding Principles A, B, C and D Submitted to the CCW GGE by Austria, Belgium, Brazil, Chile, Ireland, Germany, Luxembourg, Mexico, and New-Zealand (1 September 2020) <https://documents.unoda.org/wp-content/uploads/2020/09/GGE20200901-Austria-Belgium-Brazil-Chile-Ireland-Germany-Luxembourg-Mexico-and-New-Zealand.pdf>.

Kirsch, Philippe, 'Applying the Principles of Nuremberg to the ICC' (Keynote Address at the Conference 'Judgement at Nuremberg' held on the 60th Anniversary of the Nuremberg Judgment, Washington University, 30 September 2006) <https://www.icc-cpi.int/nr/rdonlyres/ed2f5177-9f9b-4d66-9386-5c5bf45d052c/146323/pk_20060930_english.pdf>.

Kotlik, M, 'Reviewing Legal Legal reviews: Is it Possible to Verify Compliance?', *EKIL: Talk!* (Blog Post, 19 March 2020) <https://www.ejiltalk.org/reviewing-legal-weapons-reviews-is-it-possible-to-verify-compliance/>.

Kott, Alexander 'The Artificial Becomes Real: A Back-and-Forth Interplay of Government and Commercial Funding and Research has Brought AI to the Edge of a Breakthrough', *Army Acquisition Logistics and Technology Magazine* (January-March 2018).

Lewis, Dustin A, 'Legal Reviews of Weapons, Means and Methods of Warfare Involving Artificial Intelligence: 16 Elements to Consider', *International Committee of the Red Cross Humanitarian Law & Policy Blog* (Blog Post, 21 March 2019) <https://blogs.icrc.org/law-and-policy/2019/03/21/legal-reviews-weapons-means-methods-warfare-artificial-intelligence-16-elements-consider/>.

Lewis, L, 'Killer Robots Reconsidered: Could AI Weapons Actually Cut Collateral Damage', *Bulletin of Atomic Scientists* (online, 10 January 2020) <https://thebulletin.org/2020/01/killer-robots-reconsidered-could-ai-weapons-actually-cut-collateral-damage/>.

Mines Action Canada Statement, CCW Meeting of Experts on LAWS, *Challenges to International Humanitarian Law* (April 2016).

Mola, R, 'Super Helmet, F-35 Pilots Get X-ray Vision and Other Magic Powers', *Air and Space Magazine* (online, September 2017) <https://www.airspacemag.com/military-aviation/super-helmet-180964342/>.

Montazzoli, M, 'Terrain Denial Fires on the Modern Battlefield', *Articles of War Blog* (Blog Post, 25 August 2021) <https://lieber.westpoint.edu/terrain-denial-fires-modern-battlefield/>.

New Zealand Defence Force, *Manual of Armed Forces Law, Law of Armed Conflict* (DM 69, 2 ed, Vol 4, 8 August 2017).

Office of the Deputy Secretary of Defense, *Implementing Responsible Artificial Intelligence in the Department of Defense* (Washington, DC, 26 May 2021).

OPAL Autonomous Self-healing Communications Network (Website) <https://www.dst.defence.gov.au/projects/autonomous-networking-opal>.

Permanent Mission of Austria to the United Nations in Geneva, *Contribution of Austria to the Chair's Request for Guiding Principles on Emerging Technologies in the Area of LAWS* (1 September 2020) <https://documents.unoda.org/wp-content/uploads/2020/09/20200901-Austria.pdf>.

Report of the 2018 Session of the Group of Governmental Experts on Emerging Technologies in the Area of Lethal Autonomous Weapons Systems, UN Doc CCW/GGE.1/2018/3 (23 October 2018) <https://undocs.org/en/CCW/GGE.1/2018/3>.

Report of the 2021 Session of the Group of Governmental Experts on Emerging Technologies in the Area of Lethal Autonomous Weapons Systems, UN Doc CCW/GGE.1/2021/CRP.1 (8 December 2021).

Roff, H and R Moyes, 'Meaningful Human Control, Artificial Intelligence and Autonomous Weapons'. Briefing paper prepared for the Informal Meeting of Experts on Lethal Autonomous Weapons Systems, UN Convention on Certain Conventional Weapons (April 2016) <https://article36.org/wp-content/uploads/2016/04/MHC-AI-and-AWS-FINAL.pdf>.

Saliba, A and L Barbosa, '"Like a Dog Chasing Its Tail": Group of Governmental Experts on Lethal Autonomous Weapons', *International Law Agendas* (Blog Post, 25 March 2022) <http://ila-brasil.org.br/blog/like-a-dog-chasing-its-tail/>.

Sanders, L and D Copeland, 'Holding Autonomy to Account: Legal Standards for Autonomous Weapon Systems', *West Point: Articles of War Blog* (Blog Post, 15 September 2021) <https://lieber.westpoint.edu/holding-autonomy-account-legal-standards-autonomous-weapon-systems/>.

Scharre, P, *Killer Robots, and Human Control in the Use of Force – Part II* (Presentation, 9 July 2014) <https://www.justsecurity.org/12712/autonomy-killer-robots-human-control-force-part-ii/>.

Sparrow, R, 'Ethics as a Source of Law: The Martens Clause and Autonomous Weapons', *ICRC Humanitarian Law and Policy* (Blog Post, 14 November 2017) <https://blogs.icrc.org/law-and-policy/2017/11/14/ethics-source-law-martens-clause-autonomous-weapons/>.

Stop Killer Robots, 'The Problem' (Web Page) <https://www.stopkillerrobots.org/learn/#problem>.

Switzerland Statements, CCW Meeting of Experts on LAWS, *Challenges to International Humanitarian Law* (April 2016).

Switzerland, *A 'Compliance-based' Approach to Autonomous Weapon Systems*, UN Doc CCW/GGE.1/2017/WP.9 (10 November 2017) <https://docs-library.unoda.org/Convention_on_Certain_Conventional_Weapons_-_Group_of_Governmental_Experts_(2017)/2017_GGEonLAWS_WP9_Switzerland.pdf>.

Tadjdeh, Y, 'Algorithmic Warfare: Russia Expanding Fleet of AI-Enabled Weapons', *National Defense* (online, 20 July 2020) <https://www.nationaldefensemagazine.org/articles/2021/7/20/russia-expanding-fleet-of-ai-enabled-weapons>.

United Kingdom Government, Ministry of Defence, Joint Doctrine Publication 0-30.2 *Unmanned Aircraft Systems* (August 2017) <https://assets.publishing.service.gov.uk/government/uploads/system/uploads/attachment_data/file/673940/doctrine_uk_uas_jdp_0_30_2.pdf>.

United Kingdom, 'Proposal for a GGE Document on the Application of International Humanitarian Law to Emerging Technologies in the Area of Lethal Autonomous Weapon Systems (LAWS)' (GGE LAWS, March 2022) <https://reachingcriticalwill.org/images/documents/Disarmament-fora/ccw/2022/gge/documents/UK_March2022.pdf>.

United Nations Office for Disarmament Affairs, 'Convention on Certain Conventional Weapons (CCW). Legal Autonomous Weapons Systems. National Commentary – Australia' (20 August 2020) <https://documents.unoda.org/wp-content/uploads/2020/08/20200820-Australia.pdf>.

United Nations, *Report of the 2017 Group of Governmental Experts on 'Lethal Autonomous Weapon Systems' (LAWS)*, UN Doc CCW/GGE.1/2017/CRP.1 (20 November 2017) <https://docs-library.unoda.org/Convention_on_Certain_Conventional_Weapons_-_Meeting_of_High_Contracting_Parties_(2017)/2017_CCW_GGE.1_2017_CRP.1_Advanced_%2Bcorrected.pdf>.

United States Chairman of the Joint Chiefs of Staff, Instruction CJCSI 3160.01D *No-Strike and the Collateral Damage Estimation Methodology* (13 February 2009).

United States Department of Defence, Joint Doctrine Manual, *Law of Armed Conflict at the Operational and Tactical Levels*, B-GJ-005-104/FP-021 (13 August 2001).

United States Department of Defense, Directive 3000.3 *Policy for Non-Lethal Weapons* (9 July 1996).

United States Department of Defense, Directive 5000.01 *The Defense Acquisition System* (12 May 2003) <https://www.esd.whs.mil/Portals/54/Documents/DD/issuances/dodd/500001p.pdf?ver=2020-09-09-160307-310>.

United States Department of Defense, Directive Number 3000.09 *Autonomy in Weapons* (21 November 2012, updated 8 May 2017) <https://fas.org/irp/doddir/dod/d3000_09.pdf>.

United States Department of Defense, Instruction 5500.15 *Review of Legality of Weapons under International Law* (16 October 1974).

United States Department of Defense, *Law of War Manual* (Office of General Counsel, June 2015, revised December 2016).

United States Department of the Navy, Instruction 5000.2E *Implementation and Operation of the Defense Acquisition System and the Joint Capabilities Integration and Development System* (1 September 2011).

Velez-Green, A, 'The Foreign Policy Essay: The South Korean Sentry – A "Killer Robot" to Prevent War', *Lawfare Blog* (Blog Post, 1 March 2015) <https://www.lawfareblog.com/foreign-policy-essay-south-korean-sentry%E2%80%94-killer-robot-prevent-war>.

White, SJ, 'The Legal Review of Weapons, Means and Methods of Warfare' (Presentation, September 2020) <https://documents.unoda.org/wp-content/uploads/2020/10/Weapons-reviews-2020-Australia.pdf>.

Index

www.ingramcontent.com/pod-product-compliance
Lightning Source LLC
Chambersburg PA
CBHW071247230926
51849CB00001B/262
9789004707030